California's Spanish Place-Names

San Rafael
San Anselmo
Lagunitas Lk.
San Pablo Bay
Pinole Pt.
Pinole Va
El Sobra
Castro
San Pablo
San Quentin
El Cerrito
Corte Madera
Potrero Pt.
Solano Ave.
Lake A
Tiburon
Marin
Angel Island
Sausalito
Yerba
Buena
Temescal
Alcatraz
Pt. Bonita
Presidio
Embarcadero
Pt. Lobos
Mariposa
Merced Lake
San
Francisco
Alameda
Visitacion
Valley
Junipero Serra Hwy.
San Francisco
Sierra Pt.
Pacifica
San Bruno
Laguna Salada
Coyote Pt.
Pedro Pt.
San Andreas
San Mateo

Martinez

Pacheco Paso Corto

Alhambra Valley Rd. Contra Loma

Briones

By
Barbara and Rudy Marinacci

California's Spanish Place-Names:

WHAT THEY ARE AND HOW THEY GOT HERE

Presidio Press
San Rafael, California

Moraga

Las Trampas Tassajara

Santa Rita

San Leandro Arroyo

Estudillo

San Lorenzo

Palomares Rd.

Coyote Hills Vallecitos

Peralta Blvd.

Alvarado Sunol

Published by
Presidio Press
San Rafael, California

Library of Congress Cataloging in Publication Data

Marinacci, Barbara.
    California's Spanish place-names.

    Bibliography: p.
    Includes "dictionary/index."
    1. California—History, Local. 2. Spaniards
in California—History. 3. Names, Geographical—
California. 4. Names, Geographical—Spanish.
5. Historic sites—California—Guide-books.
6. California—Description and travel—1951–
—Guide-books. I. Marinacci, Rudy, 1928–
joint author. II. Title.
F861.M32   979.4   80-11381
ISBN 0-89141-102-X

Designed by Hal Lockwood
Composed by Helen Epperson
Printed in the United States of America

For MIKE, CHRIS, and ELLEN —
who, traveling with us,
have often asked,
"What's a ———?"

Contents

Acknowledgments

THE AUTHORS wish to give special thanks to these people who have been helpful: Gretchen Trevisan, our initial place-name assembler; Marilyn Clements of Mission Viejo, a professional maker of Hispanic street names; Pete S. Torres, Jr., of Los Angeles County's Mapping Division; Mexican-American educator Ramon M. Moreno; and copy editor and book designer Hal Lockwood. The entire reference staff of the Santa Monica Public Library has surely provided assistance at one time or another. Above all we are grateful to senior editor Joan Griffin at Presidio Press for her close and enthusiastic involvement at each step of the way.

Spanish Names
All Over the Place

PRESIDIO, ARROYO SECO, CONEJO, La Brea, El
Monte, Los Gatos, Carpinteria, Laguna, Encino,
Salinas, Embarcadero: Hundreds of Spanish names
and words flash by as you travel the freeways, cities, and
backcountry of California. You notice them too when
reading newspapers and magazines or watching television:
Sacramento, Soledad, Redondo, Tiburon, Goleta, Santa
Cruz, Alcatraz, San Mateo, Fresno, Borrego, Los Angeles.
Or you spot them while jogging along neighborhood streets:
Oso, La Sierra, El Mar, Via del Sol, Puerta Real, Venado,
Cuenca, Morena, Cordero. Looking at maps when planning
some trip, you'll encounter a flock of new ones.

If you already know Spanish, you're ahead in any
guessing game you might play as you travel through the

An Introduction   1 state. Yet you may not know why and when our Spanish place-names actually came about. Californians—there are more than twenty million of us—use these geographical words daily, rarely thinking about what they mean or how they got there. If any seem odd-looking at first, we lose our surprise as we learn to pronounce them (or properly *mis*pronounce them) and use them when needed. But we may be neglecting an open storehouse of information that is interesting, intriguing, and entertaining.

Place-names, of course, don't just happen by themselves. People put them there, usually for good reasons. And succeeding generations may keep them and use them. From the beginning, people have created sounds—words— to represent places significant to them: places where they dwelled, or got food and water, or obtained useful materials for tools and shelter; or places they passed through on the way from one spot to another, or places they met dangers. Other groups moving into the same territory might have taken over these early place-names out of convenience; if they spoke different languages, they might never have learned the meanings of these words. But even if the same tribe stayed on the ancestral land for centuries, in time its members could forget the old stories that explained place-names.

Human populations are migratory. Invaders bring in new words, and emigrants take their language with them to foreign regions. Eventually, most regional maps become veritable polyglots. California has been a thoroughfare and a homeland to many peoples—representatives of almost every race, nationality, and area. First to arrive and longest staying were the tribes of American Indians, who spoke perhaps a score of quite diverse tongues and left abundant evidence of them upon the land in the form of place-names. Then came the Spanish-speaking explorers, missionaries, soldiers, and colonists from Spain and New Spain, or Mexico, who recorded a good many names they heard from the Indians—and added a great many more of their own, an amazingly large number of them still in use today, often in altered forms.

Later groups of immigrants to California, especially following the American takeover and the Gold Rush, caused new names: Russian River, French Gulch, Chinese Camp, Dutch Flat, Negro Canyon, Italian Swiss Colony, Chileno Valley, Swede Creek, Portuguese Bend, Yankee Hill. Other localities show residents' foreign origins in that they bear the names of faraway people and places, or words from another language, such as Millbrae (Scottish), Solvang (Danish), Modjeska (Polish), Downey (Irish), Anaheim (German), Kanaka (Hawaiian), Wakamatsu (Japanese), Sonora (Mexican).

The Hispanic place-names, though, are the most prevalent and distinctive of all names for California's settlements and geographical features. You'll find Spanish-looking names for counties, cities, and towns; islands and bays, lakes and rivers; mountains and valleys; deserts, forests, swamps, and springs; dams and recreation areas; schools and libraries; roads and superhighways; shopping malls, marinas, and suburban developments; and also apartment houses, restaurants, motels, and neon-lit cantinas. Sometimes these names are Spanish surnames like Martinez, Vallejo, Gonzales, Amador; or first names like Benicia, Ricardo, Adelaida. Since Hispanic surnames are frequently words with meanings, it is sometimes hard to know when a place-name was given to commemorate a personage—usually someone connected with California history—and when to record a description or an event. (Cabrillo, for example, is a small goat; Guerrero a warrior; Pico a peak, pick, or beak; Verdugo an executioner.)

An Introduction   **3**

If you have never learned Spanish, you might find California's place-names a good way to start. Or if you've forgotten much of the Spanish you once knew, you can revive it quickly and add to your vocabulary by figuring out the meanings of place-names. (In either case, a notepad, pencil, and Spanish-English dictionary are helpful companions.)

If you are already fluent in Spanish and can readily translate most place-names and street-names, there is still an area that probably could use some filling in: explanations for all those Hispanic words and names—the "stories behind them." Why a town was called Corte Madera (Cut Wood). Why a major city's name means The Angels. Why a large river, the Merced, seems to honor the quality of mercy. Why a pleasant town, Atascadero, was christened Mudhole. You can also entertain yourself by noticing the many names that are improperly constructed (Mar Vista, Oro Linda, Terra Buena) or downright silly (San Hacienda —St. Farm, and Paseo Cerveza—Beer Boulevard, in Orange County; Alameda de las Pulgas—Mall of the Fleas—in San Mateo) or redundant (El Cerrito Hill—Little Hill Hill—and Lago Lake—Lake Lake, and Potrero Meadows—Meadow Meadows).

Even the Spanish-looking names that are mistakes or fakes or nonsense tell us something important about Californians. Assigned to localities and new streets during the century and a third since Spanish stopped being the territory's official language, they are here for a purpose. Nostalgia for a lost Hispanic ambience and shrewd real-estate "boostering" combined to create a self-image that many Californians seemingly wish to perpetuate. In spite of freeway congestion, computer-age technologies, drive-in churches, super-supermarkets, garish billboards, spread-out housing tracts engulfing citrus groves, and hyped-up media events, California's residents like to feel that somewhere in

Spanish Names All Over the Place

their lives an element exists that is relaxed and carefree, passionate or purposeful, even exotic. They want to relate back to a simpler existence—in which a man and his family could own a vast tract of land that spread from one side of the horizon to the other. Where human activities had made only a small dent in the natural landscape of California. And where there was a commonly held value system that worked—if only for a while.

Whether born Californians or recent arrivals, whether or not a drop of Latin blood flows through our veins, we are responsive to a sentiment that harks back to the age of the fruitful missions along El Camino Real—that royal road—and to those idyllic, pastoral "days of the Dons" on the sprawling ranchos. Signposts bearing Spanish-looking names may constantly revive and nourish this yearning. Only vicariously can we enjoy this lost age now in our tile-roofed and stuccoed suburban *ranchitos* placed communally close on streets given Hispanic words whose meanings few may recognize—or even want to know, for fear of spoiling the dream. (Would a somber housebuyer in Orange County really like to learn that he has just purchased property on Nada Street—Nothing Street? Yet many are the name-makers' blunders, jokes, and ersatz-Spanish products within the state.)

Somehow the "Spanish style" suits us. But only occasionally do the suburbanized Anglos make any direct connection with the burgeoning population of Chicanos— Mexican Americans—living in the barrios of our cities and rural towns. (Los Angeles is the second largest city in the world containing people of Mexican ancestry, with well over one million of them.) Ironically, the Mission, Neo-Spanish, Monterey, California Ranch-House, and Modern Mediterranean building designs that have been popular for many years, and the Hispanic place-names that go with them, testify to the reality of the Spanish and Mexican entry into California. The presence of Spanish-speaking peoples, too, is a continuing association with a rich and unique cultural heritage. Approximately one-third of our place-names are Hispanic: the most prevalent ethnic ones, except for the usually amorphous Anglo-Saxon words. Some Hispanic elements came early; others came late. And more are added all the time, in a process that has deep roots within layers of California ground and time.

The many thousands of geographical features and settlements that carry Spanish names overwhelm any quick and easy explanation for their existence. It involves looking at different periods of time, exploration, and settlement. Also, it requires consideration of some basic things about the place-naming process itself. For example, what makes certain names "stick" while others change forms so as to become almost unrecognizable, and still others vanish (though not necessarily forever if people resurrect them when creating new place-names).

All Hispanic-looking words used in place-names originated in one of seven distinctive yet overlapping periods in California history. Toponymists—place-name scholars— cannot always determine the exact time in which a particular name was given, or offer indisputable explanations for why it was chosen, or produce infallible translations. Usually, however, they can at least trace the Spanish place-names to a general time when the words began to be used.

Indian habitation. The California Indians, with an estimated population of 250,000 before the Spaniards' arrival, had the densest settlement of all American Indians within the area of the present-day United States. Consisting of many tribes and main language groups, as strictly hunting and gathering cultures they lived in small units, usually

Spanish Names All Over the Place

within well-defined territories. Some led nomadic lives, traveling from one place to another as plant foods came into season and when animal prey were available. Others lived in huts in permanent villages: what the Spaniards called *rancherías*. Since these settlements were usually located at good water sources and in prime lands, many sites were eventually occupied by missions, *pueblos* or towns, *ranchos* or ranches. A number of today's cities sit upon former rancherias. Although the Spanish-speaking explorers and colonists bestowed many place-names of their own, they often recorded and used the Indians' words for their villages and for geographical features or tribes. Their word-sounds were recorded on maps and in journals and documents, using the Spanish phonetic system. This is why so many basically Indian place-names "look" Spanish. Frequently, too, the whites did not hear the words correctly or understand their meanings, resulting in endless riddles for place-name historians and linguistic anthropologists.

Coastal discoveries by Spanish mariners between the sixteenth and eighteenth centuries.   During these two and a half centuries, the Spaniards took their time in getting to know *Alta* (Upper) California. Because of adverse winds and currents and the seasonal problem of hurricanes, voyages to the north along the Pacific Coast were hazardous and long—with the dread scurvy always taking a heavy toll on the crew. Cabrillo's initial survey in 1542 was supplemented later by more observations and place-names from the voyages of Manila galleons on their return route from the Philippine Islands. Sent out in 1602, Vizcaino ambitiously renamed almost everything previously discovered and added many new names of his own. When Spain began colonizing Alta California in 1769, the trips of supply ships and new naval expeditions resulted in more names for bays, rivers, and promontories along the coast. Even a few foreign navigators like Vancouver added some Spanish place-names.

Early overland explorations by Spanish-speaking soldiers and priests. From 1769, the date of the founding of the Spanish settlement at San Diego Bay, the interior regions of California began to be explored, mapped, described, and named. The earliest and most numerous contributions to place-naming were made by the famous Portola expedition, the thousand-mile round trip, lasting a half year, across unknown land between San Diego and San Francisco bays. Everybody in the party participated in creating names, and of the hundred or more proposed and recorded en route, several dozen remain today, mostly in altered versions, yet preserving their origins. Gradually, as the hinterlands beyond the various early Spanish settlements were traveled, maps filled with regional place-names. Two significant expeditions were led by Anza in the mid-1770s. He came across the desert from northern Mexico, bringing in much-needed colonists and livestock. Other important explorations during the Spanish period were undertaken by early governors like Pedro Fages and Fernando Rivera y Moncada, and included priests, who were usually responsible for giving the sacred and saintly names, and who themselves became experienced explorers.

The first Spanish settlements. From the founding of San Diego and Monterey until the end of Spanish rule in 1822, there were twenty-eight official establishments: four *presidios* or forts to fend off foreign invasion by sea and Indian attacks by land; twenty-one Franciscan missions, first presided over by Father Serra, built to convert the Indians to Christianity, teach them the rudimentary skills of civilization, and become self-supporting colonies; and three *pueblos* or civilian towns that were to promote family life and practice agriculture and useful crafts. The names of most of these settlements—whose titles mostly began with the saints' *San* or *Santa*—are familiar because they are still with us today. They were centers for future developments in agriculture, industry, and shipping; some figured prominently in social, political, and cultural activities.

The Spanish and Mexican land-grant ranchos. The Spanish court authorized about twenty concessions of pasturage lands or ranchos to retiring soldiers who had served in California and wished to remain there with their families. Livestock—cattle, horses, and some sheep—roamed freely and multiplied, forming the basis for a new California economy and way of life. Under Mexican rule, California governors dispensed such land grants far more generously to the *Californios,* the by-then-indigenous white settlers who within a generation became landed gentry and who called themselves *la gente de razón*—"the people of reason" or "civilized people." Some of these ranchos, given freely or sold for a nominal fee, had a maximum size of 11 square leagues —about 48,000 acres. Family members, however, could add new grants or holdings to the total acreage. When the vast mission lands became available after the secularization of the missions in 1834, the pace and quantity of the land-grant largesse increased. By the end of Mexico's control over California, about seven hundred of these land grants had been handed out to colonists, many of them foreign settlers who had acquired Mexican citizenship in order to qualify. As feudal-style landowners, each *ranchero* was addressed with the dignified title of *Don* preceding his first name. The ranchos were a major source of many present-day place-names, in areas once encompassed by them. The land-grant *diseños* or maps recorded and thereby preserved

Spanish names for local geographical features and Indian rancherias. The ranchos' titles themselves generally used existing place-names. Some were Indian, some Indian-Spanish hybrids, some religious, some story-telling (the last often odd and tantalizing, such as *Rancho de Carne Humana*—Ranch of Human Flesh). Many are perpetuated in contemporary settlements: Tiburon, Sausalito, Los Gatos, Pinole, Santa Anita, Los Cerritos. The surnames of the ranchero families themselves frequently appear in towns' and geographical names; also on local street-names.

The American takeover of California. The *Yanquis* came first by sea and later overland. Actively engaged in the lucrative hide and tallow trade with the Californios (including the mission padres, who could be shrewd businessmen), the men from the New England ships took appraising looks at the charming but backward province of Alta California. Some stayed on as trading agents and merchants in the pueblos or ports to which rancheros brought their raw products: untanned hides ("leather dollars"), bags of tallow fat, jerked beef. In exchange, they shopped for manufactured goods from the United States and luxuries from South America or the Orient. Other Americans opted to become rancheros themselves, obtaining land grants after converting to Catholicism and becoming naturalized citizens of Mexico. They also tended to marry heiresses among the Californios and take up the Hispanic lifestyle, to which they added Yankee ingredients.

The American ranks grew as men increasingly came cross-country, through the mountain passes, into California. Some began as fur trappers; others as traders from Santa Fe or as surveyors from Washington, D.C. (like Fremont, who had America's Manifest Destiny in mind). Then there was the Bear Flag Revolt, the local skirmishes of the War with Mexico. By 1848 California belonged to the United States—just in time for the Gold Rush, which flooded the land and its small population (perhaps twelve thousand whites) with Argonauts from everywhere, but especially Americans, who all too often believed that the Hispanic settlers should have no rights to land at all, whether as gold claims or ranchos. The mass migration quickly overwhelmed the Californios. In many places the newcomers eradicated, translated, or otherwise altered the original Spanish words. Comparatively few genuine, newly made Spanish place-names happened from then on, although many old ones have been revived.

Hispanic survival and revival. The brash Americans displaced the Spanish-speaking Californios as fast as they could. Forty-niners called all Hispanic peoples "greasers" and treated them with the same contempt shown to Indians ("diggers") and Chinese. Some Mexicans who fought back became *bandidos* and earned place-names on new maps. But the old order was passing. The land grants, disputed in the courts, were sometimes overruled. Ranchos were illegally divided by trespassing squatters. The rancheros mortgaged their only large assets, their lands—and often lost them to Yankee land grabbers. Some were developed into new cattle kingdoms, like those of Miller & Lux, Irvine, Bixby, and Hope. Many were subdivided into small farming tracts and hundreds of new settlements made possible by radical changes brought about by railroads and water control. Tourism and "boostering" became large California enterprises.

At first it looked as if Spanish names would fade from view. But a surge of new interest in the Spanish past began in the 1880s, inspired by the enormous popularity of the novel *Ramona.* Land promoters saw commercial benefits in giving Spanish—or, more often, Spanish-looking—titles to localities old and new. California architecture incorporated elements of the mission and rancho adobes. Spanish "revival" became fashionable.

In a very different channel, the state began to receive a new wave of Mexican settlers: contract laborers or *braceros* to work in fields and factories. The Chicano culture of today exerts its own energy, ideas, and needs regarding both language and land use—already affecting the place-naming process in California by producing new words and new places of Hispanic origins. Spanish names will remain with us forevermore.

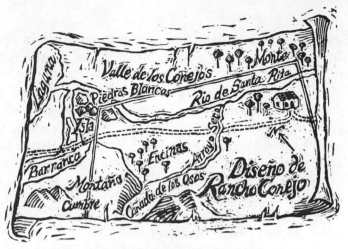

Some Words About
Spanish Words

I F YOU HAVE NEVER really thought about the pre-
ponderance of Hispanic place-names in California,
consider this: Of the state's fifty-eight counties, thirty-
two of them have Spanish titles — and three more started out
Spanish. There are Alameda, Amador, Calaveras, Contra
Costa, Del Norte, El Dorado, Fresno, Los Angeles, Madera,
Marin (an abbreviation), Mariposa, Mendocino, Merced,
Monterey, Nevada, Placer, Plumas, Sacramento, San Benito,
San Bernardino, San Diego, San Francisco, San Joaquin,
San Luis Obispo, San Mateo, Santa Barbara, Santa Clara,
Santa Cruz, Sierra, Solano, Tulare, Ventura. Kings, Stanis-
laus, and Trinity are translations of the original Spanish
names for the rivers that flow through them: *Los Santos
Reyes, Estanislao,* and *Trinidad.* Imperial County might
be considered bilingual. (A number of other titles look

Spanish but are actually Indian names recorded in Spanish, like Colusa, Inyo, Modoc, Mono, Napa, Shasta, Sonoma, Tuolumne, Yolo, Yuba.)

Then there's the matter of cities. Of our sixteen largest metropolitan areas, fourteen have Spanish names, either exclusively or included within their scope: Fresno, Los Angeles, Modesto, Sacramento, Salinas, San Bernardino, San Francisco, San Diego, San Jose, Santa Ana, Santa Barbara, Santa Rosa, Vallejo, Ventura. (Oakland actually occupies a locale originally named *Encinal* — Oak Place.)

California itself is a Spanish place-name. And its capital, Sacramento, is Spanish too.

Even people who don't know much about pronouncing Spanish may know more than they think they do simply by living in California and regularly saying its place- and street-names. One begins almost automatically to apply the necessary sounds to new situations. For example, having learned that the *j* in San Jose and San Juan sounds like the English *h,* you may find that, when confronted with a name like San Jacinto, the *h* comes readily. The same thing happens with the double *l,* as in the *cholla* cactus, where the *ll* is pronounced like *y.* A place-name like La Jolla follows both rules. Then there's the *ñ* with its tilde, a sound like *n'y* in canyon — the English word derived from *cañón,* which is a relative of the *cañada* (glen between mountains; glade) in La Canada. The town's name is rarely spelled with the original tilde, but the *n'y* sound belongs there anyway. (On the other hand, Los Banos has shed both its tilde and its proper pronunciation.)

Some Spanish place-names in California are deliberately mis-said, the best example being Los Angeles. In Spanish, *g* before *e* or *i* makes an *h* sound, but Americans have made it a hard *g* or a *j:* "loss ANG-less" or "loss ANjuh-luss." Non-Hispanics who go around saying "lohs AHN-

Some Words About Spanish Words

hay-lace" run the risk of being ridiculed for their affecta-
tion. In fact, few Spanish place-names are *ever* pronounced
quite properly by any but purists and Latinos.

An approximate melding of the two languages'
phonics is the usual result in dealing with place-words.
Most modify the original Hispanic vowels, clipping their
sonority, but preserve generally the consonants, syllable
divisions, and accents. Words that end in vowels or *n* or *s*
regularly receive stress on the next to the last syllable;
those ending in consonants except *n* or *s* have the last syllable stressed. (A terminal *y* is classified as a consonant.)
Any exceptions should really have an accent (') written
over the vowel of the stressed syllable to indicate that it
must be emphasized. However, place-names in common
usage—like Los Ángeles, San José, Santa Bárbara, Santa
Mónica, Tiburón—don't wear accents anymore. It's assumed that everybody knows how to handle the syllable
stress. Sign makers and typographers don't like to be bothered with them. The same situation pertains to presenting
various Spanish Christian names and surnames: such as
José and Luís, or Junípero, Portolá, and Vizcaíno.

Since this text adopts a simplified approach to using
Spanish words, place-names, surnames, and frequently used
terms (like *ranchería*) will not show accents except when
italicized as newly introduced words or archaic place-
names. The dictionary-index provides their correct written
forms, along with pronunciation guides.

For the novice Spanish speaker, a brief section preceding the dictionary-index introduces some basic information regarding the pronunciation of Spanish vowels and
consonants, the placement of stress, the function of gender
in Spanish nouns and their modifiers, and the formation of
number (singular and plural). Since most place-names are
essentially nouns, with the longest ones strung together

using articles, prepositions, and sometimes conjunctions, only limited attention to points of grammar is given. (The early Spanish explorers excelled in constructing elaborate place-names, which were trimmed later in ordinary usage even before the Americans arrived. Notable are *El Río de Nuestra Señora de la Merced* and, better yet, *El Pueblo de Nuestra Señora la Reina de los Angeles de Porciúncula.* Now we just have Merced River and Los Angeles, or plain "L.A.")

One big tip-off in spotting pseudo-Spanish place-names and street-names is that ill-informed place-namers have constructed ungrammatical combinations, such as Oro Linda or Mar Vista or El Bonita. (The first combines a masculine noun with a feminine modifier. The second puts two nouns together: properly, it should be Vista del Mar. The third makes a feminine noun out of an adjective and then attaches a masculine article to it.)

A person with little or no knowledge of Spanish might be consoled at the onset that its pronunciation and grammatical rules are far easier and more regular than English. In fact, most people already have an unconscious familiarity with it not only through the often-said place-names, but also through a great many Spanish words that have been incorporated into the English vocabulary. Words like these probably require no assistance in saying or translating: cargo, bonanza, fiesta, siesta, hacienda, loco, patio, plaza, mesa, pueblo, señor, arroyo, sierra, padre, madre, hombre, macho, incomunicado, aficionado, temblor, armada, machete, junta, guerrilla, politico, chili, condor, bronco, pinto, burro, rodeo, gaucho, corral, mosquito, poncho, mantilla, sombrero, chino, chaparral. Some basically Spanish words are pronounced somewhat differently in English but spelled the same: tornado, silo, cordillera, placer, cafeteria, vigilante, albino. Others were changed slightly: *rancho* to ranch, *mulato* to mulatto, *desesperado* to desperado, *bar-*

bacoa to barbecue, *cincha* to cinch, *lazo* to lasso, *la reata* to lariat, *guitarra* to guitar, *filibustero* to filibuster, *mustango* to mustang, *cañón* to canyon, *el lagarto* to alligator.

Often, English equivalents of Spanish words have slight variations in vowels. You can easily figure out such words as *palma, lima, aire, pino, fruta, centro, fortuna, isla.* But you can't always count on such similarities. *Plata* doesn't mean plate, *oro* isn't ore, *trampa* is not a tramp. Many Spanish words, though, do have close English relatives: *asilo* for refuge (like our asylum), *azul* for blue (azure), *feliz* for happy (felicity). This likeness came about whenever English adopted a Romance-language or Latin-derived word, or from some other source common to both English and Spanish forms. (Spanish, of course, has often borrowed English words too, especially for technological things like inventions, or special activities like *béisbol*— baseball.)

Spanish has taken many words from other tongues: whenever its speakers were exposed to other languages and peoples, as during invasion, immigration, or colonization. Modern Spanish was much affected by the Arabic language brought by the Moors from North Africa in the eighth century. Their military might and advanced learning dominated Spain's cultural life for hundreds of years. Examples of Arabic-Spanish words now in the English vocabulary too are adobe, alfalfa, and alcalde. The basic earth-clay, sunbaked building block of Spanish America originated in both term and technique in the Arabic *at-tob*. The forage food for livestock was a Moorish introduction to Spain, *al-fasfasah*. And the chief official of the Hispanic town or pueblo in the New World, the alcalde—a combination mayor and judge—got its name from the Moors' *al-qadi*.

In the Americas, Spanish eventually changed considerably from the original, "pure" Castilian tongue spoken by the *conquistadores* and the ranks of officialdom, including the padres who came to administer the new colonies. New World Spanish is very different indeed in pronunciation, vocabulary, and sheer style. It pronounces the *c* before *e* or *i* as *s*—not the *th* sound of Castilian. And *ll* becomes *y*, not *l'y*.

Old Spanish words changed their meanings or got lost. (This can be a problem to California place-namers who conscientiously craft words for street-names from complete, basically Castilian dictionaries prepared for translating Cervantes or Lope de Vega. Their selections may have no contemporary relevance whatsoever.)

The biggest changes to the living language came as the Spanish emigrants on both continents in the New World and in the West Indies adopted the Amerindian names for things new to their experience. Exotic foodstuffs usually received names similar to the Indians' words, and when the English-speaking peoples used them too they coined facsimiles of the Spanish-Indian names: *cacao* (cocoa), *chocolate, vainilla, chile, tomate, maíz, pimiento, patata* (potato), *cazabe* (cassava), *panoche* (penuche), *tapioca*. The New World bean, so dear to Latin American cuisine, was called *frijol* (plural, *frijoles*)—common lingo in the U.S. Southwest.

The Indian-become-Spanish words, entrenched after several centuries of colonization, were transported into California by the Spaniards in the latter part of the eighteenth century. They were applied to things identical or similar to those seen or experienced elsewhere in Spanish America. And when English adopted them too, later on, it was sometimes forgotten that they were Indian, not Spanish, in origin—from languages as different and widely separated as those spoken by the Aztecs, Mayas, Incas, and Caribbean tribes. *Canoa, caníbal, huracán* became canoe, cannibal, and hurricane. Tule, mescal, saguaro, mesquite,

Some Words About Spanish Words

ocotillo and tuna (prickly pear) are only a few of the native plant names that came to California from New Spain. Animals too: like condor (which means vulture in Spanish), coyote, puma, chinchilla, nutria, abalone. The Aztecs' habit of cleansing and invigorating themselves in a sweathouse introduced the word *temescal,* which was then brought to California, where Indians had the same practice. A number of these bi- or trilingual words can be found now in place- and street-names.

All place-names may be classified in five basic groups, which cover their origins or the reasons why they were given. They can be descriptive, dramatic, commemorative, transported, or contrived. Some names actually straddle several categories. These are the earmarks of each type of place-name, with some Hispanic examples:

Descriptive. This is the simplest and most direct type of place-name. It may state the kind of place it is geographically: *bahía* (bay), *río* (river), *boca* (river "mouth" or outlet), *estero* (estuary), *cabo* (cape), *costa* (coast), *punta* (point), *mar* (sea), *marina* (shore), *lago* (lake), *laguna* (lagoon or small lake), *arroyo* (creek), *ciénaga* (swamp), *salina* (salt flat), *brea* (tar pool or spring), *llano* and *vega* (plain or flatland), *barranca* (gulch or gully), *cañón* (canyon), *cañada* (small canyon or dell), *val* or *valle* (valley), *prado* (meadow), *montaña* (mountain), *cumbre* (peak), *cuesta* (ridge), *monte* (woods or tree-covered mountain), *paso* (mountain pass or ford in river), *sierra* (mountain range), *playa* (beach), *arena* (sand), *desierto* (desert), *malpaís* (badland), *loma* or *cerro* or *colina* (hill).

Frequently, Spanish name-givers gave diminutive forms to geographical words used, indicating either a small size comparatively or a particular fondness: hence Lomita, Cerrito, Vallecito, Montecito. The diminutive form usually adds *-ita* or *-ito* as a suffix (converting consonants like *c* or *g* to *qu-* or *gu*), though *-cito, -illo, -ejo,* etc., also occur. A curious variation on diminutive-making is with saints' names, like San Francisco, San Luis, and San Miguel: all of which were converted to Francisquito, Luisito, and Miguelito creeks. The Spanish intended the *arroyo* named to be considered small, not the saint himself!

A crudely made map by an explorer or traveler indicating various features or landmarks would be exceedingly helpful to anybody using it to follow the same route in the future. By attaching descriptive words—mainly adjectives—information could be conveyed: *Loma Prieta* (Dark Hill), *Arroyo Seco* (Dry Creek), *Sierra Nevada* (Snow-covered Mountains). In California, which has sections without rainfall or easily found water sources throughout much of the year, notations for *agua* could be vital. Thus there are numerous place-names connected with Agua: Caliente (hot or thermal pools), Dulce (sweet), Fria (cold), Hedionda (stinking, probably sulfurous), Tibia (warm). *Ríos* might be Hondo, Bravo, Amargoso, Colorado. Water words like *aguaje* and *aguajito, ojo* or *ojito*—for springs of fresh water—were also given to places. *Escondido* would refer to a "hidden" (hard to find) spring or creek. Many names originated with some wayfarer's naming of an arroyo campsite.

A remarkable feature on the landscape might be pointed out for bearings, such as a tall tree (Palo Alto), a cluster of white rocks (Piedras Blancas), the juncture of two rivers (Dos Rios). Or some overall characteristic, like the presence of some kind of animal or plant—possibly edible or dangerous—would make up a name: *Cañada de los Osos* (Bear Canyon), *Valle de los Conejos* (Rabbit Valley). Sometimes the descriptions were metaphorical, as in San Diego County's Ballena Valley, named for a hill that looked like a whale *(ballena);* it was too far inland and too

Some Words About Spanish Words

elevated to accommodate an actual one. Trees and plants were recorded: Los Alamos (poplar or cottonwood trees), Sausalito (small willow grove), Los Pinos (pines), Las Encinas (live oaks), Los Robles (deciduous oaks), Fresno (ash tree), Palos Verdes (green branches, or the paloverde shrub), Aliso (alder, but in California the word usually means sycamore).

Warnings can be conveyed as in Lomas Muertas ("dead" or dry hills), *Río Amargoso* (a river whose alkaline water tastes bitter), or the once-prevalent *Salsipuedes* (get-out-if-you-can). Actually, few early descriptive place-names used eloquent or flattering words. (Buena Vista is about as good as they got.) Explorers were brief and to the point in descriptive geographical names, bypassing the compliments that later were gladly taken up by the real-estate boosters, who would be responsible for Spanish place-names like Chula Vista and Loma Linda (Handsome View and Pretty Hill) or Asilomar (Refuge-by-the-Sea).

Dramatic. These essentially "tell stories" by compressing events into several words. They may contain an observation of some peculiarity (usually involving humans)—such as *Cañada Verruga*, where the local resident was unusually warty. Or they may record a happening: the Portola soldiers' killing of a seagull (Gaviota) and, later on, a lean bear (Oso Flaco). Dramatic place-names can be comic, tragic, odd, or simply matter-of-fact and on-the-record. They are conferred by blunt travelers in a hurry to get somewhere else or by busy newcomers—each noting down or remembering something significant to them. California's best name suppliers of this type were the Spanish soldiers and Indian fighters, and, later on, the inventive Yankee gold miners. Both tended toward the macabre: like *Calaveras* (skulls) with the former, when they encountered human skeletons—the remains of an Indian battle (in Calaveras River)—or ceremonial objects (in Calaveras Creek in Alameda County); Deadman Creek and Bloody Island with the latter. Many of their dramatic name creations often stayed in usage because they were, and are, provocative, strange, and memorable.

Commemorative. A place-name was given to honor, impress, please, placate, or simply recall and record somebody mortal—or often, in the case of Spanish place-namers, immortal. More than any other type, these names contain an element of incantation—as though the place-namers were requesting benevolent supervision or protection of the premises. (There may even have been a ceremonial christening if the place's importance warranted it.)

The largest number by far of Hispanic place-names in California fit into this category. Geographical features, settlements, and streets commemorate people of the past: explorers, priests, governors, military men, gracious señoras, rancheros. Some recall Indians good and bad, as well as Mexican *bandidos.*

The great majority, however, are the religious names —the Sans and Santas in particular. They are the male and female forms of "saint." (San, though, is actually a contraction of *Santo,* used in names like Santo Domingo.) The Spanish and Mexican explorers and colonists were religious and often followed the convention of giving sacred names to places discovered or soon to be settled, occasionally combining them with a geographical generic term like *río, arroyo, cañada,* or *laguna*—plus the useful *de.* This eagerness to commemorate and venerate led to confusing duplications in place-names honoring favored saints. For example, Santa Rosa appears in such widely separated and distinctive locales as an offshore island, a city and creek in

Sonoma County, a mountain range stretching between Riverside and San Diego counties, an Indian reservation near Palm Springs, and an arroyo with surrounding hills near Santa Barbara. (St. Rose of Lima, a Dominican, was popular because she was the first, and for a long time only, female saint created in the New World.)

Other saints' names ended up being utilized for a variety of purposes within the same area. San Gabriel, starting out as the name for a Franciscan mission commemorating one of heaven's archangels, spread out to encompass a mountain peak, then the whole range, a river, a canyon, a dam, a valley, and the town that grew up close to the mission.

Whenever two saints had the same Christian name, each could be further identified by role, place of origin, or work: such as San Luis Obispo and San Luis Rey de Francia (St. Louis the Bishop, or King of France), San Juan Bautista and San Juan Capistrano (St. John the Baptist, or of Capistran), San Francisco de Asis and San Francisco Solano (St. Francis of Assisi, or of Solano).

Most English equivalents of saints' names are similar to the Spanish forms. Mateo is Matthew; Marcos, Mark; Lucas, Luke; Juan, John; Jose, Joseph; Miguel, Michael; Felipe, Philip; Rafael, Raphael; Vicente, Vincent; Carlos, Charles; Antonio, Anthony; Pablo, Paul; Simeon, Simon; Pedro, Peter; Fernando, Ferdinand; Jacinto, Hyacinth; Benito, Benedict; Ines, Agnes; Catalina, Catherine; Ana, Anne; Ysabel, Elizabeth. And Santiago is actually a saint's name too, for St. James. The name got contracted during the Spaniards' campaign against their Moorish overlords. Since St. James was their patron saint, they cried out *"Santiago!"* as they launched their attacks.

There were several Santa Marias or St. Marys. But usually when the Virgin Mary appeared in a place-name, it was given to commemorate one of her many manifestations and was as *Nuestra Señora de* ——— (Our Lady of ———). In different guises, such as the Mexicans' idolized *Virgen* de Guadalupe, she served as the patroness for special needs, and exploring and founding priests had many anniversaries to remember her by.

Transported.   These place-names were brought from somewhere else, usually geographical locations that meant something to the place-namers, who may have felt nostalgic or may have intended that the new locale live up to the reputation or merits of the original. Various cities and towns in Spain and Mexico received California namesakes: Alhambra, Cordova, Malaga, Almaden, Cadiz, Sonora, Zamora. There are also numerous names "transported" from literary works or legends—the prime example being California itself. It was featured in a popular Spanish novel of the 1500s as a legendary island of riches. Many rather Hispanic-looking place-names given after the American takeover were brought in by American settlers. Arcadia, Pasadena, Saratoga, and San Marino are among them. Few are genuinely Spanish.

Contrived.   These consist of hybrid, manufactured, or abbreviated place-words that may have stories behind them. Others originated simply because the place-namers liked the sound and appearance of a proposed name; it did not matter to them that it was meaningless. After Spanish names again became customary, even fashionable, new place-names were contrived to "look Spanish." During the railroad-building and land-selling "boom" years of the last part of the nineteenth century, when hundreds of names were urgently required for railroad stations and sidings, for subdivided land-tract settlements, and new post offices, some very curious and amusing fake-Hispanic titles were given. The same phenomenon goes on now in the street-naming of some of the Spanish-style planned communities in suburbia, which sometimes require exclusively Hispanic-looking titles to maintain the right aura.

If you can't find particular place-words in a Spanish-English dictionary, consider these explanations:

- The word may be archaic or obscure, slang, or strictly regional or dialectal—beyond your dictionary's scope.
- It might not be properly spelled. This actually happens often, because consistency in spelling was rare in past centuries, among Hispanic Californians as well as foreigners or other Americans (who often did not know Spanish and just wrote what they heard). An error on some map or document could be perpetuated and finally officially "frozen."
- It could be an Indian word, either native to California or brought in from elsewhere.
- It might be a Spanish surname or personal name.
- It could be a word from another Romance language, like French or Italian; or a name from literature or legend; or a transported place-name.
- It may be a pseudo-Spanish name: a euphonious fake or even some name-maker's little joke.

The following chapters, all relating to periods in California history, will show how time, place, circumstances, and people combined to produce a cornucopia of Spanish place-names in California.

Naming by Sea

AS NAME AND IMAGE, California began as just another golden dream. The most alluring place-names ever contrived are those for the promised lands; idyllic places that offer peace and plenty, a life of ease, perpetual youth, and vast riches. Such paradises are portrayed as an eternal life hereafter, like the Christians' heaven. Or they may be rumored to exist on earth, and to be found by a fortunate few; or conceived as a utopia, an ideal community yet to be achieved by mortals.

Believing in the make-believe makes life's drudgeries and sorrows bearable. But the promise of paradise can also motivate ambitious or idealistic people to go forth and try to find or found it. To many generations of seekers, California has been all three types of enticing, never-never lands: a tangible, sensuous, earthly domain; a future society awaiting perfect creation; and a means of entering God's immortal kingdom. For almost five centuries, explorers, missionaries, pioneering settlers, and other immigrants have repeatedly sought to enter California—with variable outcomes.

What became the real geographical domain of California started out as a fictional place concocted by a Spanish writer named Garci Ordonez de Montalvo in a bestseller of the early sixteenth century. *Las Sergas de Esplandián* (Esplandian's adventures) introduced a terrestrial paradise called California. This wondrous island east of the Indies, possessing great wealth in precious metals and pearls, was protected by tall rocky cliffs and by its sole inhabitants: Amazon-like black women who were fierce, ardent, and beautiful—and who wore gold armor and rode wild beasts. The Spanish reading public found the place irresistibly attractive. (Oddly enough, the origin of this important place-name got lost for several centuries. Speculation ended in 1862 when the literary scholar Edward Everett Hale happened upon Montalvo's novella, shifting the search then to linguistics, to how he happened to contrive the name. Montalvo has been commemorated by a town in Ventura County—a railroad stop. It is also the name of a luxurious estate in Saratoga once owned by banker-politician James D. Phelan, now a center for the fine arts.)

Spaniards seemed more susceptible than other Europeans to believing in fabulous territories, probably because of their nation's already sensational New World experiences. Ponce de Leon, De Soto, and Coronado, hearing rumors of great cities of gold, launched large expeditions to search for El Dorado, Quivira, Cibola. Doubtless hoping to get rid of these greedy and ruthless invaders, wily Indians told tales of vast treasurehouses well beyond their own lands.

Naming by Sea

In vain quests for these gloriously rich places in North America, early Spanish explorers traversed, discovered, mapped, and named a *terra* no longer labeled *incognita.* The unknown was becoming known.

In Mexico, conquistador Hernan Cortes did find gold and silver, gems and dark-skinned slaves, and a New World smorgasbord of foods and spices, and he sent back generous samples to the Spanish court. But the loot from the conquest of the Aztec empire did not satisfy either his wishful dreams or the avid demands of the Spanish treasury for more.

So in 1534 Cortes sailed off to colonize the mysterious "island" to the northwest of New Spain (Mexico) that was already being called California. His colony, close to the southern tip, near present-day La Paz, soon foundered because the new settlers expected to reap the riches, even obtain basic provisions, without having to work at all. This, in a harsh, arid land where the aborigines searched incessantly for edibles. Cortes, disgraced and bankrupt, returned to his homeland in defeat, an outcast like others who had furnished fortunes to Spain's royalty and ruling classes. Their own earthly Edens—rent by savage rivalries and power struggles—were short-lived.

Early maps portrayed *Baja* (Lower) California as an island. Mariners first traveled along its eastern shore, opposite the Mexican coast. They came to a wide river delta at the northern end of the Gulf of California (also known as the Sea of Cortez) and observed the torrential flow of water laden with reddish silt: thus *El Río Colorado* (Red River). In future reconnaissance voyages, Ulloa showed that this California place was an island, and Alarcon sailed some distance up the Colorado River—and therefore is sometimes considered the true discoverer of Alta California. Still, many Spaniards wished to believe it was an island, and maps often portrayed it as such, inserting a purely mythical waterway that led from the western or Pacific side of California into the interior of the continent, possibly to the Colorado River. This Strait of Anian, which of course was wide, deep, and navigable, would furnish easy access to those ever-alluring cities of gold that nobody had located as yet.

Like the other European maritime and colonial powers, Spain also wanted to find a Northwest Passage that would link the Atlantic Ocean to the Pacific—that gigantic ocean which Balboa had named *El Mar del Sur,* the southern sea. The Spaniards continued to use this name for several centuries, ignoring the Portuguese Magellan's new appellation, *Océano Pacífico,* following the first circumnavigation of the world. Their experience had shown it was scarcely pacific.

The Spaniards began to conduct various searches toward the north for a conveniently placed waterway that would be a passage for further conquest of North America as well as a route for transporting treasures from the Pacific area directly back to Spain without requiring an overland journey across New Spain or the perilous voyage around the Horn.

Juan Rodriguez Cabrillo, a Portuguese navigator in the service of Spain, was the first explorer to venture beyond the west coast of Baja California itself and travel northward along the coast of what became known as Alta California. Commissioned to locate Anian, Cabrillo and his crew set out in two caravels in 1542. They named islands, bays, mountain ranges, and capes or points along the way. Occasionally they anchored in natural harbors and went ashore to get fresh water and food. Usually they were greeted in a friendly manner by the natives—which started the California Indians' unfortunate early reputation for docility. Trinkets were exchanged for provender, and the Spaniards gave names to various rancherias there.

Cabrillo sailed perhaps as far north as Monterey Bay, when adverse winter weather sent the boats southward. They retreated to an island off the Santa Barbara coast—probably the one now known as San Miguel—and there Cabrillo died from an infected broken arm. Obeying his dying captain's instructions, the pilot Ferrelo continued the expedition when the weather improved. The Spaniards probably got up to the Rogue River outlet but then turned back, without having found Anian.

Later mariners fared no better. And however attractive parts of Alta California had seemed to Cabrillo's men, the region fizzled as a prospect for conquest and colonization. Spain's rulers concentrated on holding together their far-flung New World possessions while warring with neighbors and trying to settle political strife at home. Besides protecting vessels carrying precious cargoes from Peru and Mexico on their way to Spain, however, the Spanish fleet was developing a lucrative trade with the Orient across Pacific sea lanes from Acapulco to the Philippine Islands in the annual Manila galleon voyages.

The passages of these treasures on the western coastline of the Americas naturally attracted privateers and pirates of many nationalities—including the clever and notorious Francis Drake in his *Golden Hinde*. After sacking several Spanish ports in 1579, he went north and roamed the Alta California coast. Deciding to return to England via the Pacific, he took his ship into a sheltered bay and careened it for extensive repairs. During the month spent there, he socialized with the Indians and nailed up a brass plate on which was engraved a brief report of Drake's stay as well as an official claim to this domain, named *Nova Albion* (New England, in Latin), for England.

On his return, having completed the second global circumnavigation in history and bringing back considerable spoils and information, Drake was knighted by Queen Elizabeth. Afterwards, he and other English navigators were occupied elsewhere (as in defeating the Spanish Armada) and therefore neglected to follow up this potentially valuable land claim. The site of his California visit is usually held to be the small bay east of Point Reyes and thirty miles north of the Golden Gate, now called Drake's Bay. It became known to sailors and cartographers as *La Bahía de San Francisco* (Bay of St. Francis), named by the Spanish navigator Cermeno, whose Manila galleon was shipwrecked there in 1595. The barren Farallon Islands *(Los Farallones),* thirty miles due west of Golden Gate, were visited and marked on charts as rocky hazards to mariners.

Meanwhile, the huge natural *puerto* or port of San Francisco—encompassing over four hundred square miles of water, with further inlets to California's interior—apparently went unseen and unentered by any mariners for several centuries. Had the astute Drake visited it, as some historians have asserted, he surely would have induced England to seize and settle it quickly, disregarding any vague Spanish claims to the whole Pacific Coast of North America.

Prevailing winds and the Japanese current propelled the Manila galleons back across the Pacific along a latitude ending close to northern California's westernmost promontory, *Cabo* (Cape) Mendocino (named after Mendoza, an early viceroy of New Spain). From there the Spanish shipmasters headed southward, hoping to make Acapulco without mishap. For their bearings they used various landmarks, such as the tall Santa Lucia Mountains (part of the Coast Range), which had first been named *Sierra Nevada* by Cabrillo.

After a long and difficult voyage across the Pacific in heavily laden vessels, tempest-tossed and suffering invariably from the horrors of scurvy, the Spanish sailors made poor defenders. In coves in Baja California and along the western coast of Mexico, freebooters' ships waited, poised to plunder the passing galleons of their Oriental treasures. Clearly, it was in Spain's interest to make California safe for commerce.

The first genuine California land promoter entered then: the merchant-turned-mariner named Sebastian Vizcaino. Already involved in the Manila trade and occupied with ventures like pearl fishing in Baja, he was hired by Spanish authorities to take an official exploratory trip up the coast of California. He was asked to make detailed maps and to locate a few suitable harbors where Spanish settlements could be started to provide water, fresh food, shelter, and a much-needed rest to the debilitated crews returning from the Orient, before they undertook the last leg of their year-long, round-trip excursion.

In 1602, outfitted with three ships, Vizcaino commenced his California reconnaissance. In Alta California he made his first stop at a bay visited a half century before by Cabrillo, who had called it *Bahía de San Miguel*. Disregarding orders telling him to use any place-names previously given by earlier voyagers, Vizcaino renamed it to honor *San Diego de Alcalá* (St. Didacus of Alcala), the patron saint of his expedition; also the name of his flagship. And as San Diego Bay it is known today.

Cabrillo and other mariners had bestowed numerous names for geographical features, and these were well described in ships' logs and clearly depicted on charts. Most were renamed, however, by the industrious Vizcaino. Eager to be put in charge of colonizing California, he apparently wanted all of his activities to show in the form of place-names of his own devising. Whenever and wherever they went ashore, Vizcaino "took possession" of the land they stood upon, claiming it for Spain—even though it obviously belonged already to the Indians, groups of whom frequently came out to greet the white men, little suspecting what schemes lay in the offing.

Padre Antonio de la Ascension, one of several friars taken along on the voyage to serve as chaplains and physicians, kept a detailed journal of the nine-month expedition —which included horrendously graphic accounts of the scurvy that beset most of the crew. Many died. During one pleasant sojourn on shore, Vizcaino honored his Carmelite friars by naming a river emptying into the Pacific *Río Carmelo.* They conducted a Mass there, and another one beneath a huge spreading oak tree at a bay to the north that the captain called *Bahía de Monterey,* to honor his sponsor, the Count of Monterey, the current viceroy.

A religious fellow, Vizcaino primarily selected commemorative place-names with saints' names, usually to mark one whose feast day fell at the time of discovery, doubtless trusting in their spiritual intercession at improving his chances of being selected Alta California's first *gobernador* or governor. Many coastal names in existence today came from Vizcaino: *puntas* (points) like *Los Santos Reyes, Año Nuevo, La Limpia Concepción, Pinos* (commemorating the Three Holy Kings, the New Year of 1603, the Immaculate Conception of Mary, and the pine-tree covered promontory at the southern tip of Monterey Bay). He named, or renamed, some of the offshore islands, calling them Santa Barbara, San Clemente, Santa Catalina, San

Nicolas. (All other coastal islands that he named were re-named later.) He also originated the name for the Santa Barbara Channel *(Canal de Santa Bárbara),* used in later settlements there. And he renamed Cabrillo's Sierra Nevada with his own *Sierra de Santa Lucía.* Cabrillo's almost poeti-cally descriptive *Bahía de los Fumos y Fuegos* (Bay of Smoke and Fires)—where Indians on the shore apparently had set the brush to flame—was turned into *Bahía de San Pedro:* San Pedro Bay today. (Its Cabrillo Beach would at least offer a remembrance of his brief visit there.)

The place that most impressed Vizcaino was Monterey Bay, a *puerto famoso* (famous or worthy port) "shaped like an O." He judged the area ideal for future settlement. It had, he claimed, abundant timber for both buildings and ships, plenty of fresh water, a pleasant climate, a perfectly protected harbor for anchoring vessels.

Alas for the ambitious Vizcaino. In spite of all his vigorous discoveries and some years of conferences and campaigning through correspondence, the colonization plan went for naught. Spain, embroiled elsewhere, declined to exert further effort and expense on Alta California. Why should she? The northern part of New Spain—known as *Pimería Alta,* consisting of present-day places like Sonora, Arizona, and New Mexico—and even the Baja California peninsula had begun to be colonized by missionaries and soldiers, partly to pacify the ferocious tribes like the Apaches and Yaquis. These provinces had proven more nuisance than asset, except in places where gold and silver were mined. There was no reason to believe that Alta Cali-fornia would be worth such trouble and expense, particu-larly since no returned mariner ever reported that Indians wore decorations of gold, silver, or gems, indicating a natural wealth with strong appeal to the Spanish treasury.

California waited for 167 years before showing now

promise to paradise-seekers. And of course Spanish settlement did come in time, to place innumerable names upon California's terrain. Later Spanish voyagers would bestow still more names on the thousand-mile coast. And many landsmen—explorers, priests, colonists, and official name givers—would also provide coastal features with Hispanic names. Many of the first-given ones were changed, sometimes to new Spanish names but more often to new English ones, or to English translations.

Toward the end of 1769, that first fateful year of Spanish colonization and exploration by land (to be covered in the following chapter), the magnificent San Francisco Bay—its existence heretofore unsuspected—would be found. And six years later Juan Manuel de Ayala, aided by his pilot Jose de Cañizares, under instructions from the viceroy of New Spain would locate the mile-wide entrance to the bay (named the Golden Gate by the American John C. Fremont in the next century).

The first boat to enter San Francisco Bay was the small redwood dugout *cayuco* built at Monterey as a launch for Ayala's *San Carlos*. Piloted by Canizares and bucking the strong push of the outgoing tide, it arrived within the bay itself on August 5—to be joined the day after by the larger vessel. Their first anchorage was at Angel Island, which they named *Isla de los Ángeles*. Ayala was handicapped by a gunshot wound in his foot; so he stayed on board much of the time while Canizares and the crew went about on various shores. At one place they noticed a group of weeping Indians, apparently terrorized by the very sight of these white men and their "houses with wings." They named the cove *Los Llorones* (the weepers). A large island was called *Isla de los Alcalaces* (Pelican Island). (Later on, in 1847, when the town of

Yerba Buena got its name changed to San Francisco, the discarded name was given to this *Alcatraces,* which was then passed on in a singular form, Alcatraz, to a small rocky protruberance in the middle of the bay—which one day would achieve notoriety as the Federal penitentiary.) The white cliff where a *castillo* or fortress would be built was named *Cantil Blanco.* (Worn down by the Americans later building Fort Winfield Scott—now Fort Point—the tip of this peninsula juts out into the Golden Gate directly below the Golden Gate Bridge.) A large inlet in the north-western arm of the bay was recorded on their charts as *Bahía de Nuestra Señora del Rosario la Marinera,* which seems the source of Marin County's name. For about six weeks, the Spanish mariners sailed around the immense virginal puerto, taking different anchorages while they sounded the depths and made charts and named geographical features. "It is not a port, but a whole pocketful of ports," Ayala concluded.

Ayala's exploration was one part of a three-pronged naval expedition. The other two captains, Bruno de Hezeta and Juan Francisco de la Bodega y Cuadra, went farther north: one to go as far as Nootka Sound, discovering the Columbia River on the way; the other to find and name Trinidad Bay, probably also putting in at a small harbor named afterwards, in his honor, Bodega Bay.

Many of California's bays have Hispanic titles: San Diego, San Francisco, Monterey, San Pedro, Santa Barbara, Santa Monica; among smaller bays, Bodega, Lunada, Morro, Trinidad. Of the eight Channel Islands, only one—Anacapa—is non-Hispanic. Along the coastline remain many Spanish-derived names for puntas: Points Ano Nuevo, Avisadero, Buchon, Cavallo (from *caballo* or horse), Conception, Delgada, Goleta, Gorda, Lobos (from the term *lobos marinos*

—sea wolves, the Spanish alternative to our sea lions), Loma, Lopez, Medanos, Pescadero, Piedras Blancas, Pinos, Pitas, Purisima, Reyes, Rincon, San Mateo, Sur.

Many points of land have long histories. The great English seafarer George Vancouver sailed into California ports several times during the early 1790s on his official explorations along the Pacific Northwest coast for the British crown. Despite Spain's decree prohibiting the entry of foreign vessels in Spanish ports, Vancouver was graciously received by most officers and priests in the California colony. As tributes to men he particularly liked, Vancouver named, or renamed, various California points: three for mission priests—Fermin (to honor Fermin Francisco de Lasuen, *padre-presidente* of the Franciscan missions and Junipero Serra's successor); Dumetz (later pruned to Dume) and Vicente, co-padres at Mission San Buenaventura; and three for the *comandantes* of the Monterey, San Francisco, and San Diego presidios—Arguello, Sal, and Zuniga. Vancouver also originated Point Arena, which he called *Barro de Arena* (sand bar).

Point Bonita across from San Francisco evolved from *Punta de Bonete* (Priest's Bonnet Point, because it had three tips). San Diego's *Punta de los Muertos* (Deadman's Point, so called because a ship's crew had buried victims of an epidemic there inside the harbor) was erased when the site was chosen for New Town. On narrow Point Loma peninsula that protects San Diego Bay a smaller side point juts out into the strait. It was once known as *Punta de Guijarros* (Cobblestone Point) because Spanish sailors stopped to take on rocks as weights. A Spanish fort was built there using the name. Today, suitably, it is called Ballast Point. Dana Point in Orange County, just north of a new yacht harbor, fittingly remembers Richard Henry Dana, author of *Two Years Before the Mast,* that classic

American account of life in Spanish California in the early 1830s, as experienced by a Yankee. On leave from Harvard to work as a supercargo (the word comes from the Spanish *sobrecargo*) in a Boston ship, he recorded the way that the dry cattle hides from the local ranchos were delivered to his vessel anchored in the small port then called San Juan because of its proximity to Mission San Juan Capistrano. One by one, these stiff "leather dollars"—the rancheros' main currency—were hurled, or sailed, from this point's high cliff down to the men waiting on the rocky beach below, who would catch or retrieve them and pile them into a launch.

We have kept Cape Mendocino (which is one of California's earliest Spanish place-names still in use), and now have Cape Vizcaino too. Cabrillo, whose many place-names were replaced by Vizcaino's, except perhaps for Cape San Martin and Point Mugu, has been honored by two points called Cabrillo. But the most impressive tribute to him is the Cabrillo National Monument placed at the southern end of Point Loma, with a commanding view of the land and sea which he was the first European ship captain to behold.

Names Sacred and Profane

T HE THREAT OF COMPETITION usually arouses
sudden interest in a possession previously ignored or
uncoveted by others. In 1768 Spain belatedly turned
her attention to Alta California. The Russian fur trappers
with their Aleut Indian assistants, moving south from
Alaska to obtain prized sea otter pelts, began to poach on
the Spanish preserves. Now that Canada was theirs, the British fur traders examined the Pacific Northwest and were
reminded of Drake's old claim on California. The Dutch
and the French likewise showed curiosity about the vast
area supposedly under Spanish dominion but not yet
colonized.

Carlos III of Spain decided now to occupy Alta California, to prevent other nations from doing so. Spain had
never wanted cold-climate territories, and in the past Cali-

fornia's coast had displayed to mariners a moderate temperature range that Hispanic settlers would be able to endure. Nothing was known of the interior regions, but once the Spaniards had established a foothold or two along the coast, explorations could be made to the east, beyond the coastal sierra. The inland area might be revealed as desert wastes, or a series of jagged mountains, or diabolical badlands—as much of northern New Spain seemed to be. But here and there it could have fertile lands suitable for cultivation and cattle raising, so that this faraway colony might someday manage to support itself. The urgent quest for paradise and precious metals was dimming. Spanish administrators were becoming more cautious and practical.

Jose de Galvez, the *Visitador-General* (inspector-general) of New Spain, was appointed to oversee this colonization of *Nueva* (New) California province. He realized that it would be necessary to involve a group of men already well experienced in setting up posts in the wilderness. Besides the conquistadores and their armies of soldiers, a very different type of enterprising person had come early to the New World: men drawn not to material plunder of the Indians' realms but to creating within them earthly utopias in which Christianized heathens, *neófitos,* or neophytes, would learn civilizing skills while preparing for their reception in heaven. These priests and friars, *padres* and *frailes,* belonged to the powerful mendicant orders within the Roman Catholic Church: Jesuits, Franciscans, Dominicans, Carmelites. They undertook perilous journeys and were often intrepid, superb explorers, like the Jesuits' Father Eusebio Kino. Risking martyrdom, they manned lonely missions in the harsh northern reaches of New Spain, surrounded by hostile tribes.

Sustained by a proselytizing fervor and radiating *caritas,* true Christian charity, these hardy frontier evangelists

　　　　　　　　　　　　Names Sacred and Profane

were the vanguard of Western civilization. They transformed the Amerindians' hemisphere. Preaching Christ's Gospel on its simplest level, they gave gifts of beads and cloth. Most of the missionaries had received classical educations in European colleges. Now they squatted in the dirt and unrolled amazing pictures that depicted the Virgin Mary with her infant Jesus, or horrific visions of the agonies of hell awaiting the unbaptized. They allowed the *gentiles* (the pagans) to examine small statues of saints and the crucifix *(la santa cruz)* on which the Son of God was suspended.

Such padres had proved to be Spain's cheapest and most effective means of subduing and controlling the tribes, particularly those that were initially friendly and basically tractable. A good priest did far better than an entire garrison of rough and unruly *soldados de cuera* — ("leatherjacket soldiers") who got their name from the thick, arrowproof vests made from layers of buckskin or hides.

The colonization technique was patterned after previous expansions of New Spain. Three distinct divisions — military, religious, and civilian — theoretically and ideally cooperated in settling a region and pacifying its aborigines. The soldiers, supervised by a *comandante,* erected a presidio. With their help and protection, the padres — usually there were two at each place — built the mission, which contained a chapel, simple living quarters, and workrooms in which neophytes learned useful crafts. Eventually, civilian settlers, including the soldiers' families, would come to live in nearby pueblos. The government's administration in New Spain provided the wherewithal — transportation, food, clothing, and other supplies — supplemented by money from the missionary orders' Pious Fund.

The earliest settlements used whatever building materials could be quickly gathered. Usually forests of heavy timber were remote from these localities, so branches, sticks, and brush were assembled, bound together with rawhide, and plastered with mud; a thatched roof was made from reeds and bulrushes. Forts and missions at first resembled the natives' huts. Permanent structures were put up later, when there was time and plenty of human labor available from the neophytes. The fundamental building material was the sun-baked adobe brick, made from clay soil.

Each base of operation was laid out according to official instructions as to-building plans and dimensions, and the size and types of outlying lands. Presidios, including permament armaments and barracks, were surrounded by stockades or *palizadas*. Missions were designed as self-contained rectangular units that could keep its resident Indians within, and unwelcome Indians—and soldiers—out. Each pueblo was to be built around an open plaza, with its church at one end and the settlers' *casas* all facing the square. There were lots designated for growing vegetables and for communal pasturelands.

In July of 1768 Jose de Galvez established headquarters near La Paz in Baja California, from which he intended to launch this *Expedición Santa*. He began to plan the details of colonization. A skillful executive, he set up the stages so that, with any luck, the Sacred Expedition would succeed. If California can claim an original founding father, it would be Galvez. Yet he never actually set foot in the colony he was carefully creating. He prepared the harbor at San Blas along the Mexican coast, east and south of Baja, to serve as the supply base for Nueva California. He arranged for three ships and crews to transport supplies needed in establishing two sets of missions and presidios, the first to be at San Diego Bay, the second at Vizcaino's much-praised Monterey Bay. He obtained several dozen Catalonian soldiers—crack riders, ropers, and blunderbuss shooters—to become California's first colonists. He got permission to collect neophyte assistants, pack mules, horses, cattle, and more supplies from the missions on both sides of the Baja California chain established during the previous century by the Jesuits but recently turned over to the Franciscan Order.

In his most historically significant move, Galvez selected two supremely capable leaders to carry out the expedition itself in its secular and sacred aspects: its co-mandante, Don Gaspar de Portola, age forty-six; and the padre-presidente, Fray Junipero Serra, fifty-six. Together they would carry the sword and the cross into Nueva California. Certainly, had their purpose failed, the history of the state would have been very different indeed, for Spain probably would have withdrawn her intention to colonize California.

In the spring of 1769 four separate parties, consisting in all of several hundred men, set out for San Diego Bay. Two went by sea and two by land. The ships *San Carlos* and *San Antonio*—both to play important roles in the Spanish colony—set out first and arrived first, their crews nearly wiped out by scurvy and shipboard contagion. The two overland expeditions, the first headed by Captain Fernando Rivera y Moncada, the second led by Portola and accompanied by Serra, arrived toward the end of May. Upon what is now called Presidio Hill they hastily put up the presidio and the beginnings of a mission. When the third supply ship, the *San José*—named for the patron saint of the expedition—failed to arrive, Comandante Portola sent the *San Antonio* off to San Blas to bring back more supplies. He had hoped to sail north to Monterey Bay, there to establish the second part of the fledgling colony. Now he decided to take a large contingent overland, a distance of about five hundred miles, and try to find the site from the landward side. In doing so, the Spaniards would learn a great deal about the terrain.

The historic Portola expedition is the earliest and richest source of place-names ever given by explorers in California. From the four diaries or reports submitted, historians and toponymists have located the main routes of this ambitious journey. Some names have vanished entirely; others left various traces; still others remain almost exactly as given. The trail blazed through the wilderness stretching from San Diego Bay to San Francisco Bay became the main public road—*El Camino Real* (the Royal Road or the King's Highway)—for the numerous Spanish settlements that would branch off from it in the coming years. Following the Portola expedition, one can begin to sense how place-names are created and connected to an unfamiliar land.

• July 14, 1769. The Portola expedition departed from Presidio Hill at the newly founded settlement of San Diego de Alcala. The plan was to travel northward to Monterey Bay by skirting the coast, staying on the western side of the Coast Range that mariners had reported running alongside the Pacific, yet avoiding the beaches since sand dunes, estuaries, and lagoons would make passage slow and difficult. The party numbered over sixty men—most able-bodied, yet many not recovered from illness. There were officers—Fages, Rivera y Moncada, and Ortega—in charge of several dozen soldiers; an engineer-surveyor, Miguel Costanso, handling the charts and reckoning; two priests, Padres Juan Crespi and Francisco Gomez, to serve as chaplains and diarists; a few muleteers or *arrieros* and some neophytes from Baja to function as helpers and interpreters. Crespi's and Costanso's journals kept track of the various place-names proposed by both priests and soldiers.

• July 16. The party passed through a valley where live oaks grew close to a creek. They named it *Cañada de los Encinos.* A land-grant rancho there much later took the title *Los Encinitos,* and later still the settlement in the area became today's Las Encinitas.

Later on, the men camped at a small valley close to a lagoon, calling it *Cañada de San Alejo* (St. Alexius's Canyon). The spelling evolved into the present-day San Elijo Valley.

• July 20. Camped by a river. Since it was St. Margaret's feast day, the rio was called Santa Margarita. The name is still there for the river and canyon.

• July 21. The abundance of fragrant, pink wild roses in a vale reminded the Spaniards of the Rose of Castile. Nostalgically, they added *de los rosales* to the commemorative name *Cañada de Santa Praxedis.* Although the whole title has faded away, it was replaced by Las Flores Canyon, where a few wild roses still bloom.

• July 22. Padres Crespi and Gomez were permitted to baptize two dying Indian babies—thereby conducting the first baptismal rites in Nueva California (to Serra's everlasting sorrow, when he heard of it later, for he had yearned for that honor). The valley was called both *Los Bautismos* (the baptisms) and *Los Cristianitos* (the little Christians). The last one prevailed.

Farther along, Trabuco Creek and Canyon received their names from Portola's soldiers, who lost a blunderbuss here.

• July 27. A creek at this spot was named Santiago because it was close to St. James's feast day. A tributary of the Santa Ana River, it is still known as Santiago.

Next evening, the expedition camped by a large river which the padres christened *El Río del Dulcísimo Nombre de Jesus* (River of the Sweetest Name of Jesus). During their stay the men were subjected to a terrifying succession of earthquakes; so they added *de los temblores* to the already lengthy name. Portola's group were the first white men to experience one of California's notorious seismic dramas. The river eventually became known by the soldiers' preferred name, the Santa Ana.

• July 30. The expedition passed through an opening *(la habra)* in the hills. La Habra Valley and its town continue the spelling (which in modern Spanish has dropped the *h,* becoming *abra*).

Farther along, the men built a temporary bridge or *puente* by placing poles across an arroyo. The surrounding plains were then called *Llano de la Puente.* A land-grant title picked this up later. La Puente is now the name of a town and its surrounding hills.

• August 2. They stayed at another riverbank close to an Indian rancheria called Yang-Na. Because it was the Virgin Mary's feast day, Crespi named the river *El Río de Nuestra Señora la Reina de los Ángeles* (the River of Our Lady, the Queen of the Angels). The appendage *de Porciúncula* was attached because on this day priests at St. Francis's chapel-shrine at Porciuncula could grant communicants absolution. Since this power was also granted to traveling Franciscan friars, the padres used it when administering a special Mass for their companions. Close to the site of their ceremony California's largest city was founded in 1781. It picked up the long title to follow *El Pueblo de* ———. It was shortened in time to Los Angeles, ultimately to the abbreviated "L.A."

Scouting for the best way to cross the Santa Monica Mountains, the men came across large bubbling pools of liquid tar or *brea.* Periodically, the earth still shook with tremors and aftershocks. Even the travelers' Indian hosts seemed uneasy. Some men declared that the mountains they had to cross had volcanoes ready to erupt, for surely the brea was an underground stream of lava.

• August 5. The party finally crossed the barrier to the north, probably through Sepulveda Canyon or Pass (where the San Diego Freeway now runs). The first Europeans to behold the wide San Fernando Valley, they assigned to it the name *Valle de Santa Catalina de Bononia de los Encinos* (St. Catherine of Bononia's Valley of the Oaks). The town of Encino is just to the left of where they emerged from the mountains. Going northwest, they climbed the Santa Susana Mountains to head back toward the ocean. They found and named the Santa Clara River, and pursued its downward course to the Pacific.

• August 14. At the coast they came upon a large and friendly Indian rancheria. Costanso recognized it as Cabrillo's *Pueblo de las Canoas* (Canoe Town), so named because a flotilla of them had gone out to greet his boat. The natives had retained objects and tribal stories from that much earlier visit. The place probably had not changed much since 1542. Crespi named it *La Asunción de Nuestra Señora* (Our Lady's Assumption — or ascent to heaven) and noted that it would make an ideal spot for a future mission. ("The Indians here have no fault except that of being very nimble with their fingers," he said.) In 1782 Mission San Buenaventura was founded there, and the town that grew up around it is familiar to us now as Ventura.

• August 15. The party bedded down a few miles from a rancheria where all night long, apparently celebrating the Spaniards' arrival, the natives blew on reed flutes, keeping the tired travelers awake. The soldiers' name for the spot, *Los Pitos* (the whistles), has endured as Pitas Point.

• August 17. Here they encountered a group of Indians efficiently building a large seagoing canoe, using for caulking some brea obtained from a nearby pool. The Chumash were the only California Indians who took boats into the ocean, to trade with related groups who dwelled on the various offshore islands. (The largest and closest one had recently been visited by a Spanish ship from the Sacred Expedition, which had gone too far north. Since a padre had dropped a crucifix there, which an Indian returned, the island was called *Santa Cruz* (Holy Cross), a name which it still bears today.) Crespi called the boat-building community San Roque, but the religious name eventually gave way to the soldiers' choice, *Carpintería* (Carpenters' Shop).

• August 19. The expedition camped close to a large Indian settlement at a lagoon. The Chumash were the most prosperous of California's Indians because they had seafood in abundance, along with acorns and many other wild foods. Some of their rancherias contained as many as a thousand people. Given much fresh fish and other treats, Costanso remarked, "Nowhere had we met natives so affectionate and good-natured." They seemed ripe for conversion. The Portola party's place-name, *San Joaquín de la Laguna* (St. Joachim of the Lagoon), was replaced later by Santa Barbara when the presidio and mission by that name (picked up from Vizcaino's channel) were founded there.

• August 24. In spite of the priests' preference for the name San Luis, the area was afterwards known as *La Gaviota* to recall the seagull killed there by the soldiers. Today we have Gaviota Beach and Gaviota Pass.

• August 26. The local Indian chief had a game leg, so inevitably the soldiers called his place of residence *Cañada del Cojo* (Lame Man's Canyon)—a name that survives as Cojo Valley.

• August 27. An Indian stole a sword or *espada* from a soldier's belt, but his peers took it away from him and brought it back. Thus the village was called *Ranchería de la Espada,* now remembered in Espada Creek.

• August 28. Here the soldiers found many flints *(pedernales)* which they needed for their flintlock guns and for fire making. Their *Ranchería de los Pedernales* is now Pedernales Point.

• August 30. Wanting to avoid steep mountains along the coast, the men followed a river inland for a while. They called it *Río de Santa Rosa.* It later took the name from the mission founded alongside it: *Santa Inés* (variously spelled as *Inez, Ynés, Ynez*).

• August 31. The men stayed overnight next to a lagoon, where the native women entertained them by dancing. The soldiers were impressed. Some named the spot *Baile de las Indias.* Others called it *Laguna Graciosa:* whether for the gracefulness of the dancers or the attractiveness of the lagoon itself it is not known. The Graciosa epithet persisted, attaching itself eventually to a canyon and a ridge, then a nearby railroad station.

Next night they camped alongside a lake they called *Laguna Larga* (Long Lake) or *Laguna de San Daniel.* It is now known as Guadalupe Lake.

• September 2. While in a valley, the soldiers managed to kill a bear for their evening meal. It was lean but tasty. Padre Crespi awarded another of his holy names. Some men wanted the place to be called *Cañada de las Víboras* (Viper Canyon) because of its many snakes. But the name that endured was *Oso Flaco* (Lean Bear).

• September 4. Here the Spaniards arrived at an Indian settlement whose people were generous and gentle. The chief had a huge goiter or tumor on his neck, so the soldiers nicknamed him *El Buchón.* Although Crespi had named the rancheria San Ladislao, it was afterwards known, of course, as Buchon—continued today in Point Buchon.

• September 7. In a valley the men were mystified by many odd holes scratched into the ground. They soon saw that both bears and Indians dug there for edible roots or tubers. Although awed by their first view of grizzlies—*brutos ferocísimos*—several Catalonian soldiers went on a hunt. After many shots and considerable danger to themselves and their mounts, they bagged a large, ferocious bear to grill for dinner. This *Cañada de los Osos* (Bear Canyon) was remembered later as a source for food when the Spanish settlements were close to starving. The locale became the site of Mission San Luis Obispo, and its name continues in Los Osos Valley.

• September 8. Camping along a creek close to the ocean, the group admired the great, rounded (*morro*) rock at the bay's entrance. Thus, both Morro Rock and Morro Bay.

• September 13. Realizing that they were nearing the latitude given by Vizcaino for Monterey Bay, the Portola expedition tried to hug the coastline, although this meant hacking their way through the dense growth on the steep slopes of the Sierra de Santa Lucia. Having no local guides and certainly no maps of the area, they did not realize that they could have headed inland to the Salinas Valley and come out at the Monterey Peninsula, as later travelers did when going along El Camino Real.

• September 21. Arriving at a river, Crespi named it *Nacimiento,* believing that its source (one meaning of the word) was nearby. But a later expedition assumed that the title had been given to honor the Nativity. This was one of the few instances in which Crespi had selected a nonsacred geographical name!

Names Sacred and Profane

The group passed through a pleasant, oak-dotted valley nestled in the midst of the mountains. They named it *Los Robles*. A few years later it was selected as the site for the third mission, San Antonio de Padua.

Veering inland as they plodded northward through the rugged mountains, the expedition came to a desolate-looking place some miles south of a sluggish river. A few natives approached the men. Attempting conversation, Padre Crespi thought he heard the word *soledad* (solitude) and judged it a suitable name for the place and its Indians. The mission founded there later picked up his title: *Nuestra Señora de la Soledad*.

• September 26. The sluggish river was believed to be the Rio Carmelo that Vizcaino had named as it debouched on the sea at the Monterey Peninsula. But since they were unsure, Crespi called it *San Elizario* whereas the soldiers preferred *Río de Chocolate* because of its brownish color. It was later renamed Salinas River for its saline flats. With their bearings confused, their health poor, and their spirits low, the Portola party followed the river northwest. They eventually ended up at the coast, close to the latitude given for their objective.

• October 1. Looking at the coastline, they thought they recognized *Punta de Pinos*, but little else conformed with Vizcaino's description of Monterey Bay. (This was partly because they approached by way of the Salinas River to the north, rather than the Carmel River to the south.) The trees were twisted, poor for lumber. There were brackish lagoons, not pools or streams of fresh water as promised. Costanso and Crespi—good astrolabe reckoners both—mistrusted the old figures given for the place. Worse, this puerto was hardly famoso; it was really a barely protected roadstead filled with sand. Boats would have to anchor far from shore. And it was crescent-shaped anyway, not a large wide O as on the old map. Portola, tired and discouraged, called a meeting of the officers, who all decided that they had somehow missed Monterey during their inland trek, or else it still lay to the north.

• October 8. After a brief, well-deserved rest—during which a scouting party went south to reconnoiter but saw no sign of Monterey, only sheer cliffs overhanging the sea—the men moved inland again, following the upward course of the river they named *Río de Pájaro* (Bird River). The soldiers had been intrigued with a giant stuffed bird that looked like an eagle which the Indians had set upon the riverbank as a totem. Measuring its wingspan, they found it to be about seven feet. Pajaro River and Pajaro Valley are still there today.

A few days later, camping at a small lake, they constructed a makeshift fence of branches between the water and a small hill, to pen in the mules and horses at night so as to let most of the weary watchmen sleep. This *Laguna del Corral* later evolved into present-day Corralitos.

• October 18. Here another arroyo was named Santa Cruz. Close to it some years later the Mission Santa Cruz would be built, the start of the city of today. They also named another local river San Lorenzo, which is still there too.

In the area now known as Soquel (an Indian name), the Spaniards came upon stands of forest trees taller, straighter, and wider than any ever seen before. Amazed and admiring, they joined hands to measure the circumference of the largest trees. One could not be girded even by eight men. Portola's party was the first white group to behold such wonders. Unable to identify the trees, they simply called them *palo colorado,* literally meaning "red wood." These coastal redwoods, or *Sequoia sempervirens,* thrived from there as far as the northern reaches of Alta California.

• October 20. As they struggled northward through the Santa Cruz Mountains, trying to stay within sight of the sea (and hence the sought-for Monterey), the men suffered from the sores, weakness, and pains of scurvy as well as the increasing cold. Crespi remarked that they "missed the comfort of seeing the natives." As rain fell, they made a forlorn camp next to an arroyo. After a two-day rest almost everyone felt miraculously better. Their *Cañon de la Salud* (Good Health Canyon) is known as Waddell Creek today.

• October 27. Continuing its trek, the party spotted what appeared to be Vizcaino's *Punta de Año Nuevo* jutting from the shore. By now the officers were near certain that they had somehow missed Monterey but still hoped to locate another bay suitable for the second settlement if Monterey could not be found. Almost everyone was sick again; even the stalwart Portola had to be carried on a litter strapped to a mule. Seeking shelter, they occupied some huts in an abandoned Indian village on Purisima Creek. A few minutes later the soldiers ran out, crying, *"Las pulgas, las pulgas!"* Fleas had attacked them in force. (Indians normally cleaned house when bugs and garbage became unbearable simply by burning their dwellings. Here they had apparently fled.) The rancheria site of course acquired the name Las Pulgas; so did a rancho encompassing the area later on, in turn causing the name to creep into local names, such as the grandiloquent street-name Alameda de las Pulgas (Mall of the Fleas) in present-day San Mateo.

• October 31. The men made camp at a place called *Punta del Ángel Custodio* (Guardian Angel Point) by Crespi and *Punta de las Almejas* (Mussel Point) by the soldiers, who feasted on the abundant bivalves. (It is now called Pedro Point, having dropped its original "San.") When the expedition moved on, they traveled along the hills that rose steeply from the beach. The weather had turned dramatically clear, and from their new vantage point the men could view, unmistakably, the Farallon Islands to the west, and far in the northwest they could see Point Reyes and Cermeno's Bahia de San Francisco. It was obvious now that they had gone well past Monterey Bay. Portola, who knew that another presidio and mission were being planned for San Francisco Bay, whenever that would be located from the land, and when the time was ready, now determined to march onward to this quite visible goal and place the second settlement there instead of at the elusive Monterey.

• November 1. Sergeant Ortega was sent off with a few others to the north to scout out a route for the rest of the expedition. Meanwhile, a group of soldiers went into the hills to the west to hunt for deer. They soon returned, reporting that they had seen an amazing sight: a great sheet of water, perhaps a lake, to the east. Portola waited for Ortega's return. He revealed that he had been unable to proceed toward Point Reyes because a large body of water, an *estero,* blocked the northern route.

• November 4. The party was ready to move inland now and reconnoiter. Reaching the crest of a mountain (now believed to be Sweeney Ridge in present-day Pacifica), they looked upon the view that the hunters had described: an estuary or an "immense arm of the sea" lying to the east. Ortega's path had been halted by a bay, and this perhaps was a branch of it; so they were actually standing on a long peninsula. The vast spread of water, of course, was San Francisco Bay—not Cermeno's modest-sized bahia (now Drake's Bay), but the most impressive harbor or port ever devised by nature. Again Ortega was dispatched, this time to try to skirt the estero by heading southeast and then north. Encountering hostile Indians on the way, he got as far as the juncture with the westerly bay that had stopped him before—and saw that still another branch of this gigantic estero (San Pablo Bay) would make it difficult indeed to reach Point Reyes. Told by Indians that something—was it the Spanish ship *San José?*—lay in the harbor, he saw no sign of it.

• November 10. Portola, receiving Ortega's discouraging report, felt no thrill of pride over their discovery of San Francisco Bay. It seemed to him an immense and impassable watery barrier that prevented them from fulfilling Galvez's explicit orders to establish a presidio and a mission in the northern region. Their supplies by now were perilously low, and winter was upon them. Although Crespi seemingly realized that they had found a "very noble and very large harbor"—one that could accommodate all the ships of all the world's nations—they could do nothing about settling it now. Nobody had the strength to muster up any enthusiasm for new plans. Most of the men were undernourished, cold, exhausted, disgruntled, and very sick. They would have to go back and look for Monterey again to the south. Defeated in its goal, Portola's expedition began its return journey.

• December 9. They paused again at what was indeed Monterey Bay, still searching for signs that this was unequivocally Vizcaino's overpromoted port. "The best and most careful conclusion that we could come to is that Monterey has been lost or the land swallowed up," wrote Crespi. They planted two large, rough-hewn wooden crosses: one at the beach at Punta de Pinos, the other at the mouth of the Carmel River, to notify any mariners that might come this way, searching for them, that "the overland expedition from San Diego returned from this place, starving."

Then the sorry group retraced most of its steps south. They were glad for any food given to them by the Indians, for free or in exchange for articles of clothing or anything else of value. El Buchon and his people furnished acorn cakes and other native provender. Meanwhile, to make up the evening meal, almost every day a mule was slaughtered and barbecued in a pit. Experienced travelers now, and knowing far better where and how they were going, the men doubled their pace as they hurried back to the northernmost outpost of Spanish civilization—unsure whether anyone would still be there at San Diego to greet them.

They were less interested now in bestowing place-names, but they did make a few as they wended their way south.

• January 13, 1770. They camped at a valley which Crespi named *El Triunfo del Dulcísimo Nombre de Jesus* (the Triumph of the Sweetest Name of Jesus). It exists today in Los Angeles County's Triunfo Pass and Canyon. The expedition may also have traveled through Cahuenga Pass, the scene of future battles between Californios and governors, and also the scene of the Californios' surrender to the American general Fremont, which ended the War with Mexico. Apparently, too, the party crossed the San Gabriel Valley—another "first."

• January 24. The entire expeditionary force—there was not a man missing or dead—straggled into the new *Misión de San Diego de Alcalá* and the presidio. Unkempt, ill-clothed, and "smelling frightfully of mules" (as Portola put it), they were met by a disconsolate Fray Junipero Serra. Hearing that they had neither seen Monterey nor founded a presidio anywhere in the north, he told them,

"You come from Rome without having seen the Pope."
Serra had his own story of woes to tell of experiences in
San Diego (to be presented in the following chapter).

Portola's great march, however, scarcely proved futile.
Gone for six and a half months, the party had traversed
more than a thousand miles of Alta California. It had gathered much knowledge of its coastal regions and some of
the interior. Through Father Crespi's clear perception, it
had selected the sites for at least a dozen future missions.
And ironically, because the men had not found Monterey
Bay, they had discovered San Francisco Bay, the implica-
tions of which would soon be evident.

There was yet another vital outcome of the Sacred
Expedition. It concerns the soldiers themselves, many of
whom figured later in California history and place-naming.
The two senior officers, Lieutenant Pedro Fages and Captain Fernando Rivera y Moncada, soon became, in succession, comandantes and acting governors of Nueva California. Sergeant Jose Francisco Ortega—who sometimes is
called the true discoverer of San Francisco Bay—went on to
higher rank. Responsible and well-liked, he helped to establish several presidios and missions. He also founded California's notable Ortega family, which had a large rancho, *El
Refugio* (or *Nuestra Señora del Refugio*), north of Santa
Barbara. Both Refugio and Ortega appear in various local
place-names.

Among the regular soldados who had come north with
Serra and Portola from New Spain were the progenitors of
other worthy Californio families: Jose Raimundo Carrillo,
the brothers Bernardino and Juan Bautista Alvarado, Manuel Ramirez Arellano (later changed to Arellanes), Juan
Ismerio de Osuna, Jose Maria Soberanes, Juan Jose Domin-

guez, Jose Joaquin Espinosa, Mariano de la Luz Verdugo, Pedro Amador, and Jose Antonio Yorba. Their surnames appear in California place-names to mark indelibly places on the land eventually inhabited by these soldiers or their descendants, or to honor them. Thus we have Carrillo State Beach, the town of Alvarado, Soberanes Creek, Dominguez Hills, Espinosa Lake, Verdugo Canyon, Amador Valley and County, and the city of Yorba Linda.

Portola's soldiers—who seem to have differentiated themselves, at least later, as *soldados de cuera* (leather-jackets) or *soldados distinguidos* (distinguished), meaning Catalonians from Spain or from direct Spanish ancestry with military stature—were the first wave of colonists who came in on a tour of duty and ended up staying. California was regarded by New Spain as a rude and remote region. But to most of those who actually saw it, the territory was good and became their new homeland. Exiled there by assignment, economic necessity, or punishment, the soldiers and civilian settlers found opportunities that most of them would never have had in Spain or Mexico.

Portola's immediate successors in office, Fages and Rivera y Moncada, each had reason to explore regions in California that were unknown or barely known. They and their friar-companions, Crespi and Francisco Palou (who would spend his last years in Mexico writing a biography of Serra and the first history of California), and undoubtedly some of their soldiers, gave many a place-name in areas where they traveled. Fages briefly visited San Francisco Bay in 1770, and in 1772 undertook a tour of the East Bay area. On the first trip he was the first white exploration leader to see the Golden Gate entrance. On the second, he and Crespi traveled on the eastern side of San Pablo Bay, saw that they could not cross the Carquinez

Strait to go north, and so journeyed for some distance along Suisun Bay (called *Agua Dulce*) and the lower Sacramento River (named *Río de San Francisco*), aware that the water flowing into the bay was no longer brackish. They visited the slopes of Mount Diablo, at the head of the Diablo Range, and glimpsed an impressive mountain range in the distance (later to receive the name Sierra Nevada) as they began to head southward through the marshland in the San Joaquin Delta, "a labyrinth of lakes and tulares." *Tule,* that Aztec-derived word for the vegetation abounding in wet areas, was much used to describe swampy places, as Tulare—a place where bulrushes grow. They traversed part of what is now Contra Costa and Alameda counties before returning to Monterey.

Later in the year, Fages did considerably more exploring. Initially leaving San Diego to pursue a group of hostile Indians, he crossed the southern branch of the Coast Range into part of the Colorado Desert. On his way back to Monterey, he decided to take an alternate, more inland route than Portola's, and therefore was the first to find Cajon Pass in the San Bernardino Mountains, Tejon Pass in the Tehachapi Mountains, and Buena Vista Valley.

Rivera y Moncada, coming up from Baja California in 1774 to assume the post of comandante at Monterey, which was virtually the governorship, brought with him various supplies, including livestock, as well as some new soldiers and settlers. (Two men were founders of future dynasties, Francisco Salvador de Lugo and Vicente Ferrer Vallejo.) Obeying the viceroy's orders, he went off to locate sites for a presidio and mission at San Francisco Bay. He considered the place a dreary one, covered with hills and damp sand dunes, unfit for white habitation. On the way to and fro, he and Palou did set some names familiar today: San Andres Valley (now Andreas, the home of the notorious earthquake fault), San Bruno, Palo Alto (named for a tall tree, still a living landmark), and Las Llagas and San Francisquito creeks.

The most famous of all expeditions after the Portola one were the two undertaken by Juan Bautista de Anza, a third-generation officer in the Tubac area of New Mexico (near present-day Tucson). Responding to the viceroy's request that he try to reach the new Spanish settlements in California by going overland from the east—an ambition both he and his father before him had longed to fulfill—Anza and some thirty men, including the experienced explorer Padre Francisco Garces and an Indian guide named Tarabal from Mission San Gabriel, set off across Padre Kino's *Camino del Diablo* (Devil's Highway), a two-hundred-mile long trek through parched wasteland. Fording the Gila and Colorado rivers with the help of the Yuma Indians, whom Garces and Anza adroitly befriended, the group struggled through dunes, badlands, and waterless terrain in the Colorado Desert area of southeastern California. Reaching Borrego Valley in March of 1774, they saw the San Jacinto Mountains in the north. Knowing now that water and forage lay ahead, they crossed the desolate land, went through Coyote Canyon and the Royal Pass of San Carlos (an Anza name), and at last arrived at the San Gabriel Mission—much to the padres' amazement. Having proved that the route into California could be taken directly from Mexico, Anza returned in the following year, bringing with him 240 soldiers and colonists and hundreds of cattle: human and animal populations that would make all the difference to the survival and eventual well-being of the precarious Spanish colony.

Before returning to his post in New Mexico, Anza and

his padre-diarist, Pedro Font, made a lengthy exploration of the San Francisco Peninsula, completing the site-finding work that Rivera had failed to do. Then they took a route through the East Bay similar to Fages's journey four years before, except that they went farther in their search for a *Río Grande de los Misterios,* as Crespi had called it: a great, mysterious river arising in the tall, snowy mountains in the distance (which Font now named Sierra Nevada), which sounded rather like the Strait of Anian sought by Cabrillo. Baffled by the soggy Sacramento-San Joaquin Delta area, the explorers finally turned south and headed back toward Monterey. In April of 1776 Anza took a tearful farewell from many of the colonists who had traveled safely with him to California. Between them, Anza and Font originated many California place-names, such as San Mateo, Natividad Valley, Lake Merced, Cupertino, Rinconada Creek, Guadalupe and Coyote rivers, Paso (de) Robles.

Like the Portola expedition, Anza's brought in a number of colonists in the form of soldiers. His *pobladores* (pueblo settlers), including wives and children, were the vital additions needed to complete the Spanish plan of colonization. Among them were these founding fathers: Luis Maria Peralta, Santiago de la Cruz Pico, Joaquin Ysidro Castro (the first of two Castro branches), Nicolas Antonio Berryessa, Domingo Alviso, Hermenegildo Sal, Domingo Alviso, Juan Francisco Bernal, Jose Vicente Feliz, Juan Salvio Pacheco, Jose Sanchez, and Jose Joaquin Moraga. A "merry widow," Doña Feliciana—who had offended the good Father Font with her ribald singing at the campfires —married Pico; a *mulata,* she was the grandmother of the well-known Californios Andres and Pio Pico. (Through amalgamation with African and Indian mates in Mexico, a number of California colonists arrived with already-mixed ancestry.) Again, as with the Portola contingent, California land is studded with the names and contributions of such settlers as these.

Anza's erstwhile traveling companions, Padre Garces and Tarabal, who had accompanied him on the second trip as far as the Colorado River, spent almost a year as freelance explorers. Garces went several hundred miles northward on the Colorado, then turned west to cross the Mojave Desert (the first white crossing) and followed the Mojave River into the San Bernardino Mountains, from which he descended to Mission San Gabriel. He named San Antonio Creek, which later extended the name to the high peak in the San Bernardinos, San Antonio, better known now as Old Baldy, because its wind-whipped slopes are bereft of vegetation. Garces was determined to locate a more direct route from the New Mexico region to the California settlements, but hostile Indians in the Santa Fe area blocked his plan. (About a half century later, various American mountain men—trappers and traders—utilized parts of Garces's itinerary on the Sante Fe or Old Spanish Trail.)

The Spanish-speaking explorers of 1769 and the 1770s, Portola and Anza in particular, are remembered in an assortment of places and place-names. Portola's main tributes are Portola State Park in the redwood country of San Mateo County and the settlement of Portola Valley. Anza's principal places of geographical commemoration are the Anza-Borrego Desert State Park and the town of Anza in the San Jacinto Mountains (Riverside County)—territories he passed through on his way to the California colony.

When San Francisco changed from streets designated by numerals and letters of the alphabet in 1909, a respectful board of supervisors encouraged street-names to honor a number of Hispanic explorers, missionaries, and settlers. Among the former are these: Portola, Crespi, Ortega,

Rivera, Palou, Anza, Font, and Garces. Galvez is here. And so is Tarabal, as Taraval. Conspicuously missing, however, is Pedro Fages, perhaps because of the awkwardness of pronouncing his name (FAH-hace)—he who traversed so much of unexplored California and was apparently the first white leader to behold the Golden Gate.

Fages, however, is commemorated elsewhere. A number of his geographical discoveries and campsites—notably those undertaken in the Contra Costa area in the spring of 1772, and in San Diego, Imperial, and Riverside counties, and in the southern San Joaquin Valley in the autumn of the same year—are now official California historical landmarks, bearing plaques to inform visitors of the significance of his trailblazing journeys. Similar trail landmarks have been established for both the Portola expedition and the two Anza expeditions (including his extensive survey of the San Francisco Peninsula and the "opposite coast" in the East Bay and into the Sacramento-San Joaquin Delta east of the Carquinez Strait). Points along Padre Francisco Garces's routes through the unknown southeast portion of Alta California have also been noted and honored. Although dedicated professional and local historians for many years made special projects out of resuscitating traces of the state's Hispanic past, it seems that the national bicentennial celebration worked wonders in establishing landmarks dating back even before 1776. (People are often reminded, for example, that San Francisco was officially settled during the same summer that spawned our nation's Declaration of Independence.)

The names and stories attached to the earliest Spanish expeditions in Alta California convey reminders of both the trials and the fascination, even the glory, of exploring a new terrain awaiting settlement—and more Spanish place-names.

First Overland Expeditions   **65**

Saints Along the Highway

"WHERE'S THE OLD MISSION?" visitors to California sometimes ask when arriving at a city or town with a "San" or "Santa" name. But there were only twenty-one Franciscan missions scattered along a seven-hundred-mile route between San Diego Bay and the region north of San Francisco Bay, within a hundred miles of the coast. The dozens of settlements whose saintly names commemorate missionaries, leaders, martyrs, and miracle workers in Catholic hagiology usually acquired their titles from geographical features or Indian rancherias in the area that were named long before a modern town was established.

A mission was a most particular institution. It was founded to minister to the local Indians: to attract them, to Christianize them, and to teach them the rudimentary skills of Western civilization. In the process, the neophytes were to assist the Spaniards in making their California colony productive—in agriculture, animal husbandry, and other basic industries—so that it could be nearly self-sustaining. Its padres were friar-missionaries, not secular priests who devoted their efforts to serving a parish of regular Christians. They had different interests, training, and duties. And they had chosen the kind of life they led in the New World. Almost all early padres had been born in Spain.

A town bearing a saint's name does not guarantee the presence of a mission within its boundaries. Nor does a mission necessarily have a "San" or "Santa" starting off its name. Two California missions—La Purisima Concepcion and Nuestra Señora de la Soledad—are exceptions. (The first, though, adds *de María Santísima*—of Holiest Mary.)

Furthermore, there are various Sans and Santas in California place-names that scarcely qualify as bona fide Hispanic-style saints. There was nobody named San Ardo. The name was originally San Bernardo, but when this caused confusion with the post office at San Bernardino, the residents obligingly clipped it. San Marino is a transported name; the town's founder used the title of his family's manor in Maryland, which in turn had borrowed its name from the tiny European principality. San Ramon, San Anselmo, and San Quentin got their "Sans" attached later, after being named for Indians who at baptism assumed Christian names of saints. (The Americans also managed to misspell Quintín!) Then there's the transsexual, transcultural Santa Claus, a burg along Highway 101 south of Santa Barbara that tries to keep Christmas going all year round by erecting large plaster statues of the Germanic version of the Asia Minor bishop, Saint Nicolas, the patron saint of children, and by selling tourist wares and date milkshakes. More peculiar still are such post office names as San Lawrence Terrace, San Augustine, and Santa Western.

Another source for occasional confusion is the city of San Jose and Mission San Jose. The city began as California's first official pueblo, close to the already established Mission Santa Clara. Saint Joseph, always a favorite saint, as well as the patron saint of the California colonization, was given his own mission later on, some fifteen miles to the northeast. In the city of San Jose, located within the Santa Clara Valley and Santa Clara County, at the heart of Computerland's "Silicon Valley," one visits Mission Santa Clara. *Misión* San Jose de Guadalupe is located in Alameda County.

Since explorers on both land and sea took priests or friars along with them on expeditions to serve as chaplains, tenders of the sick, and diarists, an essential part of their baggage was a calendar book that listed feast days: dates of births, deaths, or other significant events in saints' lives or afterlives and church history itself. Any geographical feature or human settlement that seemed to require naming might be awarded a "San" or "Santa" according to the approximate date of discovery or the name maker's predilection for a particular saint.

The abundance of these Sans and Santas make California look like a land inhabited by people saintlier than the rest of Christendom. There are probably more commemorative holy names here per square map-quadrangle than anywhere else in the world. But ours is not an especially religious age, and the saints go marching across the landscape as unnoticed and as anonymously as the rest of our place-names, Hispanic or otherwise.

California has not yet produced her very own saint, but there is still time for that. Canonization into sainthood is a long and complicated procedure. Several padres who devoted their lives to the California missions may someday achieve this highest honor that the Catholic Church can confer upon a mortal.

Ever since the 1930s Father Junipero Serra has been a candidate for sainthood. Martyrdom is the most direct route, but even though Serra fully expected it during his California trials, he died of natural causes. If he ultimately satisfies the Church's requirements—strong evidence of good works done in his lifetime and convincing proofs of miracles achieved afterwards by his spiritual intercession— we may someday have a San Junipero. Then the zealous little padre who rode mules or walked on a painfully ulcerated leg up and down El Camino Real, founding and then inspecting his missions, will be elevated higher in humanity's eyes than his namesake peak in the Santa Lucia Range that he passed through on his frequent missionary *jornadas*.

On becoming a friar, Serra took the Christian name of Junipero, a sturdy follower of St. Francis, who said he wished he had "a whole forest of such junipers." Serra was a hard worker who constantly practiced humility. His burning devotion to the cause of saving the Indian heathens warmed him as he lay in his cell on a narrow cot that had planks instead of a mattress—often blanketless because he had given away his only covering to some shivering *indio*. (Serra's cell is still on view at Mission Carmel.)

Men with such extreme dedication combined with organizational abilities and physical fortitude were what the Spanish colony in California needed, whether as military commanders, civilian leaders, or missionaries. Since the early settlements depended increasingly on the sustenance provided by the missions and on the padres' efforts to pacify and train the Indians within each area, it is almost certain that the California colonization itself would have failed, despite Jose de Galvez's careful preparations, if the missionary aspect of the venture had been less successful.

Father Serra was no saint as far as the comandante-governors were concerned. He was ever a nagging thorn in their sides. He demanded permission for more and more missions and would rarely listen to their reasoning. If they had no soldiers to spare as guards for these new missions he wanted, he was prepared, he said, to get along without them. The soldados de cuera misbehaved anyway and stirred up trouble with the Indians, teasing and tormenting them and abusing their women. The soldiers were indolent, rude, bestial, drunken, he said, and they set bad examples of Christian behavior. The comandantes did not deal with them strictly, as Portola and then Anza had done. . . .

Nevertheless, the missions and missionaries were required to have soldier-guards, an *escolta:* a half dozen at least, with a corporal in charge. The soldiers made servants out of the neophytes; many became too lazy to put on their own boots. But when the Indians ran away from the mission life, often taking horses and cattle with them, or when wild tribes raided, the soldiers proved useful in punishing them and in providing protection. On their parts, the padres fed them and heard confessions and gave them Communion. And when the vineyards began to yield their Mission grapes, to produce the essential sacramental wines, the soldiers began to get *vino* and *aguardiente* (brandy) with their meals.

The half century of Spanish dominion in California, from 1769 to 1822, when Mexico took over the often burdensome territory, is essentially the story of the mission chain stretched out to the right and the left of El Camino Real, established and maintained by the gray-frocked Franciscan Order. (The friars changed to brown robes at the end of the nineteenth century, by the Pope's ruling.) Almost all were set in prime locations that had good water sources, farmlands and pasturage, pleasant surroundings, and a population of Indians. Local Indian groups were often given new names based on the missions nearby, whether or not they trafficked there. Thus there were Diegueños, Gabrieleños, Barbareños, Luiseños, Juaneños.

Some missions were located at the ocean, alongside harbors. Others, farther inland, occupied fertile valleys and had routes that led to the sea and to the closest presidio and pueblo. It is no wonder that many of them remained central to California's development. Some of our largest cities and most prosperous or fastest-growing towns began as mission settlements.

There were other important Spanish settlements, secular ones—the four presidios and the three pueblos—making a total of twenty-eight official colonizing units established by order of the Spanish crown through the viceroy of New Spain. The padres themselves did not choose the names for the missions in the beginning. These and the names and locations of presidios and pueblos were decided by the administrators, acting through the *gobernador* of the Californias, both Baja and Alta.

Most of these early settlements bore the name of a saint. At three sites, eventually, both a presidio and a mission shared the same name: San Diego, San Francisco, Santa Barbara. Of the three pueblos, one honored a saint (San Jose), and one the Virgin Mary (Nuestra Señora la Reina de los Angeles). Two places—the Monterey Presidio and the pueblo called Villa de Branciforte—commemorated viceroys of New Spain. All told, twenty-six out of the twenty-eight place-names were religious in intent. Of the twenty-three that commemorate particular saints, three were nonmortals—the Archangels San Gabriel, San Miguel, San Rafael. There were two kings—San Luis Rey

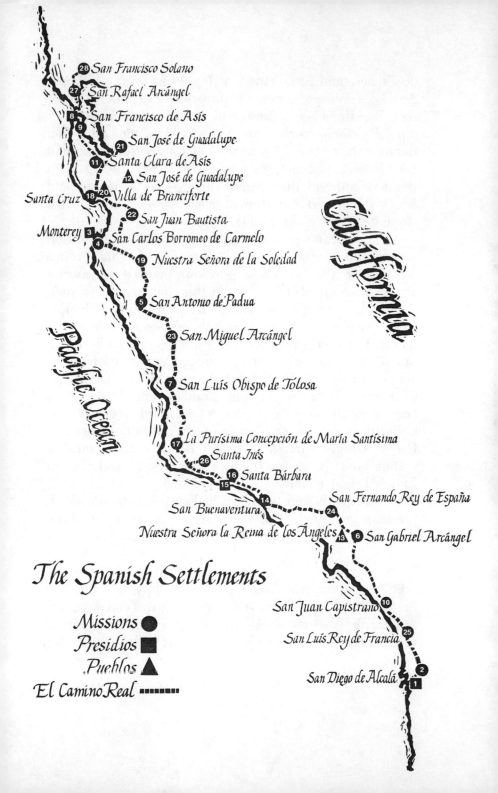

28 San Francisco Solano
27 San Rafael Arcángel
8 San Francisco de Asís
9
21 San José de Guadalupe
11 Santa Clara de Asís
12 San José de Guadalupe
Santa Cruz
18 20 Villa de Branciforte
22 San Juan Bautista
Monterey 3
4 San Carlos Borromeo de Carmelo
19 Nuestra Señora de la Soledad

5 San Antonio de Padua

23 San Miguel Arcángel

7 San Luis Obispo de Tolosa

17 La Purísima Concepción de María Santísima
26 Santa Inés
16 Santa Bárbara
15
14
San Buenaventura
San Fernando Rey de España
24
Nuestra Señora la Reina de los Ángeles
13 6 San Gabriel Arcángel

California

Pacific Ocean

The Spanish Settlements

Missions ●
Presidios ■
Pueblos ▲
El Camino Real ▪▪▪▪▪▪▪

San Juan Capistrano 10

San Luis Rey de Francia 25

San Diego de Alcalá 2
1

de Francia and San Fernando Rey de España; a bishop—San Luis Obispo; three missionaries—San Francisco de Asis, San Francisco Solano, and San Diego de Alcala; two scholarly theologians—San Antonio de Padua and San Buenaventura; two reformers—San Carlos Borromeo and San Juan Capistrano; two relatives of Jesus—San Juan Bautista and San Jose; three women—Santa Barbara and Santa Ines (martyred Roman maidens) and Santa Clara (founder of a religious order).

Like stepping-stones, these outposts of civilization were placed sometimes singly, at other times in small groups —whenever the California governor granted permission along with a squad of soldiers. As this chapter's map shows, there was a certain pattern to the placements: attempts were made to "fill in" gaps between established settlements. However, the process was not necessarily harmonious. Church and state, as institutions and as individuals, almost perpetually feuded in California, though the tenure of Serra's successor, Fermin Francisco de Lasuen, was comparatively calm and productive, partly because the California colony was no longer precarious but also because Lasuen's diplomatic skills served the Franciscan mission system well. (Between them, Fathers Serra and Lasuen founded eighteen missions: nine apiece.)

Now, taking up the individual settlements—missions, presidios, and pueblos—step by step, here are some of the stories involved. (Numbers correspond to map.)

1 *Presidio de San Diego de Alcalá:* July 1, 1769. The first foothold of Spain in Alta California was ceremoniously proclaimed a few weeks after Portola and Serra's arrival at San Diego Bay, which Vizcaino in 1602 had named for St. Didacus, a fifteenth century missionary of Alcala, Spain.

Saints Along the Highway

Temporary buildings were constructed on Presidio Hill, and some of them served as hospital quarters for those colonists who had come by sea and were afflicted with scurvy. (The Sacred Expedition lost half its original contingent through death or desertion.) Presidio Hill, east of the city of San Diego's Old Town, is now occupied by the Serra Museum, which houses displays and literature on the early period of Hispanic settlement, especially in this region.

❷ *Misión de San Diego de Alcalá:* July 16, 1769. Two days after Portola and his men left to locate Monterey Bay, Junipero Serra dedicated the first Franciscan mission site in Alta California. Taking charge of the rustic premises that combined presidio and mission, Serra lured Indians with gifts of beads, cloth, and metal knives. When he persuaded them at last to allow him to baptize an infant, he took it in his arms and began to sprinkle holy water. The horrified parents snatched away the baby and ran off, leaving the frustrated padre weeping, since this act had great symbolic meaning to him in the fulfillment of the Sacred Expedition. The Diegueños at first were affable and curious, but childish pranks turned into greedy thievery as they grabbed blankets off invalids and cut pieces from the sails of the anchored *San Carlos.* Hostile after being denied goods and scolded, the *gentiles* attacked, wounding several men and killing Serra's own servant, a young neophyte from Baja, before gunfire frightened them away.

Portola's return in January, after he failed to find Monterey Bay in the north, delivered another blow. They could not survive on their food supplies unless the *San Antonio,* sent off to San Blas a half year earlier, soon returned. Portola now declared that if it did not arrive by March 20, they would all have to retreat to Baja. Padres Serra and Crespi prayed incessantly for rescue. On the nineteenth—San Jose's feast day—a ship's sails were seen on the horizon. Although it was obviously heading north to Monterey, Portola counted on its return and granted a reprieve. Several days later, the *San Antonio* came into San Diego Bay; its crew had heard from Indians that the white men had returned from the north. Bolstered with food, tools, clothing, weapons, religious paraphernalia, and trinkets for the Indians, the first Spanish settlement survived—barely. Though in coming years it would suffer famine, contagion, neglect by New Spain's administrators, frustrated missionary efforts, and an Indian attack (1775) which massacred several colonists and martyred Padre Jayme, San Diego was never forsaken. After a while, the mission was moved to a valley area about five miles northeast of the presidio, not only to enjoy better land and water sources, but also to put distance between the neophytes and the soldiers. For the rest of his life, Padre Serra celebrated a Mass on the nineteenth of every month: a thanksgiving for the salvation of the little colony vital to Spain's—and the Church's—interests in California.

3 *Presidio de Monterey:* June 3, 1770. Their morale and provisions boosted, Portola and Serra resolved to attempt anew to locate Monterey. Portola set off by land with a smaller force, while Father Serra sailed on the *San Antonio,* figuring that the bay might be easier to locate on its seaward side. The swift land journey did originate at least one new place-name: that of Santa Monica, supposedly given by Crespi first to a group of pools where he took a refreshing bath, *Los Ojitos de Santa Mónica.* Later, the saint's name (she was St. Augustine's mother) was applied to the Santa Monica Mountains and to the large open bay where they terminated.

Again Portola descended to the coast via the Salinas River, but this time the coastline looked to them more like Vizcaino's description. At Punta de Pinos they found the large cross they had planted decorated by Indians' offerings. Their growing conviction that this indeed was Monterey got confirmed a week later when the ship came into the bay with Serra aboard.

Working quickly to construct presidio and mission shelters, by early June the men were ready to dedicate the new settlement to God and to the king of Spain. In a double christening, the padres prayed and the soldiers shot off noisy fusillades (which scared the local Indians from coming close for some while). Portola, his duties done, boarded the *San Antonio* to sail back to New Spain—and out of California history forever.

When news of the successful colonization reached Mexico City, the former Aztec capital resounded with the caroling of church bells. Portola reported directly to the viceroy and warned that Alta California would not be easily or inexpensively settled; in fact, the venture might prove impossible. As for the Monterey mission, it was moved the following year to a site five miles south, where the climate, soil, and water were better—and the presidio soldiers were less able to bother the Indians whom Serra wished to attract. The name of this mission was transferred too; it was—

❹ *Misión de San Carlos Borromeo de Carmelo:* 1771-1772. The original name honored St. Charles Borromeo, a cardinal and reformer of the sixteenth century. (Obliquely, the name also honored the reigning Carlos III of Spain.) It now added that of the new site's Carmel River which flowed close by, named after Vizcaino's Carmelite friars. Serra made this "Mission Carmel" (as it is usually called) his permanent headquarters. His work was just beginning. He was making plans for the six new missions ordered by Jose de Galvez: five to be placed between Monterey and San Diego, and the sixth at San Francisco Bay. Ten new padres—complete with gorgeous vestments likely to impress the Indians—arrived from Spain, ready for assignment. But Serra met with resistance from Portola's successor, Pedro Fages, an officer on the expedition who was now the one in charge *(gobernante)*. Fages had only about fifty soldiers in all of California: How could he spread them in eight settlements over a distance of five hundred miles? Rather reluctantly he agreed to let Serra commence his third and fourth missions.

❺ *Misión de San Antonio de Padua:* July 16, 1771. Serra now took his first real land journey in Alta California, the precursor of many extended trips he was to take in the next dozen years. Arriving at the warm valley on the eastern side of the Santa Lucias, he hung a bell upon an oak branch and rang it loudly while calling out to the heathens to come and receive God's message. He and the other padres, a handful of soldiers, and neophytes built the basic chapel and a few other structures.

Exactly two years after the mission founding at San Diego, Serra performed this new dedication to the memory of San Antonio de Padua, a thirteenth century Italian scholar who was so devoted to the meaning of the Christ child that he was usually depicted with him in religious portraits. The name had already been given to the arroyo alongside the location. The mission ceremony was attended by one curious native spectator, whom Serra welcomed fondly and regaled with gifts. His attentions produced the intended effect, for later the Indian brought a crowd of others, carrying acorns and wild fruits to exchange for the Spaniards' trinkets. After a period of field training in which Serra prepared the novice priests in setting up the mission functions and showing them how to attract and deal with the Indians, two padres were sent farther south, to launch, with Serra's blessings, the fourth Franciscan mission. He himself returned to Carmel.

San Antonio de Padua's beautiful location is considered most representative of the original settings of the missions.

❻ *Misión de San Gabriel Arcángel:* September 8, 1771. Named after the Angel of the Annunciation, this mission began its career at the edge of the Rio Hondo. It is said that the padres, when approaching the site, were accosted by hostile Indians. One deftly unrolled a large scroll painting of the Virgin Mary, which so awed the heathens that they joined the procession. After several seasons of winter floods had discouraged their efforts, the padres moved the mission to a place near the San Gabriel River, its present location, which proved to be among the most fruitful regions in the mission system, for both agriculture and animal husbandry. Mission San Gabriel lay in a crucial spot, so that in later years it became a crossroads of three different travel routes entering the California colony: one from the south, one from the north, and one from the east. Despite recurrent problems with the Indians, often initiated by the resident soldiers' misbehavior, the mission flourished. The unusual architecture of the main building, Spanish-Moorish, is not typical of the missions in general.

(Mission visitors should realize that none of the often impressive-looking structures restored or rebuilt for this century's viewers are the originals. Usually missions began as *enramadas,* crude brush shelters coated with dried mud. They grew by stages. Little wood was used, even when available, except for supports, beams, doors, shutters, and embellishments. The material most often used was, of course, adobe. Mixing the heavy clay soil with water and plant material, like straw or weeds, the neophytes kneaded the muddy mass with bare feet. Wooden frames—commonly 10″ x 10″ x 2″—shaped it into blocks, which were set in the sun until thoroughly dry, a process sometimes taking several months. Adobe walls were characteristically very thick, as much as six feet, in order to support the weight of the upper walls and roof. They were protected by eaves from rainfall, and were usually whitewashed inside and out. Although other building materials such as sandstone and burnt brick were later used in places where they could be obtained, adobe actually proved more stable during the earthquakes that periodically destroyed or damaged the churches ambitiously undertaken by resourceful padres during the early nineteenth century, using Indian labor and imported artisans. By this time most missions were prospering, having already completed such basic work as dam *(presa)* and aqueduct and ditch *(zanja)* building: some of which were done so well they are still used by local farmers. They also built living quarters and a variety of workshops for the Indians. A few padres even constructed gristmills *(molinos)*. Standard equipment at the missions were wine presses and casks, as well as olive presses to make the oil used for both cooking and lubrication. The padres obtained tannin from the California tanbark oak for curing leather. Unlike the soldiers, they usually worked alongside their neophytes.)

❼ *Misión de San Luís Obispo de Tolosa:* September 1772. The determined Padre Serra continued to annoy Fages with his insistence on extending the missions, despite the scarcity of soldiers. In the winter of 1771/72 there was a far worse problem: various settlements were close to starving because most of their crops had failed. The padres had not yet learned how to grow crops during the wet winter season and to reserve water for irrigation in the long summer dry season. Trees grown from seeds and cuttings— oranges, figs, olives, pomegranates, peaches—were not yet bearing fruit. The supply ships had not come. Pedro Fages took some of his men bear hunting at Cañada de los Osos (visited during the Portola expedition); during several months there they managed to shoot enough bears to supply meat, fresh and dried, to the various posts. The Indians in the region were friendly, perhaps because they appreciated the white men's guns. Their own arrows could not penetrate the grizzly bear's thick coat, so they were often the bears' prey rather than their predators.

Toward the summer's end, Fages and Serra traveled together to this region to found the new mission, named for St. Louis of Toulouse, a bishop who was the son of the king of Naples and a nephew of the king of France (Louis IX, who also was canonized—and has a mission namesake). This mission is renowned for having started the use of baked-brick roof tiles, those long, slightly tapered half-cylinders telescoped end-on-end upon the sloping roofs. The padres here grew annoyed when the Indians repeatedly set their thatch roofs on fire with flaming arrows, and decided to try baking terra cotta tiles themselves, as was done in the Mediterranean area. Legend says that a neophyte's thigh served as the first form for the mold. The success of their experiment spread to all the missions and to many other Hispanic structures. Today, of course, the roof tiles are the hallmark of Spanish-style architecture in California.

San Luis Obispo is a good example of how a town eventually grew up around a mission, virtually enclosing it. Only the most remote missions now stand alone.

Four years elapsed between the founding of the first seven settlement units and the next series. Irritated over the delay in establishing more missions, for which he blamed gobernante Pedro Fages, Serra determined to travel to Mexico City to complain to the viceroy himself. Sailing on a supply ship returning to San Blas, he then traveled overland, a difficult trip during which he nearly died. He arrived with perfect timing, just as the new viceroy, Bucareli, and his council were debating whether to allow Nueva California to perish, suspecting that it involved more expense and trouble than it was worth.

Serra's presentation of his experience, his firm belief in California's potential for Spain, and his proposals impressed the administrators, who now began a series of moves intended to strengthen and improve the faraway fledgling colony. The various naval expeditions of 1774–75 were ordered; Anza was given the go-ahead to blaze an overland route from northern Mexico; the harbor at San Blas was fixed up, and better, regular supply ships were requested; and arrangements were made to send many more soldiers to the province. Bucareli wanted a presidio and a mission to be founded speedily at San Francisco Bay, whose strategic importance he recognized.

Best of all, perhaps, so far as Serra was concerned, Bucareli dismissed Fages from his post and replaced him with another California officer: Fernando Rivera y Moncada. The move soon proved unwise, for this stubborn and temperamental man, though brave and hardworking, annoyed Serra even more than Fages had, and eventually he was excommunicated by him. Rivera y Moncada also tried to prevent Anza from carrying out Bucareli's orders to select sites for and then establish the presidio and mission at San Francisco Bay. By the time of Anza's departure for Tubac, in the spring of 1776, the men were not on speaking terms. Meanwhile, Padre Serra returned to Alta California to stay, well pleased with the results of his long and arduous trip and eager to launch many new projects.

8 *Presidio de San Francisco de Asís:* September 1776. Lieutenant Jose Joaquin Moraga, who had come across the desert with Anza's second trek in 1775, remained as a colonist in California. Anza delegated responsibility for constructing the new San Francisco premises to him, and Moraga admirably discharged it within several months. However, he built the presidio not at the Cantil Blanco site that so impressed Anza but at a lower, more protected spot to the east, which also had a convenient water supply. (The area, consisting now of about 1,600 acres, has always belonged to the military—whether Spanish, Mexican, or American—and still retains the name Presidio. The oldest building in the city of San Francisco is an adobe located there, now used as the Officer's Club.) In 1794 the Castillo de San Joaquin was mounted on the white cliff favored by Anza, and fortified so as to protect the entrance to the harbor by alien vessels. The presidio comandante—a post occupied by Moraga, Jose Dario Arguello and Luis Antonio Arguello (father and son), and others—was the most powerful and prestigious person within the district.

❾ *Misión de San Francisco de Asís de Dolores:* October 1776. Here at last was founded the mission honoring St. Francis of Assisi, the founder of the Franciscan Order that administered all the California missions. *De Dolores* in its title referred to the laguna and arroyo which Anza named after the sorrows experienced by Nuestra Señora following the Crucifixion. Thus the mission is more familiarly known as Mission Dolores. The adobe chapel, begun in 1782 and finished by 1795, remains there today, in spite of earthquakes and fires. The mission area itself (which continues its name through Mission Street and Dolores Street and the entire Mission District in the city) was never highly productive compared with most other missions, almost proving Rivera y Moncada's negative appraisal of the location as too sandy and cold for Spanish settlement. Nor did the neophytes themselves prosper there, for the death rate was alarming,

⑩ *Misión de San Juan Capistrano:* October 1776. Dedicated to the memory of St. John of Capistran, a lawyer-theologian in fifteenth century Italy who became an active reformer, this mission was actually started in the previous year but was interrupted by the massacre at nearby Mission San Diego. Jose Francisco Ortega, who was in charge of building it, hurried off to the south to aid the settlement's survivors, burying the church bell until work could be resumed. A huge stone church was built here in 1797, the most ambitious architectural undertaking of all the missions, but it was destroyed by the great earthquake of 1812, during which the roof and walls collapsed on forty neophytes. The sanctuary has been intentionally left in ruins. The earlier chapel, escaping destruction, is still in use as a parish church; it is the only existing structure where Padre Serra himself is known to have held services. The swallows that have built thousands of mud nests on the mission walls and eaves are renowned for their regular migratory schedules. By propitious coincidence, most of them leave for the south on October 23, the death date of San Juan Capistrano, and return on March 19, the date on which the first Spanish settlement at San Diego was rescued from abandonment.

⑪ *Misión de Santa Clara de Asís:* January 1777. This second mission ordered for the San Francisco Bay area was founded close to the Guadalupe River. It commemorated St. Clare of Assisi, a friend and follower of St. Francis who left her wealthy family to start an order of cloistered nuns, the "Poor Clares." The first structures were built by Jose Joaquin Moraga, who had completed his work in San Francisco the previous year. The warm and fertile valley later took its name from the mission, not—as customarily happens—from the main river flowing through it. The mission is now located within the premises of the Catholic University of Santa Clara.

🔔 *El Pueblo de San José de Guadalupe:* November 1777. The governor of the two Californias, Felipe de Neve, moved the capital from Loreto to Monterey in the spring of 1777. A painstaking and intelligent man, "California's first lawgiver" traveled from San Diego to San Francisco on an inspection tour of the eight missions and three presidios, paying particular attention to food production, which was still inadequate. Neve wrote to Viceroy Bucareli requesting his permission, along with shipments of new colonists, to start civilian pueblos as farming settlements. Acting on his own, he assembled sixty-eight people, mainly soldiers and their families who had come with Anza and settled in Monterey or San Francisco, and took them to a site along the Guadalupe River about five miles south of the new Mission Santa Clara. Jose Joaquin Moraga again took charge of settlement building in this first of the Spanish towns, which were to concentrate on agriculture and certain useful crafts that would help the entire colony—the presidios in particular—to become self-sustaining. An *alcalde,* a mayor-judge, would be the local official.

San Jose, named for St. Joseph, the husband of the Virgin Mary and the foster father of Jesus, prospered from its location in the Santa Clara Valley. It is now supposedly the nation's fastest-growing city. The Alameda, the tree-lined roadway built between the mission and the pueblo to encourage settlers to attend Mass on Sundays, is still a main thoroughfare.

(Not shown on map) *Misión de San Pedro y San Pablo* and *Misión de la Purísima Concepción:* 1780. These are the two "forgotten" missions that were placed along the west bank of the Colorado River, one about opposite the present-day town of Yuma, the other about eight miles to the south. Anza and Font had requested missions to be founded among the Yumas, whose helpful Chief Palma wished to have his people Christianized. By the time the two missions—named to honor Saints Peter and Paul and the Immaculate Conception—were placed in the area, however, the move was too little, too late. Furthermore, the missions did not have the relatively "pure" form of the others; they were also garrisons and civilian residences whose inmates allowed their cattle and horses to forage on the Indians' wild and cultivated crops. (The Yumas were the only California Indians to practice agriculture before the Spaniards' arrival.)

Rivera y Moncada, bringing in a large group of future California colonists that Governor Neve had asked for, along with cattle and sheep, halted at this way station on the Anza Trail from Sonora in July of 1781. He sent some of the settler families ahead with livestock, escorted by soldiers from Monterey. The Yumas, their resentment against the whites fanned by this recent invasion of their lands, now attacked both missions and killed all except women and children. Among the dead were Rivera y Moncada and the intrepid, gentle missionary-explorer Francisco Garces. This massacre closed the Anza Trail for many years since few people risked traveling upon it to California, thus preventing large-scale population expansion.

⚜ *El Pueblo de Nuestra Señora la Reina de los Ángeles de Porciúncula:* September 1781. Spain's second civilian pueblo, founded by order of Governor Neve and taking the name given by Portola's party to a river (now the Los Angeles River) flowing through the area, consisted of forty-four settlers from the northern Mexican provinces, all of them illiterate pobladores of mixed blood. Promised land, clothing, tools, and monthly stipends for settling in California, they had not journeyed with Rivera and therefore missed the Yuma massacre, having traveled up from Baja, after crossing the gulf in boats. The beginnings of a town were laid out around a plaza, with individual *solares* (building lots) and *suertes* (farming lots) given to the heads of households. There were also communal lands for pasturage and other uses. Later on, the pueblo's population was supplemented by new arrivals and by experienced settlers or soldiers from other places, such as Santiago de la Cruz Pico, the progenitor of the whole Pico clan. An Anza soldier who moved from the San Diego Presidio, he was given outlying lands, though told to live with his family at the pueblo itself.

For some years El Pueblo (its commonly used name, before Los Angeles became customary) had a reputation for slothfulness and wickedness. Even so, by 1800 it was surpassed only by Mission San Gabriel in its agricultural productivity. The mission padres serviced the small church in the pueblo, which was considered an *asistencia*. The pueblo was dusty and nearly bereft of trees, and its main water ditch, *la Zanja Madre,* was used for drinking water supplies, laundering, and conveying wastes. The settlers had built small, one-story homes out of adobe, roofed by branches and tules plastered with the brea from the nearby tar pits. The roofs were flat; nevertheless in hot weather the black asphalt melted and dripped down the walls, giving a further disreputable look to the town. Disregarding its ignoble start, the Town of the Angels is now California's largest metropolis.

❿ *Misión de San Buenaventura:* March 1782. For many years Serra had agitated for a mission to be placed among the Chumash Indians at Santa Barbara Channel, and here at last was the first one, located at the site that Crespi had found most promising during the Portola expedition. Its name and location had been among the initial missions ordered by the viceroy, but delays and feuds had halted the project—and would have done so again had the new orders arrived in time to stop the founding of a presidio and this first of several new missions. Just as Neve and Serra had carried on in California the conflict between church and state, so did New Spain's viceroy and the College of San Fernando, which supervised the missionary work in California. Neve and the viceroy wished to control and curb the missions' landholding and involvement with the Indians, turning more of these responsibilities over to the secular administration. The padres and their *colegio* in Mexico City resented interference in their work and believed that only they could properly prepare the Indians for a future place in civilized society.

This mission, the last to be founded under Serra's leadership, was named for St. Bonaventure, a thirteenth century Tuscan follower of St. Francis, who had restored him to health and good fortune (hence, *buena ventura*). Its gardens were considered the most beautiful of all the missions'. The mission is at the center of the city of Ventura, which received a shortened version of the place-name.

15 *Presidio de Santa Bárbara:* April 1782. This fourth and last official Spanish presidio took the name Vizcaino gave to the channel and bay between the land and the offshore islands. Santa Barbara—*virgen y mártir*—was a Roman girl who had been beheaded by her father when she refused to forsake Christianity. In turn, he was killed instantly by a thunderbolt from heaven, which caused his daughter to be regarded as the patron saint of those imperiled by the threat of sudden death. She was appropriated as the special patroness of artillery men, and the word *santabárbara* was given to the gunpowder magazine in a fortress or on shipboard.

The presidio was built by Jose Francisco Ortega, Portola's one-time sergeant; it was the last settlement to be dedicated by Father Serra. Its officers, who acquired ranchos in the surrounding area, are recalled in various street-names in the present-day city, such as Carrillo, De la Guerra, Cota, and Ortega. Castillo Street got its name from the fortress constructed on a mesa at some distance from the presidio itself, where the soldiers were quartered.

⑯ *Misión de Santa Bárbara:* December 1786. The mission was intended to be founded conjointly with the presidio, but four years elapsed before official permission was granted. By then, various changes had taken place. Father Serra had died, and his place was taken temporarily by his life-long friend Francisco Palou. In 1785 Fermin Francisco de Lasuen became padre-presidente, a post he exercised competently for eighteen years, until his death. Governor Neve had been transferred elsewhere in 1782, to be replaced by ex-gobernante Pedro Fages—who stayed in his beloved California until 1791, when his notoriously difficult wife, Doña Eulalia, at last succeeded in getting him transferred back to New Spain's less rustic society.

The Santa Barbara Mission was the first of nine to be dedicated by Lasuen. It was built close to *Arroyo Pedregoso* (Stony Creek), which supplied water for a dam and a *lavandería* (laundry), remnants of which can still be seen. (Pedregosa Street and Park preserve the old Spanish name.) The mission, sometimes called "the queen of the missions," contains the official archives of all the Franciscan missions in California.

⑰ *Misión de La Purísima Concepción de María Santísima:* December 1787. The title, used first at the short-lived mission at the Colorado River, was given again to honor "Holiest Mary's" Immaculate Conception. (Contrary to popular belief, this event does not refer to the "virgin birth" of Jesus but to the Church's doctrine that Mary herself was conceived, and therefore born, without sin: escaping the taint, afflicting all other mortals, of Adam and Eve's "original sin.")

La Purisima, as it is usually called, was never a major mission. Located nineteen miles west of Buellton, it has been restored as a mission-museum, and probably more than all others gives visitors the impression of what mission life was like during the height of its power and prosperity, before Mexican rule and subsequent secularization.

⑱ *Misión de Santa Cruz:* September 1791. The complete name was *La Misión de la Exaltación de la Santa Cruz* (Mission of the Exaltation—or Glorification—of the Holy Cross). This twelfth mission was situated alongside the Arroyo de la Santa Cruz named by the Portola expedition. Partly because of conflicts with the colonists in a town located next to it in 1797 (see settlement no. 20), the mission was never successful, and frequent earthquakes in the area discouraged substantial building. The contemporary "mission" that exists in the city of Santa Cruz is actually a small replica, about half the size of the original chapel.

⑲ *Misión de Nuestra Señora de la Soledad:* October 1791. The name came from Father Crespi's notation that local Indians, when the Portola party passed through the almost barren area, kept saying a word that sounded like soledad. Padre Lasuen liked this recorded place-name and therefore incorporated it into the new mission's title. Soledad is also the name of a nearby town. This mission— located in a sparsely settled area—was the last of those in the chain to be partially restored in recent years.

⚠ *Villa de Branciforte:* June 1797. The current viceroy of New Spain, the *Marqúes* de Branciforte, ordered the founding of a third civilian pueblo at a location just on the other side of the San Lorenzo River from Mission Santa

Cruz, though it was then illegal to have a secular settlement within a league (less than five miles) of a mission. The perturbed padres prevented the settlers from acquiring much land. The pueblo took Branciforte's name but did him no honor, for its pobladores were the outpourings of jails and poorhouses in New Spain. Unlike previous new colonists, they seemed shiftless and lazy. Despite its apparent charms to those who lived there, California had a bad reputation in New Spain, so it was always difficult to persuade people to immigrate there. In order to raise troops and settlers, Spain and then Mexico frequently shipped off their undesirables to California.

Branciforte Village was a miserable place, and in time all of its inhabitants drifted away. Its name is preserved in Branciforte Creek in the city of Santa Cruz, which eventually absorbed the site. Branciforte was also proposed as a name for one of California State's first twenty-seven counties, but it was replaced, more fittingly, by Santa Cruz.

❷ *Misión de San José de Guadalupe:* June 1797. The first of five missions all founded in the same year, it took the same name as that of the pueblo placed fifteen miles to the southwest twenty years before. The mission became one of the most prosperous agriculturally. During the years it was headed by Father Narciso Duran, it became well known among Spanish settlers for its thirty-piece neophyte orchestra. Duran taught his Indians how to play and read music, and most of their instruments were handmade out of salvaged wood and metal. Although the padres remarked that the gentiles of California seemed to have no music at all in their cultural traditions (beyond the shrill blowing of their pitos), the musically inclined missionaries discovered, to their surprise, that their neophytes generally showed a greater natural aptitude for music making than Europeans and often learned readily to read music (whereas language reading was more difficult and, in any case, was rarely taught by the padres). The mission's position—the only one within *la Contra Costa* (the "opposite coast" to San Francisco, which included the whole East Bay area)—made it an escape route for runaways from the San Francisco and Santa Clara Missions as well as a vulnerable raiding spot for hostile pagans. The Indian outlaw chief Estanislao (whose name was given to the river where he was finally captured by Mariano Vallejo and is now called Stanislaus) had been one of Father Duran's talented musicians and a favorite helper, but to his great sorrow eventually took to the hills.

❷ *Misión de San Juan Bautista:* June 1797. This mission helped to fill in another of the blank spots along El Camino Real, so that each mission would be only a day's journey from the next. It was founded on the feast day of St. John the Baptist's martyrdom by beheading, and was located in an area with fertile fields and abundant woods, about fifteen miles north of present-day Salinas. As a musical partner to Father Duran's San Jose orchestra, San Juan Bautista boasted Father Tapis's choir of Indian boys; a half century after their early training, some of his proteges still sang at church services. Its most famous possession was an old hurdy-gurdy that Vancouver had originally given to the padres at Mission Carmel, and the neophytes delighted in grinding out its English folk tunes and hornpipes. One day the mission was attacked by the fearsome Tulare Indians from across the mountains, but a brave and resourceful padre brought out the hurdy-gurdy and began to crank it. His neophytes then began to sing the tunes lustily, and the raiders, flabbergasted, dropped their weapons and came forward to hear more music in peace. Some even asked to stay on at the mission so that they could remain close to this marvelous mechanism. Its termite-ridden remains are stored in the museum at the restored mission, which is now part of a State Historical Park featuring the original plaza with various shops and casas, including that of former governor and general Jose Castro—which give visitors an idea of the actual appearance of a small mission town during Mexican rule.

㉓ *Misión de San Miguel Arcángel:* July 1797. The name commemorates the archangel St. Michael—the captain of God's armies and the special protector against Satan's evil wiles. The mission church is notable for the colorful original wall frescoes and handhewn beams; also because it was the site of one of nineteenth century California's most notorious murders. William Reed—the owner of the premises after mission secularization—and his family and servants were killed by robbers. The men were caught and executed, but the mission is reputedly haunted. About equidistant between Los Angeles and San Francisco on Highway 101, it is well known to motorists who stop there for a respite.

㉔ *Misión de San Fernando Rey de España:* September 1797. Saint Ferdinand, king of Spain in the thirteenth century, was praised for the religious fervor that propelled him into victorious battles with the Moorish invaders of his land. The adobe church was almost destroyed in the earthquake of 1812, and the most recent temblor of 1971 damaged it too. Its restored form functions as a mission-period museum, indoors and out. During the secularization period, when it belonged to Andres Pico, the mission lands experienced a small gold rush after nuggets were found in 1842 in what is now called Placerita Canyon. Later on, Pico Canyon nearby was one of the first sources in California for crude oil. The large San Fernando Valley north of Los Angeles proper—much of it incorporated into the city around 1913 when the controversial aqueduct bringing Owens River water was completed—took its name from the mission, located at its northern end.

㉕ *Misión de San Luís Rey de Francia:* June 1798. Although founded later than most of the missions, this one—named for Louis IX, a thirteenth century crusader-king of France—was ultimately the most prosperous. Much of the credit was due to Father Antonio Peyri, a taskmaster apparently beloved by many of the neophytes. The statistics for its agricultural yields, its livestock, its Indian population and their low death rate, compared with those of the other missions, are impressive. When the time of the secularization of the missions approached, Father Peyri, who had devoted thirty-four years to San Luis Rey, left without warning. A group of his devoted Indians followed him all the way to San Diego in order to say good-bye; it is said that some of them even tried to swim out to the ship that was taking him back to his Spanish homeland. San Luis Rey, like San Luis Obispo, is frequently mispronounced by people who say "LOO-ee," in the Americanized French manner, rather than "loo-EES," as the name *Luís* is said in Spanish.

㉖ *Misión de Santa Inés:* September 1804. The last of the missions built in the Chumash area, this mission was named after St. Agnes, who, like St. Barbara, was martyred when she refused to give up the Christian faith despised by the Romans. A beautiful woman with many wealthy suitors, she declined to marry, explaining that she had a bridegroom in heaven. She is known as the patron saint of religious chastity. Her name was given also to the river and valley in the mission area. The mission was the scene of a prolonged revolt by the Chumash Indians in 1824. Now incorporated incongruously within the Danish-style town of Solvang, it is a major way station on the annual horseback and camp-out route taken in spring by the prestigious Santa Barbara men's club, Los Rancheros Visitadores.

❷ *Misión de San Rafael Arcángel:* December 1817. The mission was appropriately named after the archangel St. Raphael, patron saint of healing the infirm. It began as an asistencia to Mission Dolores in San Francisco, where the damp climate was so bad for the neophytes that the death rate from tuberculosis became alarmingly high. The warmer, more protected locality was chosen as a sanitorium for the ailing Indians. However, the placement of a Spanish settlement north of San Francisco Bay was also a strategic move designed to counter the Russian establishment of Fort Ross built on the coast in 1812. (The Spaniards called it *Fuerto Ruso,* from the Russians' word for themselves— *Rossaya.*) During the early years of occupation, various reconnaissance parties were sent out—notably, those headed by Luis Antonio Arguello and Gabriel Moraga—into the northern regions, mainly to gain information about the Russians' activities. (*El Río Ruso,* now Russian River, was named because it was close by.) Occasionally they encountered American and Canadian fur trappers who had worked their way down from Oregon. Thus were awarded names like *Estero Americano* (still in use) and *Río de los Americanos* (now American River). The Russians intended Fort Ross as a base for their sea otter hunting, but it also became an agricultural community that supplied food to their colony in Alaska. The Spaniards and Russians actually began trading, each supplying or bartering items that the other needed. The Russians, in fact, provided a few of the mission bells and even built several boats for Spanish use.

Mission San Rafael was never ambitiously laid out or constructed. It lacked, for example, the usual mission set-up within a quadrangle. But its location was salubrious, as the current residents of Marin County can testify

㉘ *Misión de San Francisco Solano:* July 1823. The last of the Franciscan missions founded in California and the only one launched during the period of Mexican rule, this northernmost post, in the warm and fertile Valley of the Moon, commemorated another St. Francis, a seventeenth century missionary in Peru. Its founding father was Padre Altimira, one of the second generation of priests from Spain, who had divided loyalties after Mexico won its independence in 1821. (News of the event did not reach California until the following year.)

The location of this mission became important in 1835, the year after the secularization process began. Mariano Guadalupe Vallejo was asked by Governor Figueroa to serve as administrator of the mission as well as to command a new garrison of soldiers—virtually a fifth presidio—in the northern province, to check any Russian expansion and to control hostile Indians. He fought the Soscol tribe and afterwards befriended their chief, the noble-looking Sem-Yeto, whom he persuaded to turn Christian. Baptized with the mission's name, Solano, the chief was a frequent guest at Vallejo's home in the town he founded—Sonoma, which also contained the mission. (The mission is better known as Mission Sonoma.) Once when entertaining the commander of Fort Ross and his attractive bride, Vallejo, doubtful that he had dissuaded Chief Solano from his intention to steal the female guest, himself accompanied the pair back to the Russian fort to assure their safety. (Solano Valley, his tribe's residence, was named for Chief Solano.)

Mission San Francisco Solano is now part of the Sonoma State Historical Park, which also contains Vallejo's old plaza and a monument to the brief-lived Bear Flag Republic, for it was here that the Americans hoisted the crudely made flag that furnished the design for California's official banner.

The area north of San Francisco and San Pablo bays contains many reminders of General Mariano G. Vallejo who, more than all other Californios, represented the transition between the Spanish and the Mexican periods, and then between the Mexican and the American ones. He was one of thirteen children born to Ignacio Vicente Vallejo, a Mexican who settled in California in 1774, serving as a mission guard at various posts until he obtained a large rancho in Pajaro Valley (near present-day Watsonville). As a member of the younger generation that included Jose Castro and Juan Bautista Alvarado, Mariano was a rebel and freethinker in his youth. He welcomed the secularization of the missions, for among Mexican revolutionary doctrines was one proposing to grant indios a liberty never enjoyed during the Spanish regimen. Like other Californios, he fretted over the strictures which the church also placed upon *la gente de razón*. He was among those who agitated for the release of the twelve million acres of mission-held lands.

When the padres were criticized for subjecting the neophytes to a harshly disciplined and exploitative bondage, they responded that they were preparing them for the coming of civilization but that the Indians were not yet capable of taking full charge of their own lives, or of the mission lands that legitimately belonged to them. The original plan to have a Christianizing and civilizing training period of ten years at each mission was never fulfilled. Many of the most capable neophytes, exposed to European contagious diseases against which they had no immunities, died during epidemics, or caught venereal diseases—initially transmitted by the soldiers—and had lingering and degenerative demises. Indians who survived the first years of the mission experience were apt to become either model neophytes—submissive laborers reduced to a rather childlike dependency—or else runaways and renegades, some of whom led the still-uncivilized Indians in outlying areas in attacks upon the missions or in night raids to carry off livestock and food supplies. (Flour and sugar were attractive; horses—for eating as well as riding—more so.)

Most of the governors selected by New Spain—Felipe de Neve, Pedro Fages, Borica, Arrillaga, Sola—had attempted various programs to assist in the acculturation of the Indian population in gradual and practical ways, with or without cooperation from the missionary padres. A plan was also periodically proposed by both church and state to start a new chain of missions within the interior of California, particularly in the long and narrow Great Central Valley stretching for five hundred miles between the Coast Range and the Sierra Nevada. Explorers (most of them presidio officers doubling as tough Indian fighters) and padres made periodic expeditions into unknown or little-known regions during the early 1800s, searching for new mission sites.

The most abundant Hispanic names of this final period of Spanish rule and exploration were given to this *Valle Grande* area, notably to the rivers flowing into it from the Sierra Nevada. There were some Indian names: Tuolumne, Cosumnes, Moquelumne—recorded in Spanish, combining an Indian word like *kosum* (salmon) with *-umne* (Miwok for people or tribe). The greatest name giver and Indian fighter and explorer (the first expedition leader actually to go into the Sierra Nevada region) was Gabriel Moraga, son of Jose Joaquin Moraga. As a youth he had accompanied his father into California with Anza. He was responsible for naming rivers like the San Joaquin; the Merced (originally *El Río de Nuestra Señora de la Merced*—Our Lady of Mercy —who supposedly had been merciful in quenching Moraga's thirst); the Sacramento (for the Sacrament in the Catholic Mass); the Kings (which he called *El Río de los Santos*

Reyes—the Holy Kings); and Mariposa Creek (*Arroyo de las Mariposas,* because of the thousands of butterflies that flitted around the explorers' campsite). Moraga is said to have gone on at least forty expeditions into unknown lands, dropping many a name along the way.

Despite the years of exploration, however, a second group of Franciscan missions was never launched. The early 1800s in Spain and her New World colonies were a time of revolution, of uncertainty (as when Napoleon placed his brother Joseph on the Spanish throne), of periodic political repression, and of economic distress. The California colony could not depend on support from Spain, and for its own survival learned to govern, feed, and clothe itself—with assistance from foreign ships coming in for illegal trading. It was not prepared to extend much farther into the hinterlands, to take on more lands and heathen Indians.

When Mexican independence from Spain took place in 1821, most of the Californios—the priests excepted—welcomed a closer connection with the new motherland and believed that they would obtain more self-rule, representation in the Mexican legislative body, and better opportunities for landowning. To achieve the last benefit meant, to them, stripping the missions of most of their acreage. Beneath the Californios' championship of the Indians' right to freedom lay ambition and even greed. Unfortunately, the neophytes were ill-prepared to defend themselves.

In 1834, under Governor Figueroa, the mission secularization plan requested by most Californios and enacted by the Mexican government began to take effect, in stages. The churches themselves were to become secular; that is, to serve regular parish needs of the surrounding populace, Indian or Hispanic. They were to be allotted only grounds essential to their function, which no longer involved proselytizing, housing several thousand Indian residents, operating craft industries, raising livestock, and growing food. Many of the Spanish missionaries departed before the new law took effect. The priests who stayed on were mainly born and trained in Mexico; "Zacatecans" from the College of Zacatecas, not "Fernandinos" from the San Fernando College that had more thoroughly prepared the earlier generation of Spanish padres. Some mission churches were abandoned; others were poorly tended.

The mission lands themselves were now administered by superintendents selected by the governor. In some cases, they turned the position into a profit-making venture for themselves, while declining responsibility for the Indians who remained on the premises, some of whom had received small parcels of land for their own use. Cattle were sold off all at once and by the thousands. After the hides were removed, carcasses were left to rot, causing a terrible stench and a plague of scavengers around the mission lands. The neglected grainfields now grew weeds, and from lack of irrigation the orchards and vineyards that had been the pride of the padres became desiccated and desolate. The mission buildings themselves were stripped of their roof tiles, wrought-iron grillwork, supportive timbers, fixtures, and any other useful or decorative items. Earthquakes tore some of them apart. Exposed to rain, wind, hot sun, nesting birds, and stray poultry and cattle, the adobe bricks began to crumble and wash away—adding their clumps of clay to the original soil beds.

And as the departed padres had predicted, secularization disastrously affected the Christianized Indians. If they remained close to the missions that were their homes, often the only places they knew if they had been born there, they were usually quickly cheated of both rights and lands, exploited as lowly laborers, and degraded by disease, alcoholism, malnutrition, and mistreatment. Now a new pattern of unpaid employment began in which the rancho *mayor-domos,* overseers, temporarily "bought" Indian laborers from the local jail, where they had been incarcerated after a drunken weekend, or for just loitering in town. The missionaries' strict control over their lives at least had offered them direction and protection while European civilization invaded their territories.

The Franciscan padres who were largely responsible for establishing a firm Spanish foothold in California are commemorated in various place-names, particularly highway or street-names, and on geographical features. No other tribute to them, though, is as impressive as the Los Padres National Forest, stretching in two sections across the Coast Range in mid-California, which was seen and traveled through by many a Franciscan padre wending his way along El Camino Real. The name was given to this vast forest preserve by President Franklin D. Roosevelt in 1936 to honor those courageous and dedicated men who labored in the California missions, eight of them within or close to its boundaries.

In the twenty-one missions—all of which have by now been partially preserved, restored, or reconstructed through the efforts of concerned citizens and groups—one can occasionally glimpse Father Serra's vision of a Christianized heaven-on-earth in which nobody went hungry, unclothed, unsheltered, unloved, or without some work to contribute to human society while giving devotions to God. *"Amar a Diós, mis niños"*—"Love God, my children"—was Serra's characteristic greeting to his Indian neophytes.

Junipero Serra, along with Padres Lasuen and Crespi, was interred in the sanctuary of the church at Mission Carmel and so remains with the land that he and the other early Hispanic colonists helped to shape—and name. When the California legislators were asked to furnish two statues for Statuary Hall at the nation's Capitol, they unhesitatingly selected Padre Serra for this honor. (The other was also a churchman, the influential mid-nineteenth century Unitarian, Thomas Starr King.)

As for the twenty-eight settlements that grew up around the missions and presidios and within the first pueblos, they are still growing, adding more place-names all the time.

Los Ranchos Grandes

CALIFORNIA'S GOLDEN AGE of rancho living, celebrated in picture, song, and story, flourished during the three decades of Mexican rule, from 1822 to the American takeover and the Gold Rush. That brief Arcadian existence centered around the great cattle-raising domains that had been granted to the Californios by the Spanish and then Mexican governments.

This was the era of proud and dashing silver-spurred *caballeros* astride their prancing palominos; of *señoritas* in lacy mantillas hiding dark, teasing eyes behind oriental fans; of fiestas, fandangos, and merry *meriendas;* of the fast-riding, reata-twirling *vaqueros*—those cowhands, often half-breeds, who tended the vast spreads of the family-owned ranges.

Above all periods in California history, the "time of the dons" contains the romantic and heroic ingredients for Hispanic fairy tales. The spirit is evoked in the contemporary Spanish ranch-style towns created in most parts of the state, especially those with a Mediterranean type of climate. The names of such developments and many of the street-names contrived for them reflect the vocabulary of the rancho life, probably not always knowingly. (Somehow, *Matanza*—cattle slaughtering—does not seem a suitable name for a pleasant suburban street.) Hundreds of existing place- and street-names are, however, genuine derivations from actual ranchos. The name for that very chic street in Beverly Hills (the penultimate residence of *los ricos*), Rodeo Drive, came from the title of the land grant encompassing that area: *Rancho Rodeo de las Aguas*. Here *rodeo* referred not to a cattle roundup but to the "gathering" of waters from the streams of Benedict and Coldwater canyons.

In the midst of recreating the ranchero ambience—as Santa Barbara does annually in its popular Old Spanish Days celebration—there is always a tinge of sadness, of bittersweet nostalgia for a way of life highly satisfying to the fortunate families, few in number, who participated in it for several generations.

Rancho life depended on possessing and using large tracts of unfenced California land for the pasturage of cattle, horses, and sometimes sheep. In the rather simple and leisurely ranchero economy, contented Californios produced some bare essentials on their own terrain. With the merchants in ships or towns they bartered their cattle products—hides, tallow, beef jerky—for whatever they needed or desired in the form of manufactured goods like tools, kettles, and shoes; of basic processed substances like flour, sugar, coffee, and tea; and of luxury items perhaps from Peru or China.

Unlike the mission padres, the rancheros did not concern themselves over the salvation of the Indians' souls. Nor did they try to convert the natural lands into busily productive hives of agriculture and industry. The Industrial Revolution spawned in Europe was already transforming the young American nation on the other side of the continent. The Californios at first called the U.S.A. "The United States of Boston" because their initial contact came through New England sailing ships. They dwelled in a geographical cul-de-sac, an economic and cultural backwater perhaps a half century behind the technological progress and push of the times, and they saw little need for improvement.

The *don*—a Spanish title of respect, followed by one's personal name—was a member of the new landed gentry in Alta California. He usually traced at least part of his ancestry back to Spain: the part worth talking about. He may have sprung from a father or grandfather who came to California as a soldier, but he would claim his forebear was a soldado distinguido—to differentiate him from a common soldier, the leatherjacket type. Through time and need the original Spanish strain usually combined, without show of prejudice, with other races: Mexican or Californian Indian, even African, and eventually Anglo-American.

In New Spain, as elsewhere in the Spanish empire's colonies, indigenous settlers were discriminated against both politically and economically, whether they were *creoles* (unmixed white but native-born) or *mestizos* (mixed white and Indian)—creating a restless and perturbed population. Like generations of California immigrants coming after them, the Spanish-speaking colonists hoped to find political freedom and self-determination in the new land, as well as a chance to prosper.

The Spanish roots remained dominant. Often the Castilian pronunciation of words (above all, the family name) was retained in the midst of all the New World changes. Yet the speakers themselves might not have learned how to read and write, since this remote place had no regular school system. (Those rancheros who wanted to have well-educated sons employed a tutor if they could not teach them themselves, then sent them off to schools in Mexico, the Sandwich Islands, or faraway New England.) Most of the men, however defective their hold on the Three R's, had at least perfected their signatures, giving special attention to designing their *rúbricos*, the unique, florid squiggles that defied forgery on documents or communications.

With these frontier-society Californios, an elegant style was desirable, the unassailable proof of success: in riding, roping, dancing, romancing, dress, conversing, celebrating, gambling, family life, and friendship. This easy finesse had to be displayed effortlessly. To most foreigners it conveyed the impression of great charm and warmth, but also of a pleasure-loving indolence in this land of *poco tiempo* ("in a little while"). Behind the style, however, lay a lifetime of special cultural training. The boy of four or five, placed upon a saddle, was carefully instructed in the art of conducting himself as a true caballero—who "never did anything he could not do on a horse," as one American remarked. By the time he himself became a don, the master of a rancho of his own, he had absorbed the wisdom of his forefathers, those presidio and mission guards who usually considered any manual labor beneath their dignity and so induced others—Indians mainly, but also lower-class colonists from Mexico—to perform such tasks for him as putting on and taking off his boots. The ranchero's main duty, apart from the essential social functions, was to direct the work of his mayordomo (origin of the English major-domo), who took charge of the whole rancho operation, including the supervision of the crew of vaqueros. In a few cases, the rancho *doña* herself functioned admirably as mayordomo and even part-time vaquera.

The California vaquero was frequently Indian or part-Indian because the padres—the first big cattle ranch proprietors—trained their neophytes to the task. Those with any background in *la jineta,* the Spanish art of riding, climbed upon horses, tucked their gray gowns beneath them, and proceeded to show how to ride horses and how to rope cattle with the most important tool of the rancho —*la reata* (our lariat). In New Spain, teaching Indians horseback riding was forbidden, but here the padres had no other workers available for this essential role. The California Indians, like all other Amerindians, had never seen horses until the Spaniards arrived. Now, like their cousins on the Plains, but with the special skills needed for ranchos, they soon proved themselves among the best horsemen in the world. Among Indians, the vaqueros became aristocrats and had special privileges and freedom not given to the others. It was the ideal place for a half-breed who had to straddle two cultures.

The vaqueros, both homegrown and imported from northern Mexico, were the ranchos' work force. They caught the *mustangos* (evolved from the word *mesteño*— stray), then broke them to saddle and bridle-bit. They took charge of the *caballada,* the dependable collection of horses used regularly for work or traveling. In the springtime, during the annual *rodeo,* they rounded up all the cattle and drove them into enclosures, where they separated out any needing branding or special treatment and those that belonged to the neighboring ranchos. The rodeo was a hard-working time but also a festive one, during which other rancheros would join in the fun of the "run through the mustard," flushing out any cattle hiding in the horn high fields of the yellow-blooming forage weeds, whose seeds had first been planted in California by the padres.

In the corrals the vaqueros deftly threw *lazos* (our lasso) to hobble the yearling cattle and brand them with the rancho's own *fierro* mark. Any disputes over ownership were settled by the *juez de campo* (judge of the plains). Rarely was gelding a part of the operation, since the rancheros were not interested in scientific breeding and permitted bulls to do as they would, doubtless figuring that their stock would increase more rapidly that way. (The prevalence of ill-tempered longhorn *toros,* however, made it hazardous to saunter about a rancho's premises on foot. No wonder the caballeros rode everywhere!) The casual attitude toward animal husbandry caused the perpetuation of a breed that was scrawny and gave beef of a poor quality. The meat, however, seemed good enough for its uses. Since the Hispanic cuisine used few dairy products, cows were not kept or bred for milking, either. The rancheros were mainly interested in the hides or *cueros,* for rancho usage and for trading. They did not mind if local Indians or passersby killed a steer, so long as its hide was left.

Rawhide *(cuero en verde* or *cuero crudo)* was a multi-purpose substance. It was used in making reatas: an expert could cut a hide into a long, thin, single strand that was then braided with others to make a rawhide rope, lightweight but as strong as iron, and quite malleable. Rawhide covered doorways in place of wood. In the absence of nails and bolts it held together the posts and beams of buildings. (Some can still be seen today.) It provided the "springs" for beds and the upholstery for furniture. It was often the bottom to the narrow wooden cart that was Hispanic California's only vehicle. It was used as chink-filler and even glue, and was the *bota* (bag) that held the tallow taken away for trade. It served as a measuring rod. It was even strung around posts to form corrals.

Hides and tallow were obtained during the periodic matanzas, large-scale operations conducted by the vaqueros. Cattle were driven to a special area on a rancho. Riders galloped by them, and without breaking the horse's stride and hardly leaving his saddle, a vaquero would plunge his knife into an animal's neck, hitting the jugular vein and causing near-instant death. Then the rancho's other work crew took over, most of them Indians. Men stripped off the hides, scraped them, and left them to dry in the sun. Women removed chunks of fat that were placed into vats over fires and rendered into tallow or *manteca*. It was often cooled and solidified by being poured into holes in the ground. The best pieces of beef were taken for immediate use while fresh. Other pieces were sliced into strips, dipped in brine, and hung on the poles at the *tasajera*, to sun-dry into *carne seca* or *charqui* (the origin of our word jerky). The carcasses were simply left for the dozens of semiwild dogs that always hung about each rancho, or for other local predators and scavengers like coyotes and *cóndores*. The cleaned-up cattle skulls were sometimes used as stools, indoors or out. Or they might be cemented into the tops of the adobe-walled corrals that contained the rancho's prize horses. With their sharp horns protruding, skulls would discourage entry by grizzly bears or rustlers. The horns themselves were often converted into *butanos;* after their open ends were plugged, they became canteens to be carried by vaqueros on their rounds of duty or by the don himself when undertaking a journey, which he did often.

The Californios were visiting folks. Women and young children usually rode in a *carreta*, the crudely made, narrow, two-wheeled wooden cart still familiar in Latin America, with its pair of oxen yoked across their horned heads, not their necks. In those years, before spokes came to California, wheels consisted of round cross-slices of tree trunks attached to a main axle. Rarely lubricated (and if so, by soap or tallow), the cart wheels squeaked and squawked as the carreta rolled along over the dusty or muddy, pot-holed camino on the way to the casa of some friend or relative. And as a procession of these carts approached the local church in the closest pueblo or mission or presidial town, the chorus of screeching joined in with the tolling of the *campanas*. (It was said that each family's carreta had its own characteristic "voice," so that without even looking, one could tell who was approaching.)

In the warm climate of coastal California and its interior valleys, with abundant forage and reliable arroyos and springs for water, cattle and horses thrived and multiplied, with little exertion on the rancheros' parts. Marrying young and producing many children in a healthful land (for them, if not for the Indian population), the Californios also thrived and multiplied prodigiously on their ranchos.

The first ranchos were pasturelands attached to missions as part of the land the Spanish crown allotted to them for temporary use, and as might be expected, they were usually given religious commemorative names. Among Mission San Gabriel's outlying ranchos were places called San Gorgonio and San Bernardino, both contributing geographical names and place-names to their surroundings. San Jacinto was one of Mission San Luis Rey's ranchos. The presidios were assigned *ranchos reales* (royal ranches) on which they might graze their horses and any livestock used for food.

The first California lands claimed by the Spanish empire but converted to private usage were *concedos* or concessions given to soldiers who had served the province loyally for years and now, aging and perhaps ailing, wished to retire. With permission from New Spain's viceroy, the California gobernador could make a few such usufructuary grants. These required landholders to build a structure on the premises to be used by the vaquero caretakers and to stock the rancho with several hundred cattle. (In later years, the stipulation was for several thousand, which by then amounted to the same initial investment.) The rancheros themselves were expected to dwell in the closest pueblo—which was one way to swell a settlement's population and add to its overall caliber. Generally this live-in requirement became ignored because of its inconvenience, though a family might continue to keep a *casa de pueblo* as well as their *casa de rancho*.

These early private ranchos were not given in perpetuity as possessions of ex-soldiers and their descendants, just as none of the mission lands were ever actually owned by the Franciscan Order but were regarded as being held for them for the Indians' benefit, eventually to be given back to them when they had proven their ability to utilize them for farming or ranching. The ranchos were considered public lands in the control of the king of Spain. In Mexico, such lands had been developed into extensive *haciendas* or farmlands, to which Indian populations had been attached as *peones* or bondaged laborers. California, with its cycle of wet and dry seasons, made farming difficult without the construction and maintenance of dams and irrigation channels. The padres had done this in order to feed their hundreds of resident neophytes and also to furnish food to other settlements. But the rancheros grew only as much produce as they needed for immediate family use; they relied upon their cattle herds for all else, directly or indirectly.

During the time of Spanish rule, only twenty of these

early land concessions were given. Most of them became very important historically and economically. To give some idea of the original scope of these grants and their eventual roles in California's development, here are the names and acreage of the most notable ranchos that set the pattern for future ones:

- *San Rafael* or *La Zanja*, belonging to the Verdugos. It encompassed almost 40,000 acres. Some of the domain is now occupied by the cities of Glendale, Burbank, and Eagle Rock. The Verdugo name itself is perpetuated in mountains, a canyon, and a town.
- *Santa Gertrudes* or *Los Nietos* was originally owned by the Nieto family. Eventually it was subdivided into five ranchos, including Los Cerritos and Los Alamitos. A huge acreage within the premises of Los Angeles County, it contained land between the San Gabriel and Santa Ana rivers from the mountains to the sea. Long Beach, Downey, and Norwalk all sit upon it.
- *San Pedro,* the Dominguez estate, was a triangular section that is now covered by settlements like Compton, Redondo Beach, and Wilmington. It had more than 43,000 acres.
- *Nuestra Señora del Refugio* or *El Refugio* was given to Jose Francisco Ortega, who served as sergeant on the Portola expedition and is considered the first European to behold San Francisco Bay. Lying northwest of Santa Barbara, it contained 26,500 acres. The name of the rancho continues in Refugio Pass, Refugio Beach, and Cañada del Refugio. Ortega occurs there too as a geographical name.
- *Santiago de Santa Ana* of the Yorbas was a rancho

with some 30,000 acres that are now part of cities such as Orange, Santa Ana, and Newport Beach.

- *San Antonio,* the Peralta family domain, consisted of eleven square leagues (over 40,000 acres) that are now divided into the East Bay communities and environs of Oakland, Alameda, and Berkeley.
- *El Conejo*'s premises now straddle both Ventura and Los Angeles counties in the vicinity of Thousand Oaks. It was acquired from the original grantee by the well-known De la Guerra y Noriega family. Conejo (rabbit) still appears there as a name for a mountain, a valley, and a creek.
- *San José de Gracia de Simi,* totaling more than 100,000 acres, belonged to various members of the Pico clan. The last word in the title, an Indian word meaning "village," endures in the name of the valley and the settlement, now within Ventura County.
- *Topanga Malibu Sequit,* combining three Indian names, was the Tapia family's rancho stretching along the Pacific Coast, where Malibu and Topanga canyons and settlements retain parts of the title. Tapia Canyon and Tapia County Park perpetuate the original owners' name.
- *El Encino,* assigned to a soldier named Reyes in 1785, was challenged later by the padres at Mission San Fernando, who claimed that this grant encroached upon the mission's lands and therefore interfered with the Indians' property rights. The concession was withdrawn, but after mission secularization another private rancho at the site took the same title, which now appears in the town's name in the area.

When Mexico became independent and acquired California as a territory, the nature of this landownership changed. The California governor was authorized to make permanent and no-cost land grants to Mexican citizens who applied for acreage in specific unsettled areas. Since the "cash flow" between Mexico City and Monterey was less than dependable, land grants were often used in lieu of paying salaries or discharging debts to soldiers or civilians. An applicant had to prove that he was a citizen in good standing and could maintain the land as a cattle rancho. He also had to submit a roughly surveyed map or *diseño* of the place he desired, along with a title appropriate for it. The boundaries were usually erratic, following streambeds and ridges, and using certain land features in the locality — large trees, rock formations, even cattle skulls — as markers. Vaqueros would measure the land by working as a team, one attaching a fifty-*vara* reata (about 150 yards) to a stake while his partner rode off with the other end.

The Spanish and Mexican system of recording land transactions was different indeed from the Anglo-American one involving a grid system of platting ownership divisions. A successful claimant was given a deed to the property, which could be no larger in total than eleven square leagues (about 48,000) acres). Most of it would consist of grazing land, but perhaps some of it lay alongside a river or another water source that could make it suitable as an hacienda. The rancheros who had acquired concessions under Spanish rule and wanted to retain them under the new Mexican government submitted requests for their lands and now became legal owners of their ranchos.

The pace of land granting speeded up considerably after the secularization of the twenty-one missions, which released some twelve million acres of mostly prime grazing lands into the public domain. Before 1834 there had been only about fifty grants made. By 1846 over 600 ranchos were awarded. In those dozen years Californios made many requests for sections of Franciscan holdings unoccupied by settlers. (Indians' rancherias, not considered bona fide settlements, could be included within a rancho's domain.) Both newcomers and already propertied families succeeded in gaining possession of mission-improved lands, although usually these were sold for a nominal sum—to friends and relatives of the governor or his aides.

Some ambitious rancheros, appointed as supervisors of mission lands, acquired outright ownership. Others took advantage of confused or gullible neophytes given their own plots. An unscrupulous fellow could buy them out for a collection of baubles or a keg of aguardiente—piecing these land bits together until he had a sizable tract. The dispossessed Indians could depart. Or they might be permitted to remain on the premises, living in nearby rancherias or in huts near the main casa, working as peons on the ranchland or as domestic servants—nursemaids, housekeepers, cooks, laundresses, gardeners, factotums. They were paid in food and cloth. (Only the vaqueros received small salaries for their work.) It became customary for each rancho family to have as many Indian domestic servants as its own population of men, women, and children. At best, it was a form of benevolent servitude, though the natives were mostly free to come and go at will, unlike at the missions.

Gradually the ranch houses, which were erected at those spots providing year-round water and the best vistas, were improved. At the start, just like the first crude missions, they were usually made of interwoven branches plastered with mud and roofed with tules: one- or two-room shelters. Since timber for building purposes was rarely available in rancho territories, requiring both transport and sawing, rancheros erected permanent buildings and even corrals from the adobe soil at hand, with the Indian workers—who had experience already at the missions— doing the basic brick making and construction.

Becoming accustomed to living in adobe or sometimes stone houses, the Californios saw little need for lumber, except for roof beams and posts and carved doors. Their tradition did not include making or using sawmills, so land grants in forested areas were not desirable to them. The *corte de madera* (cut-wood) ranchos usually belonged to foreigners who installed machinery to saw wood both for the Spanish-speaking population and their own purposes.

The rancho casa was added to in stages as the family grew and its assets multiplied along with their cattle and the hide and tallow trade. At the center of each casa was the traditional open-air patio, where cooking was done. Sometimes along the external walls of both patio and the outside of the casa *arcadas* or verandas were built, with overhanging eaves that protected the residents—who liked to spend as much time as possible outdoors, talking, sewing, singing, preparing foods—from both strong sunlight and rain. Some houses eventually acquired second stories, though in earthquake-prone places this was unwise. Gradually, too, the interiors and exteriors were given such niceties as a lime whitewash. Made from limestone obtained in the closest chalk or fossil beds or from shells gathered at the beach, then roasted at high heat in a limekiln, slaked lime was also used in plaster and stucco. Mixed with pure sand, it became mortar for stone and brick laying.

Tiles or planks eventually replaced the old hard-packed dirt floors. Windowglass was brought to California at first on Yankee boats. (The Vallejo family's *Casa Materna*

—mother house—at present-day Watsonville was also called La Casa de Cristal—The Glass House—because of its many and extravagant windows brought all the way around the Horn from New England.) As blacksmithing increased, new touches were wrought-iron railings and windowguards. Craftsmen who arrived in the California colony were valued by both padres and rancheros wanting to build impressive structures and then beautify them.

Like the old missions, the ranchos were renowned for their generous hospitality. Strangers were met with trustful openness, not with the suspicion and fear of later epochs. A traveler could go from one rancho to the next along El Camino Real or any other route between settlements and be assured of a meal and lodging. And he would be sent off in the morning with a fresh mount taken from the caballada. (These horses regularly ran around with long lazos hung around their necks so that they could be easily caught.) An unexpected visitor who pleased the don and his family might be invited to spend a week or two. From such guests the isolated rancheros learned the latest news and gossip. Their arrivals gave good excuses for parties, and sometimes alliances were formed in politics, business, or marriage.

The Californio families were unusually large, consisting of a dozen children or more. *Las señoras* kept busy supervising the running of the household, along with child-bearing. If a wife died young, a don most likely married again, producing another set of offspring. Since the rancho clans married among themselves, joining young people of equivalent social status, eventually most of them were interrelated in rather complex ways, and generations were close together. (This consanguinity partly explained the Californios' reluctance to carry their political squabbles into actual bloodshed on battlefields. Much as they might feud, Mariano Vallejo and Juan Bautista Alvarado were uncle and nephew, and near-peers.)

Often the young men at about age sixteen enlisted as soldiers at a presidio regiment, and quickly rose to officer rank, which they might retain for years if the position was prestigious and carried social and economic advantages. The presidial towns were centers for California's cultural life, particularly the capital, Monterey. which had about two thousand inhabitants in its Mexican heyday. An extended family often maintained a casa there. During wedding celebrations and the holiday seasons, particularly Easter and Christmas, siblings, in-laws, and cousins of all different ages would happily crowd together in one house, sometimes fifty at a time—having brought bedding with them in their lumbering carretas, perhaps traveling for a week and several hundred miles, making overnight stops at ranchos along the way.

There were the invitation-only *bailes* held at private houses, when dancing was often interrupted by the boisterous young of marriageable age, who flirted with each other by cracking *cascarones*—eggshells filled with perfume or confetti; later, sometimes with gold dust—over each other's heads. (During the pre-Lent season in Monterey, if eggs were obtainable at all, they cost as much as a dollar apiece.) And there were the communal, everybody's-welcome *fandangos,* where expert and enthusiastic dancers performed for several days at a stretch, with time out only for naps. After Mass on Sundays in the town there were meriendas or picnics attended by all, followed by horse races, bullfights, and other contests of skill and swiftness and style that were good for gambling purposes. A particularly enticing sport was the *carrera de gallo,* which involved planting a cock up to his neck in dirt, then trying to pluck him out while galloping by. The caballeros were inveterate gamblers.

These early-settler *familias* who were now California's leading citizens were inclined to forget any modest or even disreputable beginnings. They drew a sharp distinction between their grandee class and that of the lower-class pobladores and the recently imported *cholos* from Mexico, who outnumbered them perhaps by ten to one. They believed themselves qualified to run their own government and put up with the Mexico-dispatched governor only if he pleased them. Thus when the arrogant new gobernador Victoria arrived and tried to impose strict rules, the Californios revolted successfully against him at the Battle of Cahuenga Pass. Four years later, in a similar confrontation, they deposed Micheltorena, who had infuriated them by bringing in a band of scoundrels and calling them soldiers when they were obviously only cholos, who robbed the countryside of ripe fruit, roosting chickens, and even laundry hung out to dry. (A decade later, at the same Cahuenga Pass, the Mexican Californios would officially surrender to the new American regime.)

The nearly self-sufficient Californios did not like most appointments and decrees that came from Mexico. Nor did they readily put up with each other's plans and ambitions, so that the province during Mexican rule experienced a succession of feuds, *juntas* among various politicos and supporters, rebellions, and pitched battles of little consequence—giving Alta California a reputation as a stage for political comic operas. A perennial conflict also commenced between the northerners *(los arribeños)* and the southerners *(los abajeños)* with the Tehachapi Mountains considered the dividing line. Sometimes the abajeños, with the current governor's connivance, succeeded in switching the capital to San Diego or Los Angeles. (At one point, there were two governors sharing the same office several hundred miles apart.)

The ranchero class was largely drawn from the soldier-settlers who had traveled in with Portola or Anza in 1769 and 1776. Vallejo and Lugo had come up from Baja with the new governor Rivera y Moncada in 1774. Periodic reinforcements for presidio and mission squads brought in such valued men as Roque Jacinto de Cota, Jose Dario Arguello, Jose Maria Estudillo, Francisco Xavier Sepulveda, Jose de la Guerra y Noriega, and the Castro whose grandson Juan developed the town of Castroville. Later arrivals were Juan Bandini, who emigrated as a youth from Peru; Antonio Maria Sunol, who jumped ship in order to stay in California; and Francisco de Haro, who eventually became a comandante at the San Francisco Presidio and Yerba Buena's first alcalde. All in time rose to eminence in a society that appreciated the right style of self-presentation.

A Mexico-hatched immigration of 250 settlers led by Hijar and Padres, with plans to take over the soon-to-be-secularized missions, was received coldly by the Californios, who had their own designs on those lands. Disbanded, with their leaders sent back home, the colonists were dispersed among the established pueblos or sent north to the Sonoma area being developed by Vallejo. As colonists they possessed unusually valuable talents. Many were well-educated craftsmen who eventually contributed needed skills and culture to the province. Among them were the much-respected schoolteachers and civic leaders from Los Angeles, Ignacio Coronel and his son Antonio; their relative, Agustin Olvera, who later became a judge and lent his name to the old-style Mexican street at the Plaza familiar to tourists; and Jose de Jesus Noe, soon afterwards a notable landowner in San Francisco, where he served as the last Mexican alcalde.

These and others with Hispanic surnames were all rancheros, so that localities within their land-grant holdings frequently contain their names on geographical features and street-names; also for towns such as Martinez, Peralta, Sunol, Gonzales, Duarte, Serrano, Moraga, Tanforan, Pacheco, Camarillo, Yorba (with the decorative Linda added). As in Castroville, the French -*ville*, for town, was added to a surname to create a number of California settlement names from many sources. Vacaville therefore does not really mean "cowtown," but commemorates the Vaca family—Hispanic—that lived there. Los Feliz Boulevard in Los Angeles is not ungrammatical at all. (The plural *los*, combined with the singular adjective *feliz*, properly would be *felices*—the happy ones.) It commemorates instead the rancho of the Feliz children—children of the soldier Jose Vicente Feliz, who with their father had walked over El Camino del Diablo and the Colorado Desert in Anza's expedition. (Their mother had died in childbirth at the trip's start; amazingly, the only casualty on the long march. Her infant, however, survived and became a Californio.)

Hispanic settlers of the past were honored in San Francisco's 1909 name-changing-and-making burst (post-earthquake and fire). Many early residents were remembered, including senoras like Feliciana Arballo and Juana Cardenas, as well as De Haro, Noe, Guerrero, and Noriega. Here and there in cities there are also commemoratives for governors, loved and even less than loved: Neve, Borica, Figueroa, Victoria, Micheltorena, Alvarado.

An important physical outcome of the ranchos is the present course of many roads. Major routes often run along the former borders of ranchos, or at one time led to their casas from the main thoroughfares like El Camino Real. Main streets in urban and rural areas, beginning as these boundary paths or interior driveways, may now have numbers or indistinctive names, but quite a few carry on original rancho titles or their former owners' surnames.

Land-grant ranchos usually had titles attached to them that appeared on both the deed and the diseño (kept, hopefully, either in the Monterey archives or among a family's most guarded possessions). These titles often acquired alternative names when a rancho was sold to another person or was subdivided by heirs. Because the Californio families usually retained close interrelationships in their landholdings, some eventually accrued vast acreage, whether in adjoining areas or scattered in places throughout the province. In the south, the Carrillos owned a total of 320,000 acres; the Picos, 532,000; the de la Guerras, 320,000. In the north, the Peralta, Vallejo, Alvarado, and Castro dynasties had similarly impressive figures. (As an individual ranchero, the American Abel Stearns outdid them all.)

The newly acquired rancho frequently adopted the name of an existing place—a geographical feature or a rancheria—within its domain. Many of these titles therefore were basically Indian words recorded in Spanish. Among those still in use today, mainly because of preservation within rancho titles, and their disenos, are these: Acalanes, Aptos, Azusa, Bolinas (from Baulines), Buri-Buri, Cahuenga, Castaic (from Castac), Cholame, Cotati, Cucamonga, Cuyama, Cuyamaca, Guajome, Huerhuero, Jamacha, Jamal, Jurupa, Lompoc, Malibu, Napa, Niguel, Nipomo, Ojai, Orestimba, Otay, Pala, Pauma, Petaluma, Pismo, Saticoy, Sespe, Simi, Soquel, Tamalpais, Temecula, Topanga, Tujunga.

As with all place-naming, the land-grant titles came from a variety of origins, and since many were transferred from already set, partly descriptive names, they kept words like Arroyo, Canada, Laguna, Llano, Rio, and Vega at the beginning of the title: Rancho de———. Just plain *Rancho*

La Cañada became the town La Canada of today. And *Arroyo de las Nueces* was later translated into the settlement name of Walnut Creek. Arroyo, a water source, appeared in at least thirty titles, and sometimes, during the process of converting a rancho title into useful local place-names, a tautological term resulted, like Arroyo Creek. Certain words pertaining specifically to land grants appeared in some titles, such as *Sitio* (place), *Sobrante* (surplus land "left over" from an established rancho nearby), *Paraje* or *Parage* (residence or site), *Cajón* ("boxed-in" area), *Bolsa* ("pocket" of land surrounded on three sides by difficult terrain but open on the fourth), *Rincón* (portion of land), and *Rinconada* (a "corner" of land shaped by woods, hills, or roadway).

Because the rancho casa itself was likely to be located close to a water source, titles reflected this, not just in the many *Arroyos* but in words like *Ojo* or *Ojito* (here, not eyes or little eyes but springs of water), *Boca* (a river mouth or opening, such as *Rancho Boca de Santa Mónica*), *Aguaje* and *Aguajito* (spring and small spring). *Chorro* was water coming from a narrow place, *Zanja* and *Zanjón* were ditches, *Butano* in a title designated a place to drink. *Tijera* could have meant scissors, or else a channel or drain, perhaps to drain off marshland. Thus *Rancho Cienega o Paso de la Tijera* in an area now part of Los Angeles, which contained several other ranchos with *cienaga* (swamp) misspelled: hence La Cienega Boulevard. (There's also a La Tijera Boulevard.) There were various *Posos, Pozos, Pozitos* (wells, pools, puddles). The absence of water would be noted: *Laguna Seca, Arroyo Seco, Llano Seco*. Also the kinds of water available, not always desirable: Ranchos *Agua Caliente* (hot springs—these were numerous), *Agua Hedionda* (once a stinky, swampy lagoon north of San Diego), *Agua Mansa* (still water).

Another recurring descriptive term in titles was brea, the tar or asphaltum (sometimes called pitch) that oozed up from the ground in pools or from mountain springs. (It even came up occasionally from the ocean floor, close to the Ortegas' *El Refugio* rancho, where the surf sometimes carried an oil slick—a natural "spill" in an area notorious for them much later, when people learned to drill for "black gold" beneath the sea.) Brea was useful to Hispanic settlers for roofing buildings and caulking boats, so it was worth mentioning on maps—and in titles. The best-known one was, of course, *Rancho La Brea,* whose black, bubbling pits preserved thousands of Pleistocene fossils, on view today at the on-the-spot Page Museum near La Brea Boulevard. A rancho named *Pismo,* the Indian word for tar, continues now in the town of Pismo Beach.

There was only one modestly complimentary descriptive title: *Buena Vista,* used thrice. A number of plants and trees were featured in rancho names, like *Los Alamitos* (Cottonwoods), *El Alisal* (Sycamore Grove), *Llano de Robles, Paso de Robles* (Oak Flats and Oak Pass), *Sausal Redondo* (Round Willow Grove, perhaps the originator of Redondo Beach), *Sausalito* or *Saucelito* (Small Willow Grove), *Palos Verdes* (Green Shrubs), *Laguna de los Palos Colorados* (Redwood Lagoon), and *Bolsa de Chamisal* (Pocket with Thick Shrubs). The city and county of Alameda took their names from *Rancho Arroyo de la Alameda* (Cottonwood Creek).

Animals too often entered into titles: *El Conejo* (Rabbit), *El Tejón* (for the valley in which early travelers once saw a dead badger), *Los Bueyes* (Oxen), *Los Cuervos* (Crows), *Los Coyotes, Paraje del Toro* (Bull Place—now El Toro), *La Liebre* (Hare), *Cañada de Coches* (Hog Canyon), *Rincón de la Ballena* (Whale Corner), *Ciénaga de las Ranas*

(Frog Swamp), *Rinconada de los Gatos* (Cat Corner, because its discoverer supposedly saw two wildcats engaged in ferocious combat). *Punta del Tiburón* (Shark Point) eventually became the well-to-do Marin County town of Tiburon. And of course there was the Portola Expedition's irrepressible *Las Pulgas*. *Rancho Las Mariposas* recalled Gabriel Moraga's 1806 encounter with swarms of butterflies (though some say they were poppies that looked like butterflies!). John C. Fremont purchased the ranch from Juan Bautista Alvarado; and it drew swarms of miners during the Gold Rush. The name for the town and county later became singular.

There were geographical statements, like *Los Médanos* (Sand Dunes), *Montecito* (Little Woods), *Los Cerritos* (Little Hills), *Piedra Blanca* (White Rock, now plural in Piedras Blancas Point), *Arroyo de los Pilarcitos* (Little Rock-Pillar Creek). *Rancho El Sur* took its name from *Río Grande del Sur* (Large River of the South, because it was south of Monterey). The area is now known as Big Sur. There were also ranchos conveying warnings, like *Cañada de Salsipuedes* (Get-Out-If-You-Can Canyon) or *Atascadero* (Mudhole).

Some descriptive titles displayed human alterations of the landscape: *Cañada de Huerta Vieja* (Old Orchard Canyon), *Corral de Piedra* (Stone Corral), *Milpitas* (Little Cornfields), *Corte de Madera* (Cut Wood), *Misión Vieja* (Old Mission, a rancho first attached to Mission San Juan Capistrano, and now evolved into the contemporary, Spanish-style, planned community of Mission Viejo), *Dos Pueblos* (because two Indian rancherias were within the rancho boundaries). There were odd or whimsical combinations of names, mostly perhaps having to do with the names of existing sites, such as *Las Positas y la Calera*—the

Puddles and the Limekiln—probably where cement was mixed! (This rancho later became the Hope Ranch in Santa Barbara.)

Often it's hard to know whether a rancho title is purely descriptive or tells some story and is therefore dramatic (such as *Rancho Las Pulgas,* dating back to Portola's soldiers). Among the curious mixtures of title words was *Rancho Cañada de los Osos y Pecho y Islai*—Valley of the Bears and Breast (more likely courage) and Islay (a wild cherry eaten by the Indians)—the last continuing in San Luis Obispo County's Islay Hill and Creek. Or *Bolsa de Potrero y Moro Cojo* (Pocket of Pasture and the Lame Moor—though the *moro* surely carries another meaning, a dark roan horse). *Rancho Aguaje del Centinela* (Sentinel Spring) shows itself in today's Centinela Boulevard in Los Angeles. *Monte del Diablo* (Devil's Woods—now Mount Diablo) was a rancho in Contra Costa that belonged to "Dr." John Marsh, an American; it took its name supposedly from the time when Spanish soldiers were treated to a diabolical dance by their Indian foes' medicine man. *Rancho La Goleta*'s title came from the schooner that ran aground there, though some informants said that it came from the ship that was built and launched at the site: one of the first ocean-going boats built in California.

Probably the strangest rancho title was *Carne Humana* (human flesh). It did not commemorate some pre-Donner Party cannibals but was the grotesque joke of its grantee, the English physician Edward Bale, who was something of a troublemaker, having been jailed twice: once for bootlegging and once for shooting at his Napa Valley neighbor, Salvador Vallejo. Deciding that the Indians' name for his new place sounded like carne humana, he put that title on his land-grant request and it was approved. The name proved too grisly to perpetuate.

There were only a few transported names, such as *Rancho Ballona* (reputedly commemorating its owner's home place in Spain, Bayona), which continues in Los Angeles's last remaining marshland, Ballona Lagoon. And there was John Augustus Sutter's place, *Rancho Nueva Helvetia* (New Switzerland), the scene of much action in the 1840s and '50s.

Naturally among the ranchos were a good many commemorative religious names, saints' names in particular. There were eight San Antonios in various forms; numerous San Felipes, San Juans, San Joses, and Santa Rosas. Also a few San Francisquitos. (It was not the saint who was "little" but the geographical feature connected with it, usually an arroyo.) Often, of course, the rancho titles picked up an existing place-name. A number of the saints appearing in rancho titles are familiar to us because they resulted in settlement or other names: San Bernardino, San Cayetano, San Dimas, San Emigdio, San Geronimo, San Gorgonio, San Gregorio, San Jacinto, San Leandro, San Lorenzo, San Marcos, San Mateo, San Onofre, San Pablo, San Ramon, San Simeon (later of Hearst Ranch fame), Santa Anita (where the racetrack is now), Santa Margarita, Santa Monica, Santa Paula, San Vicente, San Ysidro. There was also a *Rancho Santa Ana y Quién Sabe* (St. Anne and Who Knows?), perhaps an early jokester's contribution, or maybe the product of somebody weary of thinking up place-names. (At any rate, there is a Quien Sabe Creek in the area in San Benito County.)

Religious names did not halt with the saints, for there were *Familia Sagrada* (Holy Family); *Visitación* (the presidio rancho in the San Francisco Bay area, now recalled in Visitacion Point and Valley—whose original *c* has recently replaced the Anglo *t*—honoring the Virgin Mary's visitation to St. Elizabeth); *Las Ánimas* (The Souls), *Noche*

Buena (Christmas Eve); *Loma del Espíritu Santo* (Hill of the Holy Spirit); *Natividad* (Nativity), *Las Cruces* (The Crosses), *Asunción* (Assumption, or the Virgin Mary's ascent to heaven), and *Nuestra Señora de Altagracia* (Our Lady of the Highest Grace).

The rancho titles live on in many forms in those regions of California that contained ranches created by Mexican land grants. The ranchos themselves also kept alive, through usage and on their maps, a great number of the Hispanic place-names for land features and rancherias which often dated back to an earlier time of exploration prior to settlement.

As for the ranchero families themselves, the way of life that they led, dedicated to simple pleasures and conducted at a slow *mañana* pace, could not last forever. By the mid-1840s it was clear that changes were in store for the isolated and rusticating province of California— brought mainly by the enterprising *Americanos* who came, by sea or land, from the other side of the continent.

The Yanquis Are Coming!

MI CASA ES SU CASA" (My house is your house). This traditional welcoming phrase in Hispanic countries was repeated both in the province of California and in numerous individual households when newly independent Mexico began to manage the place that Spain had been neglecting for years. One of Mexico's most popular decisions so far as the Californios were concerned was the legalization of trade with foreign ships.

Not that trade hadn't been going on briskly, despite Spain's edict forbidding it. California was too remote and too needful for the disintegrating Spanish empire to service it properly. Ships had come in periodically starting in the 1790s: English, French, Russian, Dutch, even American vessels, on scientific expeditions (the Spanish were inclined to regard them as spying trips), diplomatic or charting voyages

American Takeover

(like Vancouver's), or fur-trapping and trading ventures that came in to take on water and fresh food and make repairs. All the while, the visitors looked around to see what California might offer them—either then or in the future.

At first the presidio comandantes and the governor frowned at foreign intrusions. But then they began to realize that these visits might offer certain advantages. Not only did the Mexicans enjoy the social contact with people of culture (like the captains and officers and scientists) and the news of the world outside that they brought, but they also found that they could acquire goods they wanted or liked, unavailable otherwise. They trafficked regularly with the Russians at Fort Ross. And a busy smuggling trade went on behind Spanish officialdom's back with the Sandwich Islands (Hawaii) as a main base of operations, the offshore islands (Santa Catalina especially) as hideouts, and pick-ups and deliveries going on in the dark of night at harbors. Even the padres at the missions—many of them shrewd businessmen—entered into covert transactions. For years, a Yankee captain and his ship made regular mail and cargo deliveries among the coastal settlements.

The first American to arrive in California was either dead or dying. John Groehm, or Graham, had been a crewman on the Spanish naval expedition captained by Malaspina, an Italian navigator, who had been asked to search for the still-unfound Strait of Anian. The American was put ashore at Monterey, where Malaspina had paused for a few days, and there he was buried, in 1791. The next American entry was made by Captain Dorr in 1796, engaged in the China trade, which involved the exchange of otter skins cherished by the Chinese for porcelains and silks and tea. His ship, the *Otter,* landed at Monterey to take on provisions and discharge about a dozen stowaways from Botany Bay—survivors of the recent mutiny on the *Bounty*. (The Californians rather liked the British crewmen and were willing to keep them as settlers, but the governor had to send them south to stand trial in New Spain.)

The next historically important visit by an American ship did not go so pleasantly. The *Lelia Byrd* came into San Diego hoping to do business over otter skins. The outraged authorities jailed some sailors for a while, and the ship eventually had to fight its way out of the harbor, exchanging cannonades with the Spaniards' battery on Point Loma. (This was one of the rare occasions when California artillery was used. The Spanish defenses were of poor caliber, with the weaponry rust-corroded from lack of maintenance and disuse. During the entire Hispanic regime gunpowder and cannonballs were in short supply. Sometimes foreign vessels entering a port were asked by the presidio comandante to give their hosts sufficient gunpowder to fire off the required formal salute!)

The first Americans to settle down in California were sailors who jumped ship in 1816. They liked the look of the the place and simply deserted. By then the colony was used to foreigners. Two were carpenters from New England; the third was a black sailor. The best known was Thomas Doak, who quickly made himself useful by painting decorations at San Juan Bautista in exchange for his room and board. He then married into the local Castro family.

The next permanent American resident, Joseph Chapman, arrived in a more spectacular way: in Bouchard's notorious 1818 attack on the California settlements. Hatched in South America and launched from the Sandwich Islands supposedly to stir up the Californios to rebel against Spain, it caused the evacuation of the capital. Monterey was taken with scarcely a shot being fired from shore. After looting the town and moving southward, the raiders began to encounter resistance. Close to the Ortega rancho north of Santa Barbara a "pirate" was lassoed by the Californios. Young Chapman welcomed this rescue, for he was a Bostonian who had been shanghaied earlier by the revolutionist Hipolito Bouchard. He refused to take part in a prisoner exchange conducted shortly before Bouchard's departure from the colony that had proven its dislike for imported ideas of rebellion. Chapman became a favorite with the padres at San Gabriel Mission, where he directed the building of a boat—California's first—in 1831, from timber hauled down from the mountains; disassembled, it was carried by carretas to San Pedro Bay, where it was put together again and then launched. Chapman married an Ortega family heiress, acquired a rancho near Santa Barbara, and spent the rest of his days happily working at construction projects, for which he had special aptitude.

Americans were not the only early non-Hispanic settlers in California. John Gilroy, a Scotsman, jumped ship in 1814. He too married an Ortega girl and even acquired his own rancho, San Isidro, which eventually evolved into a settlement now known as Gilroy in his honor. Robert Livermore, an Englishman, and John Milligan, an Irishman, followed the same pattern.

When Mexico, under its own regime, relaxed the trading rules in 1822, more and more Anglo-American vessels came into California harbors. They had often started out in search of otter skins and the fur seals off the coast or were engaged in whaling, but increasingly they sought the ranchos' crudely dried cowhides and bags of tallow: the first to be converted into leather goods tanned and manufactured in New England cities (with many items like shoes and fine saddles finding their way back to California on return voyages), and the second an essential ingredient in

The Yanquis Are Coming!

making soap and candles and various lubricants, including tanning oils.

The first Yankee ships to concentrate on this California trade became department stores on water. Totaling up a ranchero's credit in hides, tallow, and perhaps some beef jerky too, the captain would invite a Californio family on board his ship to do their shopping, escorting them among the displays of fabrics from the Orient, mantillas from Peru, bolts of cotton cloth, or fashionable clothing turned out in New England's garment factories, metal pots, utensils, and tools, iron stoves, nails, bridles, guns and gunpowder, furniture (even pianos), tortoiseshell combs and other adornments, toys for the niños—and basic provisions that California could not yet produce for herself. There was something for everyone, all figured in at the exchange rate of about $2 per hide and $1.50 for a twenty-five-pound bota of manteca.

New England and British shipping companies soon saw that it would be convenient to set up permanent stores in the settlements, so that this shopping could go on all year round instead of seasonally and in bursts when news of ships' arrivals got around, bringing on a rash of local matanzas. This way, too, warehouses could be built close to the shore, where hides could be properly prepared— washed in sea water, then set out to dry in the sun—and then stored until ships were ready to take them away on the round-the-Horn voyage to New England or England. British and American shipping companies hired permanent agents to look after their interests in the California ports and function as merchants. Among the Englishmen to begin their California careers this way were William Hartnell and William Richardson: respectively, a hide trader who became a customs collector, inspector of mission properties, and ranchero; and the founder and first port captain of Yerba Buena settlement, which became San Francisco, before settling down on his Rancho Sausalito across the bay. (There the much smaller bay, Richardson, takes his name.) Hugo Reid, a Scotsman, also began as a hide trader. He married an Indian woman and eventually took over as proprietor of Rancho Santa Anita and Rancho San Pascual (covering the area now including Monrovia and Pasadena).

The best-known American merchants and ex-captains were Alfred Robinson, Abel Stearns, John Temple, Nathan Spear, Thomas O. Larkin, John Rogers Cooper, Henry D. Fitch, William G. Dana, and William Heath Davis. All of them except Larkin eventually became rancheros with considerable lands—Stearns, in fact, became Mexican California's largest landowner. They did so by becoming Mexican citizens and Roman Catholics in order to qualify for land grants. ("Leaving their consciences at Cape Horn" was how this conversion got explained by the cynical.) All of them too (as with most of the Englishmen) married into prominent Californio families: Carrillos, Vallejos, Picos, Castros, Bandinis, Estudillos. Larkin, who became the U.S. consul at Monterey, built a home that served as prototype for the Monterey Colonial architectural style, combining New England and Californio elements. These two-story casas, usually constructed of adobe, had a long balcony-walkway that used wooden posts and railings and sometimes stretched around the building, providing a former Yankee sailor with a panoramic lookout.

These *Yanqui* landholders were joined by other foreigners who came by sea and worked their way into California's landed gentry. Quickly assimilating Hispanic ways, they became dons themselves, and took new Spanish names: Juan, Benito, Esteban, Guillermo, Alfredo, Jose, Roberto. They all gave their ranchos Spanish or Spanish-

The Yanquis Are Coming!

Indian names. Those with long residence became so proficient in Spanish that they automatically talked and wrote to each other in that language.

But it took a while. One American wanting to pay court to a lovely señorita was schooled by a helpful compatriot in the appropriate phrases. Arriving at her casa and invited into the *sala,* he blurted out, *"Yo quiero té,"* which was met by a surprised look on her face as she scurried from the room. In a few minutes she returned with a cup of tea for him. Only then did he realize that he had said, "I want tea," not—as he intended—*"Yo te quiero,"* ("I love you.").

In spite of any awkward blunders, however, most Anglos in the California of the 1830s and 1840s were well received by the dark-eyed young ladies (many of whom were only fourteen or fifteen years old) and welcomed by their parents into matrimony. (One of the highlights of Richard Henry Dana's *Two Years Before the Mast* was his description of the wedding of Alfred Robinson and a De la Guerra heiress.)

Once in a while, though, there were problems, as when Governor Echeandia refused to permit Captain Henry Fitch to wed his Carrillo enamorada because he was smitten with her himself. The pair, with Pio Pico's help, simply eloped to Valparaiso in Chile, where they were married. Returning home to California, Fitch was jailed, but the San Gabriel Mission padres arranged for his release. He made amends for his offense to the province by purchasing a large bell needed for the asistencia church in the plaza at El Pueblo de los Angeles.

The Americanos found favor among the Californios. The señoras liked their manners, the señoritas their earnest and energetic demeanor, the caballeros their apparent willingness to do work that they themselves declined to do but saw value in—the supervising of details of trading transactions, the complex administration of rancho properties, the setting up of businesses useful to the province such as gristmills, sawmills, soap- and candle-making shops, blacksmiths' foundries, brick and cement works, fruit orchards, vineyards, leather-tanning and boot-making establishments. After the missions closed down, these important industries and crafts had to be continued. The Americans' work ethic —Protestants though they might no longer be—impelled them to find pleasure and profit in economic activity. No wonder, then, that the Californios opened their doors to the Yanquis. (Those with unaccustomed blue eyes and blond hair were nicknamed *huero,* meaning unfertilized egg—for obviously some element was lacking in their coloring.)

But then Americanos began to enter the province in a different way—overland across the prairies and Rocky Mountains and the Great Basin, then scaling the escarpment of the Sierra Nevada and coming through its passes; or moving down from Oregon as fur trappers; or traveling south along Anza's route or the Old Spanish Trail, from the Sante Fe area. Americans coming by sea were one thing; peculiar-looking landsmen wearing buckskin, beads, and feathers quite another. First came the fur trader and explorer Jedediah Smith, arriving at Mission San Gabriel in 1826 after crossing the Mojave Desert and descending from Cajon Pass, as Father Garces had done a half century before. Jailed by Governor Echeandia, he was released when the Yankee Californios got him to agree to leave at once—which he did, but not by the way he came. Instead, he and his companions did some beaver trapping in the San Joaquin Valley and then exited east through the Sierra: the first white men to go across the range. The following year Smith returned again, was jailed again and ousted again. This time he left from Monterey and traveled overland to Oregon, the first white man to make such a trip.

Young Jedediah Smith soon met his death from the Comanches. (He reportedly was on his way to check on gold nuggets seen near Mono Lake, on the plateau east of the Sierra.) But there were other mountain men to fill his boots. James O. Pattie and his father came in 1827 from New Mexico, and they too were jailed. The elder Pattie died there, but his resourceful son talked himself out of prison by convincing Governor Echeandia that he could inoculate the whole population against the near-epidemic smallpox disease. He apparently did so successfully—counting up some ten thousand patients; but the governor refused to to pay him in any other medium than land, which Pattie would be unable to own until he became both a Catholic and a Mexican citizen. Unwilling, he went off to Mexico to seek payment there, was unsatisfied, and returned to the States to write his *Personal Narrative* in 1831. This book caused a sensation among his countrymen, who for the first time could read in detail of the land lying far to the west.

Much as the Mexican Californians were suspicious of the motives of the Yanquis who came overland, the authorities could do little to stop them since the colonists themselves welcomed their goods and made exchanges. As the word spread among trappers and traders, different routes were developed into regular trails. Such men as Kit Carson and Joseph Walker came to explore sections of California during the 1830s. The Old Spanish Trail from Santa Fe was traversed by Jacob Leese (who built a house in Yerba Buena, married a sister of Mariano Vallejo, and acquired a rancho in Sonoma) and by William Wolfskill (who became southern California's first commercial fruit-grower). Traders William Workman and John Rowland eventually stopped trafficking in mules and bright woven wool *sarapes* and in 1841 took up Mexican citizenship so they could settle their own ranchos. In the meantime, they had brought in other industrious colonists, like Benjamin D. Wilson (Don Benito, the much-respected ranchero and agriculturist, the first Los Angeles mayor, whose name was given to the mountain peak above Pasadena), Juan Manuel Vaca, and Francis Temple (whose brother John was already here).

In the same year as the Workman-Rowland immigration came the first wagon train, the Bartleson-Bidwell party, all the way from Missouri, where the eager young schoolteacher John Bidwell had gotten others to pledge to travel with him in an army of covered wagons. At departure time, he found himself the only passenger, but he joined up with several groups and ultimately became the leader because of his common-sense intelligence and even temperament. After six months of hard journeying, during which—like Portola's party—they had to eat their mules, they crossed the Sierra just before winter set in and arrived at Rancho Los Medanos near Mount Diablo in Contra Costa County, owned by "Dr." John Marsh.

A Harvard graduate who had gotten in trouble in the Midwest by selling firearms to Indians, Marsh had settled in Los Angeles in 1836. Having studied some medicine in the past, he set up practice as California's first "licensed" physician by displaying his college diploma. He took payment in the form of "California banknotes" (cattle hides). These he converted eventually into land, and perhaps to make his property more valuable, he wrote a pamphlet that was printed back in the States and that encouraged more Americans to go west. Now, for a fee, he was willing to bail the newcomers out of jail (for entering California without the authorities' permission) and obtain settlement permits for them. Several other new settlers besides Bidwell achieved later prominence: Josiah Belden, the first mayor of San Jose; Joseph B. Chiles, a ranchero and aide to Fremont; Charles Weber, the founder of Stockton.

John Bidwell did what many another incoming American was doing: he attached himself to "Captain" John Augustus Sutter. Originally a German Swiss, Sutter had become a naturalized U.S. citizen before arriving in Alta California in 1839. Ingratiating himself with then-governor Juan Bautista Alvarado—who was looking for a way to counter the power and land expansion of his uncle and rival in the Sonoma area, General Mariano Vallejo—Sutter soon acquired a land-grant rancho of 48,000 acres in an unsettled but promising area just where the *Río de los Americanos* joined the Sacramento. Calling it *Nueva Helvetia,* he employed Indians to erect a virtual fortress of adobe and wood ten feet thick, and armed it with artillery purchased from the Russians at Fort Ross, which was being abandoned because otters were almost extinct. An ambitious man with large plans, Sutter started developing a number of enterprises at his virtual barony, including extensive agriculture—and perhaps a sawmill upriver. Recognizing real worth in John Bidwell, he employed him as an overseer. (He even tried to get him to marry his daughter, but Bidwell graciously declined.)

Sutter's Fort in the north and Jonathan Trumbull Warner's Ranch in the south, east of San Diego, were the main gathering places for newly arrived Americans. There they could purchase supplies, gain information, meet future partners, and plot ways in which the United States could take over California. Some Americans long settled in the province, like Isaac Graham (a distiller in the Monterey area) and Abel Stearns, entered into the political ups and downs of the squabbling Californios and their procession of governors. Meanwhile, the American consul, Thomas O.

Larkin, worked slowly on his government's plan of winning the Spanish-speaking Californians over to the idea of somehow delivering the slumbering province into American hands. So far, negotiations with Mexico over purchasing the whole land north of the Gila and Rio Grande rivers had gotten nowhere, and it was feared that California might be given to Britain to satisfy an unpaid debt.

The U.S. moved cautiously as a nation, but did little to discourage the guerrilla activities of some of its citizens abroad, as in the formation of the Texas Republic. And in the 1840s, under the guise of surveys, it sent into California first Charles Wilkes of the navy, who reconnoitered much of northern California, and then John Charles Fremont. Publishing an account of his expedition in 1845, Fremont brought to fever pitch the American public's cry of Manifest Destiny, that chauvinistic doctrine proclaiming America's right to own all territory across the continent within her East Coast latitudes. (Some people even wanted the whole of North America.) Land was wanted by homesteading free-soilers of the North, and it was just as eagerly sought by the slaveholders of the South, who looked upon the Southwest as suitable terrain for expanding their cotton crops and human property. Both had concluded that indolent Mexico did not deserve California.

With war rumors mounting and the less stable, more rambunctious Americans in California obviously anxious to do something, the Mexican officials considered expelling all noncitizens. They started with pathfinder Fremont, who had entered California again with a small army. He defied them by raising the Stars and Stripes at Gabilan Peak, east of Monterey, then retreated northward to Sutter's Fort, where the Yankee hangers-on were encouraged to ride off to Sonoma, make a prisoner of General Vallejo (who actually *wanted* an American takeover though they didn't know it), and raise the Bear Flag of the new California Republic. Soon afterwards they learned that war had been declared between Mexico and the United States, even before their revolt.

From his pugnacious Americans Fremont formed the California Battalion, marched south again, spiked the rusty cannons at Castillo de San Joaquin in San Francisco Bay, and combined forces with the newly arrived American officers Sloat, Stockton, Gillespie, and Kearny. The only battle that the Mexicans decisively won was at San Pascual Valley near San Diego, where they caused the Americans to overestimate their numbers by stirring up dust from their horses. The poorly organized California militia was induced to surrender at Cahuenga Pass in January of 1847. A year later, the Treaty of Guadalupe Hidalgo (named for the Mexican town in which negotiations took place) ended the Mexican War and turned California officially over to the United States, along with all the Mexican territories in the west: for a forced purchase price of fifteen million dollars.

In California, the news and particulars of this treaty — which guaranteed all Mexican residents there "free enjoyment of liberty and property," including U.S. citizenship — were very nearly ignored. For on January 24, 1848, Sutter's business partner, James Marshall, had found gold nuggets in the tailrace under construction for the new sawmill upriver on El Rio de los Americanos. The fortunate white population in California, then numbering an estimated twelve thousand, were on the ground floor for earning fortunes. Mexican Californios, American and English rancheros, *gringo* veterans of the recent war (some of whom, arriving in California, never even saw a battleground), and lowly pobladores got to the Sierra Nevada gold country early. Sailors jumped ship as soon as they heard of gold, carpenters and masons laid down their tools in the middle of a job, soldiers deserted their posts, and Indians dwelling in the locale decided to discover for themselves the whereabouts and value of these yellow rocks. Many of the first arrivals literally picked up gold from the surface of the soil. John Bidwell earned enough to purchase and stock his own rancho, *Arroyo Chico* (which gave its name to the town of Chico). Schoolmaster Antonio Coronel journeyed from Los Angeles with some friends and servants and did well at first. His account of his experiences in the Sierra and San Francisco is a minor classic that gives the Mexican side of the early Gold Rush years. He became one of southern California's leading citizens.

The news of the gold strike reached northern Mexico swiftly and precipitated the emigration of many thousands of Sonorans. Most of them came with provisions, equipment, and knowledge: things that the novice miners rarely brought at the start, in the rush to fortune. With their goods placed firmly on burros and mules, they entered *la Veta Madre* (soon translated into the Mother Lode) country to the sound of jingling bells on their pack trains. Their round-topped, wide-brimmed sombreros and *calzones blancos* (white trousers) were their uniforms. The American and Californio greenhorns looked to them for guidance, and the *Sonoreños* gladly shared their wisdom and their words.

The basic gold-mining tool and technique was the *batea,* a shallow and wide-flared wooden or metal bowl that the Mexicans filled with dirt and water from a creek or river and gently twirled, until only the heaviest bits — *oro,* or gold — remained. Panning could also be done with the Indians' tightly woven baskets. The Sonorans talked of the *placer* (a word that probably came from *plaza*), that crumbling deposit of gold dust found washed into river bars or embankments, among alluvial sand and gravel. And when they hit a rich vein, they would cry out, *Bonanza!* —

their name for prosperity. After a stint of painstaking but profitless toil, they would call their claim area a *borrasca,* a washout or failure. (Both words originated with sailors' terms for fair weather and foul.) They looked for *chispas* – "sparks" – that would indicate a good site. They sold their extra mules to the other miners (in the first five years, they brought in perhaps ten thousand of them) – and in those early months of digging, provided the main information and entertainments.

After a week of hard grubbing, on Saturday night the miners felt ready for some rest and recreation. Those from the outlying camps came into the Mexicans' places – Spanish Towns – with their huts and shacks bright with fabrics woven through poles and branches, or flying out in the breeze as streamers. Many Sonorans had brought their women along too. These were an irresistible attraction, not just for the spicy, homecooked food but for the chance to dally too. There were wine and aguardiente; music from guitars, banjos, fiddles, and improvised *tambores;* singing – or braying. A castanet-snapping fandango was always in progress, and everyone was welcome, Latin or not. (The miners became so familiar with the wild activities of this public dance that they gave the name Fandango to a valley and pass – in Modoc County now – where some Forty-niners on their way to the gold fields experienced such cold at a campsite that they could only keep warm by dancing all night long.)

Gambling went on too. The favorite card game was the fast-played Spanish *monte* (often called "monte bank" by the miners), which might be set up outside a doorway or along a path with a serape thrown down as a dealing surface. The stakes usually were small bags of gold dust.

The Californios offered other forms of gambling: horse racing, of course, and the bull-and-bear fights. The latter pastime horrified the Americanos even while they made bets on the victor. A grizzly or some other ferocious bear was captured by the reata experts and hauled into camp. A snorting bull was brought forward, and his front leg was chained to the hind leg of the bear. The two wild adversaries commenced to lunge and tear at each other until death finished off one—or both. The bear's usual fighting tactic was to crouch as low as he could, sometimes even digging a hole beneath him, so he might bring the bull down to a position vulnerable to his teeth and claws. The bull, on his part, attempted always to get the bear up on his hind legs so that he could spear him with his horns. The miners' frenetic bets on the bear's or bull's position were recalled later on in investment activities in the West's new financial capital of San Francisco. The "bear" speculator waits to buy until prices fall to his supposed advantage. The "bull" speculator, on the other hand, buys stock confident that its price will continue to rise and therefore increase in value, to his profit. These terms eventually found their way east to the American Stock Exchange.

As might be expected, the gold country—uninhabited by the white men till now—began to receive innumerable place-names, some temporary and some quite permanent. The Spanish-speaking miners contributed their share, or names were created because of them. Sonora, the seat of Tuolumne County, was founded by Sonorans. Sonora Pass led to or from Sonora, across the Sierra. Lancha Plana originated because Mexicans built a flat boat here for river crossing. Melones was a mine on a hill where Mexicans had found nuggets shaped like melon seeds. There were various Oros: Oro Fino, Oro Chino (perhaps a place worked by the Chinese), and of course Oroville. Hornitos (Little Ovens) perhaps got its name because of structures built by Mexicans for bread baking. It has been suggested, though, that the name came from many oven-shaped gravemounds of Sonorans who died in an epidemic and were given shallow burials at the locality. Camp Seco was a "dry digging," where little or no water was available for panning during the dry summer season. The Sonorans improvised at such places by putting handfuls of soil on their serapes and then hoisting them into a passing breeze that hopefully would carry off all but the gold dust.

Amador—town and county—are derived from the surname of a Californio, Jose Maria Amador, who left his Rancho San Ramon to dig for a while in the hills. Vallecito had various spellings—Vallicito, Valacito, Vallicita—until it finally returned to its correct, original form. Chili Gulch and Chileno Creek had been worked by miners from Chile. Chiquito Creek in Madera came from an arroyo named *Chiquito Joaquín,* a tributary of the main river. San Andreas was originally a gulch occupied by Mexicans. However, the place-name Pulga in Butte County did not start out Spanish. Yankees had called the spot Flea Valley, but when a railroad station was placed there much later it was considered more elegant to call it by the translated name! Placerville, using the Hispanic gold term with French *-ville,* was nicknamed Hangtown because it was probably the first place where a mob of miners lynched men they summarily declared guilty. (Since at first there were no jails, justice was meted out fast by impromptu juries.) There used to be several mining towns called *Garrote:* the Spanish word for strangling or hanging. (The usual method involved roping the necks of the convicted persons to tree branches while they stood on wagons, then driving the wagons out from under them.) A town called Second Garrote was later renamed Groveland.

For a while, the gold-mining camps were fairly peaceable. There was plenty of gold for everyone if they worked

American Takeover 145

at it. But by the second year of activity, congestion and competition among the avid gold seekers—even when they fanned out into areas farther north, south, and upcountry —caused a great change in the spirits and behavior of the men. The Forty-niners brought with them or soon picked up a violent dislike of all Spanish-speaking miners: Sonorans, Chileans and Peruvians (who had beaten most Americanos to the fields because they were closer), and even the Californios who were U.S. citizens and often more refined in their manners. All were contemptuously classified "greasers." (The term may have originally come from the Yankee sailors, who looked down upon the lower-class Mexican Californians, many of them mestizos—the hide haulers for the ranchos or the pueblo merchants.)

The new arrivals at the gold camps, considering themselves the rightful owners of California since "they" had won the war, resented the presence of any kind of "greaser" —especially since it appeared to them that the Hispanics had the best-staked claims and knew far more than they did about mining them. They took the situation into their own hands and began harassing anyone who looked and talked like a Mexican; even if he happened to be French, his life was now endangered by mobs, who forced Latins to flee their claims and their camps, and manufactured reasons to perform beatings and lynchings. A notorious early racial incident in the Mother Lode came when a Sonoran woman named Juanita killed an Anglo who had broken down her door one night during a Fourth of July binge and then returned next morning to insult her. She was dragged away by a mob and hanged. Her coolly spoken last words— *"Adiós, señores!"*—to the assembled Downieville spectators made her an everlasting heroine among her compatriots.

This was El Dorado, the long-sought-for realm of gold that had lured Spanish-speaking peoples for three centuries. The Mexicans now countered the Yankees' epithet "greaser" with one of their own: *gringo*. (Even today the word carries some of the dislike aimed at the *norteamericanos*, among whom the Latinos then had to live, and who invaded their mother country of Mexico first in war, then as *filibusteros*, finally as tourists. By now, however, gringo can be uttered matter-of-factly or even fondly but nontheless differentiates the Anglo from the Chicano in the United States.) Legend traces its origin to the Mexican War, when Mexican troops camped across the river from the Yanquis heard them singing the popular song, "Green Grow the Lilacs"—and adapted the first two words of the oft-repeated refrain. It may have come, though, from the Spanish word *griego*, for Greek: by extension, any person speaking an unintelligible or gibberish language.

The Yankees were taking over California, as the new place-names began to declare. Their creations—as Portola's soldiers' had been—were blunt, picturesque, amusing, crude, and direct, although usually descriptive and dramatic as well. Like Hardscrabble, Yankee Jims, Dirty Sock, Starve Out, Greenhorn River, Drytown, Fiddletown, Diamond Spring, Dead Horse Glen, Nigger Bill Bend, Mad Mule Gulch. Some names changed as fast as the residents; many were abandoned when the placer gold gave out and the miners moved elsewhere. They translated *los Rios de las Plumas, los Americanos, Estanislao, los Santos Reyes,* and *Trinidad* into the Feather, American, Stanislaus, Kings, and Trinity rivers. And the Moquelumne became Mokelumne—or just plain "Mok."

Shortly after the American takeover, the pueblo-port of Yerba Buena adopted the commemorative name given to both the presidio and the mission nearby—San Francisco. For a while, after the discovery of gold was announced, the place was almost deserted. But when President Polk told Congress, and the nation, about the California find, Americans came west as fast as they could: around the Horn (which took at least three months in the fastest Yankee clipper, six months in a regular boat); by a sea and then land crossing to some port in Mexico or Central America, and then a wait for a boat going to California; or by an overland journey that could take as long as five months, but that would cost less than a ship's fare and be less boring.

By the middle of 1849 San Francisco was jammed with ships of many nations, and often captain and crew deserted them along with the passengers. (Some ships were hauled ashore to be used as stores and rooming houses.) People were going to the goldfields, and people were returning from them; supplies were being sent by steamer up the Sacramento River to Sutter's Fort and beyond; and gold was coming back, with or without its finders. Drifters and ex-convicts were arriving too, figuring on taking gold rather than working for it themselves. It was convenient for them to hound the "greasers," who had few defenders. Ironically, the Mexican-American's worst enemies were the Australians and the Irish—who really *were* foreigners.

In 1849 California was still under military rule since Congress—divided over the troublesome matter of slavery —had not yet assigned it a territorial status, with interim laws and judicial and civil procedures. Part of the time Californians used the old Mexican system, including the alcalde as the town official and the *ayuntamiento* or town council; part of the time they used American common law and juries. The new residents decided to try to bypass the whole territorial period and aim directly at statehood, for by now the population, pouring in fast, was over one hundred thousand. In August a constitutional assembly was held at Colton Hall in Monterey (attended by forty-eight

The Yanquis Are Coming!

delegates, only about a half dozen of them Mexicans), a constitution was constructed, and the state's boundaries were decided—along with the scope and names of twenty-seven counties (all but two of which had Spanish or Indian titles). A year later, as part of the Compromise of 1850, California was officially admitted to the Union as a full-fledged state.

Then the new state legislature got down to work, although it moved to a succession of new capitals until it finally settled on Sacramento in 1854. Responding to the American miners' objections to competition from the foreign-born, it passed a Foreign Miners' Tax bill, imposing a $20 a month fee on them if they decided to stay. Californios had trouble proving that they were not foreigners. Most Mexicans found it easier to go home, wherever that was. Sonorans left by the thousands, only to find that when they reached the Colorado River, men took away their mules, their possessions, and their gold (if they had any left), and sent them off to trudge three hundred miles on foot, part of it total desert.

The first "anti-greaser" bill proved unpopular with the merchants of the Mother Lode country, who discovered that they had lost some of their best customers, since the Mexicans tended to spend their gold on goods rather than hoard it. Furthermore, the Sonorans were known to be the best mule skinners *(arrieros),* and they were needed to carry the merchants' supplies into high-country areas not accessible by boat, horse-drawn coach, or ox-pulled wagon. Also, mining entrepreneurs were realizing that they could make better profits by employing gangs of workers for a small salary plus perhaps a slight percentage of the take. Americans had no liking or ability to labor for a boss, whereas the Sonorans were used to a *patrón.* They showed patience, too, in working the gold-bearing quartz ore, using their *arrastre* contraptions (Yankees sometimes called them "rasters")—circular pits in which a horse or mule dragged a huge boulder over chunks of ore, crushing it fine, so that it could then be run through a Long Tom or sluice box.

The southern Sierra mines began to be worked intensively by hired crews of Mexicans after the tax was reduced to about $3 a month. Other Sonorans migrated to the recently opened quicksilver mine at New Almaden (named after the famous mercury source in Spain), which was producing from cinnabar the substance needed in purifying gold, especially now that a Federal mint was established in San Francisco to convert the precious metal into ingots and coins. (Soon, too, there would be Nevada's Comstock Lode and Death Valley's Cerro Gordo.)

In the meantime, the Californio rancheros had been converting their cattle into money. Some, especially the younger ones, had gone off to the Mother Lode, but most of them returned disgusted with what they had experienced, and advised relatives and friends to stay away. "The good ones were few and the wicked many," Vallejo concluded. The rancho itself was proving to be the best source of gold, just by selling off its herds for beef for the miners. Vaqueros were sent north and east, driving sometimes a thousand head at once to the marketplace, where a cow that had once been worth about $3 had suddenly grown in value to several hundred dollars. There was gold in the ground, but the prices that miners had to pay for grub tended to offset their earnings. A dozen eggs might sell for as much as $6, and then they might be seabird eggs obtained on the Farallon Islands—and none too fresh.

The miners wanted butter too; so the rancheros first had to learn how to milk their unaccustomed cows, a procedure that involved at least three people. When the cream was skimmed off the tediously accumulated milk supply, it was put into a leather bota and roped onto a bronco or bull, who quickly bucked it into *mantequilla,* with little effort on the ranchero's part. His main function at that time was to enjoy the money he was getting: to buy splendid things like silver-trimmed saddles and bridles, or solid silver spurs that might cost $2,000 a pair. More than ever, he wanted to impress the world with stylishness, while gambling recklessly at high stakes.

Most Hispanic rancheros paid little heed to the Land Act of 1851 passed by Congress at the urging of new Californians who questioned the whole situation of landownership. It required a ranchero to submit to a three-man commission, within two years, all proofs he possessed of his land grant from the Mexican government. In some cases, such deeds had been lost, misplaced, destroyed—or had never been received at all. It took a while for many Californios to realize the gravity of their plight: they would lose their lands if they did not produce the essential documents or assemble enough testimony that showed them to be incontrovertibly the owners of their domains. All this took time, effort, and expense: money especially, for the gringo lawyers who took on their cases. And at the same time, the rancheros were starting to face another peculiar American legality: property taxes.

The ranchos of the north, especially in the Central and Napa valleys and the San Francisco Bay area, were increasingly overrun by American squatters. As men left the gold mines, with or without gold, they saw unoccupied lands that looked promising for farming. To their way of thinking, obviously unsettled terrain was open for homesteading. In this Jacksonian democracy, a man had as much right to a piece of land as he did to the vote. But the Americans then learned that huge amounts of prime land given over only to some straying cattle belonged exclusively to Mexican Californians or others who had become Mexican citizens in the past. And whether the declared owner was a Sutter or a Vallejo, a Californio "greaser" or a Yanqui, did not matter in the least: the squatters simply moved in, built shanties, put up fences, planted some crops—and waited for the Land Commission to disinherit the ranchero family. (It did not help the rancheros when a number of land-grant claims submitted to the commission turned out to be blatantly fraudulent.) Sometimes, as with the Peralta family in the East Bay area and the Berryessas in Santa Clara and Alameda counties, the Americanos so harassed them that when their land patents finally did come through, the owners were forced to sell out at rock-bottom prices.

In southern California the rancheros' way of life lasted longer. Farther from the goldfields, and with Mexicans still outnumbering the Yankees and other newcomers by five to one, they were rarely bothered by squatters, transients, or overpopulation. They continued their rounds of merrymaking, gambling, horse racing. To sustain themselves in a grand style and to pay lawyers to handle their legal business, they borrowed large sums of money at usurious rates, which were compounded monthly, so that in less than a year the original principal doubled. Their debts mounted; mortgages were undertaken on their lands; creditors' loans made to friends and relatives were naively cosigned, using their rancho property as collateral.

The old grievances between the arribeños and the abajeños continued, but now it was more the Mexican Californians vs. the sharp gringo politicos in Sacramento and their associates, the shrewd financiers of San Francisco. Even before statehood, the abajeños had tried to separate from the north: to remain in a territorial status as part of

Colorado Territory, or even to become a separate unit using the Mormon name of Deseret. This, however, was not permitted them. Grudgingly, they paid their large property taxes on their expansive but undeveloped acreage, far greater than their "fair share" in assuming the new state's expenses. But their representation in the legislature was pitifully poor because of low population and the fact that the southern region was divided into only six counties— "Cow Counties," they were dubbed, whereas the gold-country area north and south of Sacramento, temporarily overpopulated, was split into numerous small-sized counties. (This issue has never been resolved, though in subsequent years a few more counties were formed in the south from existing ones. Yet the tiny counties of the northeast remain, some with total populations less than that of a southern California apartment complex.)

Having usually a better sense for business and a stronger suspicion of the motivations of their ambitious countrymen, the Mexican rancheros' American in-laws tried to advise them wisely; but their warnings often were disregarded, or else they themselves became snared in similarly complex and hopeless financial tailspins. Until the rancho lands were cleared by the commission—or, failing that, given a final patent by a superior court or even the Supreme Court, a process that in some cases took almost thirty years—any land-grant property could not be sold outright. Rancheros paid off debts by deeding future rights to their land, so that by the time a patent came through, it was much too late to rectify their indebtedness.

Furthermore, the Californios seemed never to have heard of the inexorable law of economic supply and demand. No longer were their cattle of much value. In 1848 there had been three hundred thousand; by 1860 the figure had grown to three million! Americans had brought in great cattle herds from the Midwest, and thousands of sheep had been driven into California from New Mexico, swelling the figure in a dozen years from twenty thousand to one million. The Californios also had sold off so many of their cattle that their herds were depleted. And having neglected selective breeding, their longhorns were no longer desirable as beef or milk cows as soon as superior breeds became available. Their sheep yielded inferior mutton, and the wool that had been acceptable in weaving the coarse *serga* blankets of the mission years was not wanted. Still, the cattle were worth something, if just for their hides. But then came the year of the great flood in 1862, when the whole Central Valley became a lake and many valleys in southern California filled with water, isolating ranchos and communities for weeks. (Almost with glee, newspapers in San Francisco and Los Angeles reported the other settlement wiped out.) First the weather drowned the cattle; then in the following year it brought total drought that denied water and forage to the survivors. The great rancho lands became littered with thousands of cattle carcasses. In a vain attempt to save sustenance for some of the cattle, vaqueros stampeded whole herds of mustangs over cliffs. All assets, present and future, were gone.

Not until the land booms brought on by the coming of railroads to particular areas, notably to southern California in the late seventies, did California land begin to accelerate remarkably in value. A property that in the 1860s might have sold for twenty-five cents per acre skyrocketed by 1885 to $2,000 per acre. By then, however, few Californios had managed to hang on to what was once theirs in order to profit from the increase. In past transactions too they had tended to devaluate the land, since usually it had cost their families nothing to obtain it to begin with. Their inability to speak or read English also allowed them to be cheated. Sometimes they sold land by signing papers that they thought meant they were only leasing it for a particular price. Or they misheard or misread purchase prices that were in fact absurdly low.

Innocents and prodigal spendthrifts to the last, the rancheros saw the loan sharks (they called them *garroteros* —stranglers) and lawyers and Yankee businessmen foreclose and take away their ranchos, leaving them—if they were lucky—the family adobe casa with perhaps a few acres of land surrounding it. Nineteenth century economist Henry George stated: "If the history of Mexican grants of California is ever written, it will be a history of greed, of perjury, of corruption, of speculation, of high-handed robbery for which it will be difficult to find a parallel." Californios were left with their place-names and their memories.

A few Mexicans took to violent ways during these years after the American takeover. Whether proud and defiant, or deranged and diabolical, they became outlaws or bandidos. The most famous of all was the legendary Joaquin Murieta of the gold camps, who managed to be in so many places at once that some people declared there were *five* Joaquins. Since he seemingly sought revenge among the gringos, especially those who "deserved" it, Mexicans and their sympathizers made a folk hero out of him, a Californio Robin Hood. In 1853 the California legislature offered a large reward for his capture, and a self-appointed "captain" claimed to have killed him after long pursuit, bringing in as evidence a Mexican's head pickled in a whiskey jar. (For years afterwards, this ghastly specimen was on public display but finally met its end in the San Francisco earthquake and fire of 1906.) Place-names of

Joaquin's hideouts survive with the legend: Joaquin Ridge and Rocks in Fresno County, and Alameda's Joaquin Murieta Caves.

The Mexican backlash against the "anti-greaser" Yanquis continued for years with highway robberies and settlement raids conducted by desperado gangs (from the Spanish word *desesperado*). Often they used a trusty reata to down a man. Within fifty feet it was as accurate and fast as a gun, but near silent. A young cousin of Pio Pico, Solomon, who took up as a badman, is recalled in Santa Barbara County's Solomon Canyon and Mount Solomon. The notorious outlaw Juan Flores is memorialized in Flores Peak in Orange County. The most famed among the last of this breed was Tiburcio Vasquez. A man of curious gallantry, he held a strong attraction for women, some of whom showed up at his trial in San Jose in 1875 and wept at his hanging. One of his supposed hideouts was Vasquez Canyon and Rocks in northern Los Angeles County, now a public campground and park. Another favored den may have been a cave at Pinnacles National Monument, near King City, which was named Vasquez Monolith.

By 1870, more than twenty years after California became part of the United States, its Hispanic characteristics had faded and seemed as derelict as the old missions along El Camino Real, most of them crumbling into dust. Yet many of the old Spanish names lived on, pronounced oddly upon the American tongue. Soon, thanks to technological progress and modern salesmanship, along with a large dose of sentimentalism, there would be a whole new group of Spanish names—created mostly by people who hardly knew the language.

Boostering, Nostalgia, and Barrios

T HE HISTORY OF any region is written in the ways
people have used the land. And the names eventually
given to this land reflect the stages of its development. New and differing economies and values usually
spring from contacts with outsiders. An isolated population, satisfied with its own way of life, would be loath to
change. Things stay as they are, as they have been. When
people dwell in a place that looks promising to others,
however, they risk being overrun by invaders with better
technology, whether in tools or weapons. The newcomers
may also possess more efficient methods of doing things—
of making the land yield food and wealth, and of getting
others to perform the labor for them.

Ironically, the American invasion of California during

the late 1840s and early '50s—swelling the population from 12,000 to 100,000 in 1849 alone—was brought on by finding the very gold that the Spaniards were seeking when they discovered and claimed California. By 1852, the state had a still-burgeoning population of 250,000. This mass migration, involving other nationalities besides Americans, was the swiftest and most intensive in human history. It left no chance for any gradual accommodation between the two radically different cultures. Elsewhere in the Mexican territories transferred to the United States, the Spanish-speaking populations were able to retain much longer their lands, customs, and political power.

By 1870 the simple, pastoral, and modestly agrarian landscape of Hispanic California had radically changed, not just in ownership but in what was being done to it. The vigorous and ambitious Yanquis, aided considerably by the monetary value of the gold obtained from the Sierra Nevada foothills and by the presence of cheap labor, were rapidly transforming the terrain. They brought with them the two main features of the Industrial Revolution spawned in Western Europe and on the Atlantic shores of North America: machinery for transportation, communication, and industrialization of farming, forestry, and mining; and the concept of continual progress—an idea rather alien to the Californio.

Intolerance expressed by one group toward another frequently has an economic base. Considering the natives in some coveted area lowly and perhaps despicable furnishes the excuse for moving in and taking over their land. Continuing to regard the original inhabitants in a prejudicial way, and treating certain groups of newcomers in a similarly demeaning manner, offers the conqueror-entrepreneur the opportunity to exploit their labors. They are given menial jobs and only paid a pittance.

The Spaniards, when they came into California, had subjected the Indians to economic and spiritual (or psychological) bondage. They utilized their labor while seizing their lands. The three colonizing units—military, religious, and civil—all agreed that the Indians' most notable characteristics were negative ones. They were childish, ignorant, lazy, frivolous, deceitful, gullible, superstitious, ostentatious, violent-tempered, unclean, bestial, thievish, cruel, unambitious, gambling, dangerous. In summary, a backward and inferior race.

When the Americans began arriving in California in the 1820s and '30s, they said almost identical things about the Spanish-speaking populace. And although they were aware of the Californios' virtues—particularly if they married into one of the respected landholding families—they were impatient and intolerant of what they considered defects and vices. The Americans who published their views about the Californio population indicated that a superior race should come in to properly appreciate and fulfill the land's great potential.

Most migrating Americans therefore felt few qualms about pushing the "greasers" from their claims in the goldfields or off their ranchos. Manifest Destiny had arrived in California, and progress was its motto. Progress meant steamships and clipper ships that could transport thousands of Americans from one ocean to another, and paddlewheel ferries that would carry them up the Sacramento, San Joaquin, or American rivers to the diggings. Progress meant wagons and stagecoaches pulled by fast teams of horses, using wheels with iron spokes, not sliced tree trunks. Progress meant digging great canals for transportation, swamp drainage, and irrigation. Progress meant chopping down trees and cutting them into planks for buildings or for making flumes to carry the millions of gallons of water needed to wash down mountains and expose the gold veins buried in them. Progress meant installing telegraph wires clear across the country, so that news could be carried in minutes, not in weeks or even months. Progress meant sinking artesian wells and placing lighthouses on rocky coastlines.

Above all, progress meant railroads. More than anything else introduced by the Americans, the railroads changed California. They could link the state with the eastern part of the nation, ending its isolation. And the lack of a network of rivers navigable by oceangoing vessels could also be overcome. The first railroad line, a short one from Sacramento to Folsom, was built in 1855. Arguments went on for years in Congress over the best route for a transcontinental line, with the North and the South in a deadlock, just as they were over slavery.

San Francisco as terminus for the Sacramento-San Joaquin river system, the only seagoing one in the state, was the principal port, but Sacramento—laid out by Sutter's son upon the Nueva Helvetia rancho property where the American and Sacramento rivers converged—was the new state capital, the hub of the wheel of activity because of its proximity to the Mother Lode. There the various overland and intrastate stagecoach lines began and ended, with their livery stops and rest stations bearing many a Spanish name picked up from the locale. The Butterfield Overland Mail coach took twenty-five days to get to St. Louis. About half the names of the several dozen stops made between San Francisco and the Arizona border were Hispanic in origin, such as Pacheco Pass, Fresno City, Tule River, Poso Creek, Fort Tejon, El Monte, Chino Ranch, Laguna Grande, Carrizo Creek, Alamo Mocho.

The Civil War at least settled the matter of a main

railroad route. The precious metals still being mined in California and nearby Nevada were helping to finance the Northern cause, and Congress provided a large subsidy for the Union Pacific and Central Pacific entrepreneurs who were ready to undertake the building of a transcontinental line. The line running from the west began, of course, at Sacramento. The Central Pacific's founders—Hopkins, Stanford, Crocker, and Huntington—were promised ownership of a checkerboard of lands that covered twenty square miles on each side of the railway in progress, an inducement maintained later, when they took over the Southern Pacific, to construct lines within the state too. Like most California financiers, they had gotten their starts as merchants during the Gold Rush.

When the Central Pacific met the Union Pacific at Promontory Point, Utah in 1869, California no longer was an isolated and remote part of the United States. Joined by steel rails to the eastern markets, it could export products, raw or processed, as well as ship them in. Crops, livestock, minerals, and lumber became big industries with unlimited markets—especially as the railroad networks grew within the state, between suppliers and ports, and extended to other regions of the nation.

The Mexican ranchos had made it possible to transfer the ownership of huge tracts of land to private or corporate ownership. Agriculture was advanced not so much by individual small farmers as by large enterprises with capital sufficient to clear land, contruct dams and irrigation channels, experiment with crops and soil, employ hundreds or thousands of workers, and develop markets for produce. "Agribusiness" got its main impetus from the great Central Valley of the San Joaquin and Sacramento basins, and by the early 1900s it was converting the barren Colorado

Desert, trudged across by Anza and the early colonists, into a farming paradise through irrigation: the Imperial and Coachella valleys.

The 1870s saw the growth of the great cattle kingdoms too, mainly on lands once tenanted by the easygoing rancheros. Miller and Lux, Irvine, Bixby, Newmark, Baldwin—among the new breed of ranchers, the Hispanic names mostly disappeared. Barbed wire fences went up to encircle and protect the livestock, whose grazing fields now were often irrigated. Cattle and sheep were scientifically bred to produce improved varieties.

But still the vaqueros lingered, those Mexican-Indian cowhands who could rope anything, moving or not, with their reatas. Americanos who joined these "buckaroos" or expert cattletenders learned the Spanish style of riding and roping, and picked up a semi-Hispanic vocabulary in the process: rodeo, corral, bronco, lariat *(la reata)*, lasso *(lazo)*, cinch *(cincha)*, chaps *(chaparrejos,* first worn in California by Portola's soldiers), serape *(sarape)*, quirt *(cuarta,* or whip), hackamore *(jáquima)*, saddlebag *(alforja)*, stampede *(estampida)*, "part out" *(apartar)*. There were the names for the Mexican ranch foods: chili, frijoles, tamales, tortillas, calabash (for *calabaza,* or squash). And the campfire roast *(barbacoa,* or barbecue). Expressions like "Savvy" for *¿Sabe?* (Do you understand?). Or "Vamoose!" for *Vámonos!* (Let's get out of here!). Trouble could get one into the calaboose *(calabozo,* or jail), or an ordeal at the hoosegow *(juzgado,* or trial court). The Western saddle, bridle, bit, and stirrups were fashioned on Spanish and Mexican models that came from the Moors of North Africa and the Catalonians and the Sonoreños. The rodeos and the caballero processions in today's parades, created for public entertainment, derive from the Hispanic Californian and southwestern beginnings.

Gold was just the start of the digging into California land for silver, iron, copper, borax, cement—and that "black gold," oil, which brought a new burst of land speculation and transformation. (The biggest strike of all took place at Signal Hill, on the former Rancho Los Cerritos.) The hundreds of thousands of acres of timberlands largely ignored by the Spanish and Mexican Californians were now exploited, most significantly the palo colorado—red wood—seen first by Portola's group.

The railroads of the late nineteenth century mainly enabled large-scale agriculture, ranching, mining, and forestry to be initiated and then made profitable. There were new feudal barons: the monopolistic entrepreneurs. The Central Pacific's "Big Four" had taken over the Southern Pacific Railroad and were well on the way to great fortunes. California, for better or for worse, was promoted in the other states, and even abroad, as a wonderful place to visit, but even better to buy property in so that one might live there forever.

The portrayal of California as the pot of gold at the end of the rainbow, the Promised Land of milk and honey, or a start on Utopia was launched on the heels of Manifest Destiny and the Gold Rush. Several communities of religious or political idealists were established early. The Mormons purchased land on the Rancho San Bernardino and moved there in 1852, prepared to build an even greater kingdom than Salt Lake City, with an outlet to the ocean at San Diego. Repeated Indian raids discouraged them into finally abandoning their dream. Colonies like Holy City, Kaweah, Fountain Grove, Point Loma, and Llano del Rio were founded—to founder in time. More successful were less extremist, preplanned communities like El Monte, Riverside, Etiwanda, Pasadena, and Ontario.

The Southern Pacific and a number of real-estate

corporations would plan a new settlement, name it, and begin to divide it into smaller units that could be purchased and settled on by a group of people who would by their very presence create an "instant" community. In the East, this technique had a strong appeal. The Southern Pacific wanted to develop successful economic units employed in farming (such as citrus growing) or other product-making activities that would need transportation and therefore use their railroads—paying freight prices they alone would dictate. The company employed writers like Charles Nordhoff (founder of Ojai and author of *California for Health, Wealth and Residence,* published in 1872) to let the world know about the splendors of California. It also was the original publisher of the highly successful *Sunset Magazine.*

The railroad tried many devices to lure settlers to the Golden State, including arranging for touring-group excursion trains and providing the visitors with meals, housing, and stagecoach rides to interesting sites or beautiful vistas. On all sides were men with property title deeds ready for signatures on the dotted lines. All they needed was money down on the mortgage. Lands purchased through advertising campaigns in the Midwest by farmers eager to try California living sometimes included in the price the use of an entire boxcar on an "emigrant train" to transport the family's belongings, including pigs and chickens. They even furnished a stove on which the travelers could cook their meals while crossing the country. Tourism and real-estate promotions now took place too, as California big-business enterprises.

To make things easier for incoming Anglos, translations were made: *Punta de la Concepción* to Point Conception, *Isla de los Angeles* to Angel Island, *Cañada Verde* to Green Valley, *Río Carmelo* to Carmel River, *Isla de la Yegua* to Mare Island (where a favorite mare of Vallejo's had once been stranded). *Todos Santos* was changed to plain Concord, *Nación* to National City, *Río Ruso* to Russian River, *Cajón de las Uvas* to Grapevine Canyon. *San Isidro* became Gilroy (at least commemorating the Scotsman-turned-Mexican who had owned the rancho with that name).

Sometimes the sound of the new place-name stayed similar but the spelling and meaning altered. A canyon in Los Angeles County had been called *El Buque* (boat), the nickname of a French sailor who had settled there; somehow it got changed to Bouquet Canyon. Rancho *Arroyo del Hambre* (Hunger Creek), so named because travelers there nearly starved, evolved into the less dramatic Alhambra Valley. *Punta de Bonete* became Point Bonita, keeping a Spanish identity anyway. And there were misspellings: like Cabazon (for *Cabezón*), named after a local Indian with a huge head; Gabilan (for *Gavilán* or hawk), where Fremont first raised the American flag; Tassajara (for *Tasajera*, the place where beef jerky was made on a rancho). And Padre Dumetz's name got lost in Point Dume.

For the convenience of its many new Anglo settlers, Los Angeles's downtown streets were renamed. Some were simple translations: *Esperanza* to Hope, *Primavera* to Spring (the name supposedly came from Pio Pico's favorite granddaughter), *Loma* to Hill, *Aceituna* to Olive, *Flores* to Flower, *Principal* to Main. Others took wholly new names: *Fortín* (Small Fort) became Broadway; *Caridad* (Charity), Grand; *Calle de los Chapules* (Grasshopper Street), Figueroa, which commemorated the former Mexican governor. For a time, the Americanos called *Calle de los Negros* the blunt Nigger Alley—which during the 1850s to '70s provided assorted vices. (The only angels in Los Angeles, it was said, were fallen ones.) Then there was *Calle de los Indios*, which apparently began as a pathway from Yang-Na alongside the Los Angeles River to the Pacific's shore. Now Wilshire Boulevard, it remains the main direct artery from the downtown area to the sea, at Santa Monica.

Still, in Los Angeles, there would be various commemorative street names to recall its former, well-known Californio residents, whether Mexican or Americano, like Pico and Sepulveda boulevards, Temple Street (honoring "Don Juan"), Stearns and Arcadia streets (named for "Don Abel" and his lovely, Bandini-born wife), Olvera Street (for *Juez* — Judge — Agustin). For a long time, Chavez Ravine was settled by Mexicans. It had once been El Pueblo's potter's field, then a flourishing milpita cultivated by its first owner, Julian Chavez. Now, of course, it is the home of the Los Angeles Dodgers.

The transference of rancho lands to real-estate investors and promoters invariably brought on new settlements. Colonel Robert S. Baker — who had married Abel Stearns's childless widow, Arcadia — joined his business partner, Senator John P. Jones, in turning part of their jointly owned *Rancho San Vicente y Santa Mónica* (which had once belonged to the Sepulveda family) into the coastal town of Santa Monica. But they also contributed several hundred acres of prime land for a Veterans Home: the expanse now belongs to the Veterans Administration. Located in Brentwood, a section of Los Angeles, it is bordered on the east, appropriately, by Sepulveda Boulevard. Nearby, the second campus of the University of California occupies the former site of *Rancho San José de Buenos Aires*. Other universities and colleges in California, as well as public recreational areas — many of them expansive — exist because of previous ranchos.

Although the vast, privately held estates in California were often decried within our democracy based on small, individual landholding units, it is now apparent that there have been public compensations. The retention of large sections of former ranchos, whether by the original family's descendants or by new owners, effectively kept these lands from indiscriminate sale and development. Through the years, however, some sections have been offered up to the public, but often rather selectively—as in the case of the gigantic Irvine Ranch property in Orange County, which encompasses the Sepulvedas' former *Rancho Bolsa de San Joaquín*. Only in the past two decades has its owners' corporation begun converting areas into preplanned industrial parks and specially designed housing tracts— many of them bearing Spanish names. Another large ranch property, that owned by Henry Cowell, founder of a profitable cement company in Santa Cruz County, has benefited the public by supplying land for a new branch of the University of California and by donating the site for the Henry Cowell Redwoods State Park. Some 3,700 acres from Rancho de los Feliz were donated to the city of Los Angeles in 1896 by Griffith J. Griffith. (The park named after him is the largest metropolitan public park in California.)

Some large ranches have managed to keep the land virtually inviolate. Thus wilderness areas were preserved for a time when the new disciplines of environmental science and urban planning, along with aroused public concern and government conservation programs, could prevent irreversible and irresponsible inroads. Many acres will be spared haphazard human "development," remaining as forest preserves and habitat sanctuaries.

By the late 1870s, California's Hispanic past receded farther and farther away. Only scholarly publishers like Hubert Howe Bancroft or painters of the picturesque like Edward Deakin (who for a time specialized in depicting the ruined missions) seemed aware of the fast-disappearing heritage of Spain and Mexico in California.

Then came *Ramona* in 1884, Helen Hunt Jackson's popular romantic novel. It fascinated the entire nation, riveting attention at last upon two cultures nearly erased by then, except for their many enduring place-names. Mrs. Hunt, completing research for her book about the disgraceful treatment of the American Indians, *A Century of Dishonor,* was introduced to California. Asked to prepare a report on the condition of the Mission Indians, she journeyed around the parts of California formerly occupied by the Hispanic settlers, usually with Antonio Coronel as her guide. When she returned to the East, the impressions, stories, and materials that she had been accumulating began to take shape in fictional form. Hardly taking time to eat and sleep, she composed her story of a part-Indian orphan girl growing up on a Californio rancho who falls in love with a full-blooded Indian named Alessandro. (An Italian name, however, not Spanish—which would be Alejandro.) A relentless fate pursues them and her Spanish foster-family, the Morenos, embodied in the form of the Yankee invaders of their land.

American readers by the millions through the years welcomed Ramona into their hearts. Through the craft of the novel Helen Hunt Jackson had aroused strong interest in, as well as guilt about, California's missions and ranchos, Indians and Spanish-speaking people. Tourists went *Ramona* crazy and poured into California, eager to see the "actual" ranch where she grew up, the chapel where she and Alessandro were married, and other places that marked the steps of her life's tearstained journey. Mrs. Hunt died shortly after her book was published, but various authors supplemented it. George Wharton James's *In Ramona's Country* was essentially a guidebook to southern California.

The penchant for things Spanish had begun. *Ramona* became an annual pageant attended by thousands in the town of Hemet: it is actually a pilgrimage play, with a cast of several hundred performers. Commemorative place-names were created: Ramona, of course; Alessandro Valley; and Armona—since the other name was already used.

Bancroft, employing a whole "literary factory" of interviewers, editors, researchers, and writers, had begun publishing several dozen tomes detailing the entire history of the Pacific Coast, concentrating particularly on California. His massive collection of manuscripts, oral history, legal documents, maps, and rare publications formed the unique foundation for the Bancroft Library at the University of California, Berkeley, the primary hunting ground for students and scholars of Californiana. A set of historians now lectured and wrote to inspire the public about the fascination of the Hispanic settlement period. Most notable were Herbert Bolton at UC Berkeley (who personally retraced Anza's route through the desert) and Zoeth Eldredge of San Francisco. The latter was responsible in the century's first decade not only for suggesting the commemorative titles on his city's streets, but also for nagging communities to correct the way they erroneously ran together their Spanish words, such as Rionido, Elmonte, Dospalos, Lamesa, Elrio, Eltoro. (In at least one case, though, he himself made a grammatical error by splitting a place-name apart: Delrosa—a surname—into Del Rosa!)

Another highly useful rescue effort was conducted by various individuals and groups to raise public interest and funds in order to purchase and restore or rebuild the decaying or ruined missions and various pueblo or rancho adobe casas. The colorful, brilliant, and eccentric editor and librarian Charles F. Lummis, the "crusader in corduroy," founded the Landmarks Club, which was dedicated to preserving historical sites. The missions were in the greatest immediate need of attention, since most of those still standing had been ruined inside and out by periodic earthquakes and from usage as barns, barracks, taverns, and warehouses. Presidents Buchanan and Lincoln at least had returned many of the mission buildings and their immediate surroundings to the Catholic Church, removing them from the neglect or misuse incurred through private ownership. In places where the churches were yet cherished and used, as at San Luis Obispo, rectors' renovations had spoiled their authenticity. There was much work to be done, and it took years of fund raising and toil, plus the participation of the Catholic Church, the State of California's division of parks, private groups like the Mission Bell Association, even the Civilian Construction Corps (CCC) and the WPA labor force during the Depression. Slowly, the Hispanic past was resurrected.

A single person intensely devoted to California history could work wonders. And such a one was Lummis, who as director of the Los Angeles Public Library gathered valuable materials to be kept in a California History room there. He also arranged the start of the Southwest Museum, with its collection of Indian artifacts and its re-creation of an authentic adobe house. At his own eclectic, self-designed house nearby, El Alisal, he assembled creative and intellectual people of the early years of this century and inspired new architectural styles that incorporated elements of California's past, styles such as Mission Revival, Spanish Neo-Colonial, Spanish Californian, Monterey Colonial, and Spanish Ranch House. Now came such creations as the Panama-California Exposition in San Diego in 1915 (some of its buildings still remain at Balboa Park), the campus of Stanford University at Palo Alto, the Mission Inn in Riverside, the rebuilt Del Monte Hotel at Pebble Beach near

Monterey, and the world's first motor-hotel or "motel"—Spanish style too—in Paso Robles. The seemingly endless variations on the Spanish theme continue, and usually they are given Hispanic place-names and street-names to match.

The revolution in transportation accelerated. Los Angeles remained a fairly sleepy town until 1877, when it was joined up to the railroads in the north and thence to the eastern states. The first "land boom" in southern California began. Since the most desirable location along a major railroad line was the terminus itself, a great battle went on between the port of San Pedro/Wilmington, belonging to the city of Los Angeles, and that of Santa Monica, promoted by the Southern Pacific. The eventual winner, San Pedro, received a huge breakwater construction that turned its open bay into a semisheltered harbor, now the world's largest and busiest man-made port.

When the Santa Fe Railroad came into southern California in 1886 on the second transcontinental line, a "rate war" ensued with the Southern Pacific. At one point, a one-way ticket from Missouri, which normally cost $125, could be bought for a dollar. At such low prices many people visited California—or moved there. The Southern Pacific alone brought in 120,000 in the year of 1887. Some immigrants hit "pay dirt"; others got "taken."

The rosy glow cast by *Ramona* swiftly influenced place-naming in most parts of the state, particularly in regions where new railroad stations and new tract settlements sprouted. With or without any simple formulas for constructing Spanish-style names, they were cropping up all over, even though not a single Mexican might be living there.

Railroad stations "out in the tules" where nobody lived as yet, sidings built for future commerce and industry, and communities in the planning stage—all were recipients in this name-giving rash. Affected too were already established communities that sought to improve their attractiveness to tourists and prospective settlers by acquiring new names. (If they aimed for a Neo-Spanish appearance, they were likely to look for Spanish street-names too.)

Some were pleasantly descriptive but sometimes improperly constructed, like Rio Linda, Mar Vista, Oro Linda, Oro Loma, Costa Mesa, Vista Robles, Monte Vista, Mira Loma, Miraleste, Asilomar, Miraflores. And there were those that combined another language with Spanish: Terra Buena, El Modena, Rio Dell, Hacienda Heights, Buena Park, Hermosa Beach, Redondo Beach, Oroville, Altaville, Altadena (using the -dena from Pasadena, a Chippewa word supposedly meaning "crown of the valley," plus alta, for a higher elevation).

Then there were the advertisement names, paying compliments that the Hispanic place-namers had never done: Chula Vista, Linda Vista, Vista Grande, Alta Loma, Loma Linda. Or they sounded "poetic": Alturas, El Encanto, Escalon, La Mirada, El Verano, Escondido, Descanso, Del Mar, Playa del Rey—even Armada, in an area far from the sea.

Other towns' names had stories to tell, or at least reasons for taking on particular Spanish titles. El Segundo featured the Standard Oil Company's second refinery in the state. Los Olivos was a place with commercial olive groves. Primero occupied the first station on a new railroad line. Adelanto was a community that aimed to move ahead. Crucero lay where two railroad lines crossed, and El Centro was at the very center of the newly productive Imperial Valley. Fruto produced fruits on its outlying farmlands. Naranjo grew orange trees. Manteca was the location of a creamery where butter was produced. Moreno happened because a real estate promoter named Brown declined to have his name given to the settlement, so it was translated. At Modesto a railroad director said he was too modest to have the new town named after him. Dulzura offered sweetness to come from its new honeybee-raising venture. (The pollinizing and honey-making insect was not indigenous to North America.) El Portal stood at the very gateway to Yosemite; Cima sat on the crest of the newly built railroad line. The town of Sierra Madre, located in the foothills northeast of Pasadena, echoed Padre Font's belief that the mountains above it, which became known as the San Gabriels, were the "mother range" from which all other California sierras had sprung.

There were towns that changed their names to become Spanish: Rosena to Fontana, Fortune to Fortuna, Spottiswood to Famoso, Indian Wells to Indio, Mound City to Loma Linda, Cowell to Manteca, Dorrisville to Alturas, Port Ballona to Playa del Rey, Wineville to Mira Loma, Whitton to Planada, Marion to Reseda, Randolph to Sablon, Maizeland to Rivera, Ocean Park Heights to Mar Vista. A place settled by a man named Luce in time acquired the name De Luz!

But the most wonderful names of all were the contrived ones, made to "look Spanish": Almanor, Calimesa, Calipatria, Calistoga, Capitola, Citrona, Coalinga (from Coaling Station), Covina, Dinuba, Gardena, Glendora, Glorietta, Lamanda, La Crescenta, Silverado, Solromar (combining *sol, oro,* and *mar* to make "golden sunset to the sea," a prize winner in a contest), Tarzana (named by Edgar Rice Burroughs, a resident, after his famed character Tarzan), Termo, Urbita, Valyermo. And a whole set of hybrid names came from the words concocted by fusing parts of other states' names with *Cal-* from California, to use as border towns: Calexico (its Mexican opposite is Mexicali), Calneva, Calvada, Calor, Calzona.

Some legitimate names transported from foreign places, other states, or literary sources, not Spanish but somewhat Spanish looking, are Arcadia, Avalon, Cambria, Elsinore, Hesperia, Mendota, Monte Cristo, Olinda, Orinda, Placentia, Pomona (the Roman goddess), Rialto, Toluca, Visalia.

The railroads acquired new rivals when the automobile's popularity and prevalence in California began in the 1920s. The corduroy or plank roadways of the past were converted into concrete and macadam highways so that people could take their cars (there were 150,000 of them in the state by 1929) almost anywhere they wanted to, for business or pleasure. New towns built up along these thoroughfares in order to accommodate the travelers. El Camino Real was selected as the first major route to be given a hard surface. In a single year, a giveaway map had almost 170,000 takers. New Spanish names now joined the old familiar ones. Old-timers were interviewed and old maps consulted in order to produce accurate spellings and reasonably authentic names taken from arroyos and ridges and canyons. Mapmakers and place-namers were officially requested to honor well-known past settlers of the area—many of them having Spanish surnames.

Since the new highways needed filler for the roadbed, construction workers threw in whatever rubble they could find along the way. Sometimes the remnants of deserted casas were hauled off and dumped, adding their adobe chunks to the foundation that would provide passage for modern-day explorers and colonists traveling not by foot or muleback or ox-drawn, wooden carreta, but in gasoline-powered metal vehicles.

The need for names and more names went on. Major routes like highways could be given numbers. Roads that ran basically north and south received odd numerals (like

101 for El Camino Real). Those that went east and west got even ones. For people who resist a world in which everything and everybody is identified by a number, many of these modern routes are given Spanish names, commemorative or otherwise, such as the Junipero Serra and Embarcadero freeways in San Francisco.

San Carlos, a community on the San Francisco Peninsula, took a modern-day saintly commemorative name in 1887 because its founders believed that their hills had been the site from which Portola's scouts first beheld San Francisco Bay on November 4, 1769—St. Charles's feast day. Portola Valley, a young settlement in the small valley between Palo Alto and Skyline Boulevard, is regarded as a probable camping spot of the expedition. In the same area, the town of Pacifica was created in 1957. In Los Angeles County, two Hispanic-named communities merged their names into a confusing Pico Rivera.

Newly made names for the Spanish-style planned communities abounding in Orange County, where old Mexican land grants were often held intact for decades, have used titles from the past. Mission Viejo adapted the title for the old *Misión Vieja* rancho. Laguna Niguel combines the Indian word in a land-grant title with Laguna (already long used at nearby Laguna Beach), derived from *Cañada de las Lagunas*.

Sometimes these names are chosen for authenticity, such as Trabuco Canyon, and sometimes for their advertising potential (Casa del Sol, for a retirement community). The community names and street-names selected by developers may not always be appropriate, euphonious, or easy to pronounce. Such ungrammatical, irresponsible, or inelegant titles as Mesa Dump Road, Toto Loma, Tierra Blanco, Loganlinda, Monte Mar Vista, Paseo Mira Flores, Oro Verde, Pastiempo, Santa Domingo, and San Hacienda have been affixed to road signs and maps. English first names may have *-a, o,* or *-ita* added for Hispanic effect, as with *Nancita.* And all sorts of nouns and adjectives may accompany—with or without a *de*—the convenient variations on Spanish words for street: Calle, Camino, Paseo, Via, Avenida. There are the expectable *El, La, Los,* and *Las* combined with nouns. And some street-names aim for a poetic effect, as in Remolino Lejos Road (a faraway whirlwind, or "far from the madding crowd"!).

In Spanish-style planned communities, the naming of streets—along with concern for the overall appearance of the place with regard to signage, architecture, and landscaping—can range from the casual or uninterested to the thoughtfully and carefully prepared. One developer may turn the matter of street-naming over to "someone in the office." Another will call in a special consultant, who, after methodical research, will choose names that are grammatically correct, geographically sensible (no *valle* on a hilltop, for example), and in conformity with regional rules.

In many places, approval of street-names is no longer automatic. Various state, county, and city departments as well as the U.S. Post Office must be consulted before a choice becomes official. Duplication of names, or the proximity of similar-sounding names in a small geographic area is the main concern of fire and police departments. An emergency call to "Hurry to 714 San Carlos" could cause confusion and delay if officers must first figure out whether it's San Carlos Street, Place, Avenue, Boulevard, Lane, or Drive (or one of their Spanish equivalents).

Names now may be limited to a certain number of letters (to fit on street signs). Accent marks and other niceties are not permitted in some areas, since they make signs more difficult to read. Acceptable names must be properly spelled, grammatically correct, and in good taste.

Los Angeles County stores all street names in use in a computer and provides printouts for developers to refer to when selecting names for new streets. The county frowns upon double names and now refuses to accept names that mix languages, such as adding an El or La to an English word. It also requires that foreign-language words be spelled correctly. To those who feel that any humor in street-naming is impossible under these controls, officials are quick to point out that even within their system such whimsical examples as Jamon (Ham) Lane next to Huevo (Egg) Circle—they are in Orange County—would be approved if local residents have no strong objection.

Still, there is a curious dichotomy between the Hispanic past evoked by the largely Anglo middle-class settlements and the current reality of the Spanish-speaking population living in *barrios* in the cities or, often, as transients in rural areas. The sentimental nostalgia for the departed Arcadia of Spanish California, often exploited by land promoters, cannot easily coexist with the vibrant, assertive, and sometimes angry culture of the *Chicanos*. A slang word for Mexican American, derived from *Mejicano,* it is usually preferred by the younger generation.

The Chicano movement that started in the sixties paralleled the rise of assertiveness in other underprivileged minority groups, notably blacks and women (who, of course, are numerically a majority). Chicanos promote a new pride, frequently aggressive, in their own kind: *hijos de país,* or *la Raza.* Inevitably, California became the center for this new agitation.

Delano is a farm town now famous as the headquarters of Chicano labor leader Cesar Chavez. At least one place-name scholar proposed its Spanish origin as *de lano* (of wool), because sheep were raised there. In truth, it was the name assigned by Southern Pacific personnel to a new railroad station in Kern County, to commemorate then (1873) Secretary of the Interior Columbus Delano. Issuing forth from the town of Delano have come those new slogans and placards saying, *La Huelga!* (strike) and *Venceremos* (we shall win).

California is known not only for forward-looking ideas and behavior (including eccentric ones) but also for the significant presence of groups of people who originally came here to improve their economic lot in life. California contains the greatest Spanish-speaking population of all states in the nation, the majority of them of Mexican ancestry. The entry level of employment, and often the lifelong pursuit of a living, is usually in agriculture, which, with a low wage scale, and for stoop labor, is unattractive to other groups.

Periodically in the past, when California growers needed field workers, especially at the crucial harvest time, they imported groups of Mexican laborers on a temporary, contractual basis. These *braceros* (strong-armed ones) had their entries, working conditions, and exits regulated by state and federal authorities. Because of inevitable wage and job competition with U.S. citizens, however, this large-scale importation has mostly been discontinued. The flow goes on nonetheless with the *mojados* ("wetbacks," so called because in the Southwest many swam across the Colorado or Rio Grande to come in). Men who profit by bringing such undocumented or illegal aliens across the border, usually in small groups that can be hidden in vehicles, and then arranging employment for them, are known as *coyotes*.

As low-cost, competent domestic help and unskilled but hardy and hardworking laborers in farmlands and factories become increasingly difficult to obtain, employment of household servants and migratory workers without visas or work permits will be inevitable. A child born to a woman who is an illegal alien is automatically considered an American citizen—which makes efforts to expel the mother difficult. Arguments for and against having a fenced and heavily patrolled border, or allowing Mexicans free access to economic and living opportunities in the United States, have gone on for years, without reaching any satisfactory, practical, or humane solution. It is certain, however, that Mexican Americans will remain here and also continue to come in, with or without documents, and raise families in their land of birth or adoption. The Hispanic population of Los Angeles alone is now overtaking that of all other nationalities, including the Anglo majority; it is heavy in many other areas of California. The presence of so many Spanish place-names and street-names gives them the sense of the familiar.

Since place-names, like personal and family names, may be partly responsible for building positive self-images and affecting other people's opinions, Mexican Americans have sometimes been successful in increasing the visibility of their own chosen names to honor roles and accomplishments of noted Hispanics. One example is the naming of Ruben Salazar Park in Los Angeles, in remembrance of a respected Chicano newsman. Another is giving the name of Representative Edward R. Roybal to a new health center in East Los Angeles. Non-Chicanos wishing to upgrade the community status of Mexican Americans may also take the initiative in creating commemoratives that evoke historical Hispanic personages: as when a branch of the Los Angeles Public Library—a highly active cultural center—was named after Spanish California's first resident governor, Felipe de Neve.

Such new names or changed names can come from any concerned citizen who makes the effort to request them. Application is made to a local politician or to city or county officials. If enough public interest can be aroused, a new school, hospital, or street will receive the commemorative name. Or a change can be made if good cause for it is shown, though this process is more difficult since the old name is already established.

The Hispanic culture is also reflected in the super-graphic paintings of Chicano artists—professionals and amateurs—that sprout up to decorate the walls of permanent buildings and the wooden fences of construction sites in barrio areas. Many of them are distinctively Mexican in colors, designs (using Aztec and Mayan motifs), and the revolutionists' mural-art traditions. They often depict scenes and people in California's past or in the history of Hispanic America.

Californians can expect to see more and more Hispanic names, whether used in new settlements designed to look Spanish or proposed by a growing, increasingly self-confident Mexican-American population. Living now in a land that was once ruled by their own people, contemporary Spanish-speaking residents remind themselves and their children that they are symbolic heirs of the past. They wish to honor that past, improve the present, and prepare for the future. Many Spanish names are already there upon the California land; surely they will wish to implant more.

The Spanish language is in fact being used increasingly in the state of California. In response to both need and public pressure, the legislature enacted a bill that now requires all laws, public notices regarding safety, health, and education, and voting information and ballots to be printed in both English and Spanish. This recent stipulation actually revives a past one. In 1849 California's first constitution specified bilingual publication, but the clause was repealed in later years. It may be that California is well on

Boostering, Nostalgia, and Barrios

the way again to becoming a two-language culture, as it was for incoming Yanquis more than a century ago.

In the meantime, the established Spanish place-names will stay. They still look good, sound good, and admirably suit the California climate, terrain, and temperament.

The presence of some old Spanish names is bound to cause consternation in those with any knowledge of Spanish. Why should a heavily industrialized area in San Francisco be called the Potrero (Meadow) District? How could a fortresslike prison have the name of a pelican (Alcatraz) or a saint (San Quentin)? What can be so sacred about Sacramento? Where is the Indian food at Pinole? Or the lean bear at Oso Flaco? Or the bridge at La Puente?

But although La Cienega is a major Los Angeles thoroughfare, paved and no longer a swamp; and Atascadero a lovely city, not a mudhole; and it would be most surprising to encounter a wild bear, *flaco* or otherwise, within many miles of Los Osos Valley, the names remain to remind us that once upon a time such things were possible.

Yet some of the Spanish names are as accurate now as they were two hundred years ago. Seagulls still wheel over Gaviota Pass, rabbits hop across Conejo Valley, the Sierra Nevada glistens with snow, tar still bubbles ominously in pools at La Brea, pelicans can be seen near Alcatraz Island in San Francisco Bay and Alcatraz Point near Malibu, and many arroyos all over California are as *seco, dulce, mocho* or *permanente* as they were in Portola's and Anza's time. And, who knows? Perhaps all those commemorated saints are maintaining perpetual vigils over the terrain that has received many an immigrant with dreams and sustained a multitude of people raised upon its adobe soil.

Hispanic Places to Visit

THANKS TO STRONG public interest in California's Spanish and Mexican past aroused in the last decades of the nineteenth century and actively sustained by numerous individuals and civic-minded organizations through the years, many historical places have been preserved and set aside for posterity. Some are the original structures: usually adobe casas occupied and cared for by families, whether descendants of the original builders or later owners who took pride in maintaining the premises. Other buildings have been restored or re-created: the ruined missions particularly. There are also specifically constructed places—such as the Serra Museum in San Diego and La Casa de Adobe in Los Angeles—that recapture the architecture of the mission and rancho times. Many of these buildings, both indoors and out, are veritable museums of Hispanic California, and often include artifacts of the Indian culture and the Yankee settlers. A number are transitional, combining both Mexican and American aspects. They often display authentic household furnishings, fashionable apparel, and domestic, craft, agricultural, and cattle-tending equipment. The missions specialize in the religious, neophyte-training, and food-producing functions. Additionally, Spanish expedition campsites and important passes have been located and marked, along with the sites of early settlements and homes, battles, and other significant events.

This list of suggested places to visit is hardly complete, but it indicates many possibilities for interesting excursions, whether as jaunts into a metropolitan area or as side trips on a long drive. Most buildings mentioned are open to the public; often a small entrance fee is charged. A few properties remain private residences. Community rescue efforts, as well as the educational use of historic Hispanic sites, increasingly bring more of them into the public domain. Generally there is free access to landmark sites commemorated by the state of California. Missions have few daytime hours or days when they are closed; many conduct religious services in their chapels and churches. Some are operated in conjunction with Catholic schools. Several are attached to the State Historical Park system. Lesser-known places, especially houses built during the rancho period, are likely to have limited visiting hours or days. More detailed information about these historic spots and their exact locations may be obtained from regional guide books, tourist bureaus, visitors' centers, and chambers of commerce. At a public library, a reference librarian can be helpful in finding publications about a particular region. Local historians usually have prepared studies of a county, area, or township, and if Spanish-speaking explorers and colonists were there, their traces—including place-names—are usually discussed in detail. An excellent general reference book is Abeloe, Rensch and Hoover's *Historic Spots in California*.

The list is divided into three main sections, by region; these in turn are reviewed county by county. These are Northern California (including San Francisco and the Bay

Area, the Sacramento River region, and the Santa Clara Valley); Central California, from Santa Cruz County southward to Santa Barbara; and Southern California, from Ventura to San Diego, both along the coast and inland.

I. Northern California

San Francisco County. Because of the fast growth of the city during the Gold Rush, the destruction of many fires and the earthquake of 1906, and the lack of early concern over preserving buildings from the past, the city itself has only two original Hispanic structures: Mission Dolores, the adobe chapel built in the 1790s as part of Mission San Francisco de Asis (with its old cemetery providing a resting place for various early settlers, including De Haro, Arguello, and Noe); and the adobe Officers Club at the Presidio. The fine collection at The California Historical Society at Jackson and Laguna streets contains rare books and maps of the Californio period, plus photographs of original adobes. Fort Point within the Presidio, dating back to the Civil War and the only brick fortress in the West, occupies the Cantil Blanco site once used by Castillo de San Joaquin—at the very tip of the Golden Gate's southern end, and right below the bridge. Now operated as a National Historical Monument, it has a small museum with some artifacts from the Spanish and Mexican periods. From the roof a visitor can get a splendid view of San Francisco Bay and the city itself.

Marin County. Angel Island State Park was the site of the first anchorage in the bay by Ayala's *San Carlos* in 1775. It was once a Mexican rancho.

At Mill Valley's Old Mill Park there are the old timbers from the area's first sawmill, built by John Reed at Rancho Corte de Madera del Presidio. (Reed's house was the first one at Sausalito. He constructed the first ferryboat for crossing the bay.)

Mission San Rafael Arcangel, at San Rafael, is mostly a replica, but there was little evidence of what the original structure actually looked like.

Sonoma County. At the center of the town of Sonoma is Sonoma State Historical Park. At one end of the plaza is Mission San Francisco Solano (Mission Sonoma). The plaza, laid out by Sonoma's founder, Mariano G. Vallejo, features the Blue Wing Inn, the Sonoma Barracks, a small section of Vallejo's Casa Grande (which burned down in 1867), and his brother Salvador's casa—all Mexican-period structures; also the Bear Flag National Historical Monument, for it was here that the California Republic was proclaimed and General Vallejo taken prisoner. Nearby is Vallejo's home, Lachryma Montis, another historical monument. Although built of wood, it has inner walls of adobe, giving it better insulation and stability. An old warehouse on the site was made of lumber shipped around the Horn during the Gold Rush days, when various American buildings were "prefabricated" in New England.

At Petaluma stands General Vallejo's adobe casa on his Rancho Petaluma: the largest adobe in the northern region.

At Fort Ross Historical Park the Russian settlement on the California coast in the early 1800s has been reconstructed.

Napa County. At St. Helena is the Old Bale Gristmill, a survivor of Dr. Edward Bale's Rancho Carne Humana.

At Chiles Valley there is the Chiles Flour Mill, another historical park.

Tehama County.   In Red Bluff the William B. Ide Adobe State Historical Park is a four-acre park alongside the Sacramento River, built in 1846—shortly before Ide became the first and only president of the California Republic. The ranch house is virtually a museum. The site can also be reached by boat.

Butte County.   At Chico, John Bidwell's Victorian mansion is at the center of what was once his Rancho Arroyo Chico.

Tuolumne County.   Columbia State Historical Park has re-created the site of Marshall's discovery of gold at Sutter's Sawmill on the American River.

Sacramento County.   In the capital city, Sutter's Fort, rebuilt, is a state historical park containing a museum of period history. Old Sacramento State Historical Park is a nine-acre section of the waterfront area set aside to reproduce the appearance of Sacramento in the mid-nineteenth century.

Contra Costa County.   At Concord, Fernando Pacheco's adobe; at Martinez, the Martinez family adobe. At Moraga Valley there is the adobe built by Joaquin Moraga, son of soldier-explorer Gabriel Moraga and grandson of Jose Joaquin Moraga, the founder and first comandante of the Presidio at San Francisco.

At Los Medanos is "Dr." John Marsh's Victorian-style stone home built on his rancho. His daughter, orphaned when several of his vaqueros murdered him in 1856, turned it into a public monument.

Alameda County. Mission San Jose de Guadalupe is a reconstruction. The only authentic remnant is the padres' adobe casa, now a small museum. The pastoral setting at the base of Mission Peak is a main attraction.

At Pleasanton Valley is the Alviso adobe.

In Berkeley, the Bancroft Library at the University of California has the richest collection of written materials from or about the Hispanic period. It also houses the much-debated brass plate said to have originated with Drake's visit to a California bay.

Santa Clara County. Mission Santa Clara de Asis. The mission was moved five times. The original structures on this last site were reconstructed after a disastrous fire in 1926. The church is on the campus of the University of Santa Clara (a Jesuit institution).

Nearby is the Old Adobe Women's Club, originally one of the Indian family houses adjoining the mission. It is among the oldest structures in the Santa Clara Valley.

There are adobe casas once lived in by the Higuera, Miranda, and Sunol families.

In the city of San Jose, which belatedly turned its attention to its prominent past as northern California's first and foremost civilian pueblo, apparently only one structure remains from its early days: the Peralta adobe casa. Within Pioneer Park there is the restored De Quevedo adobe. San Jose, however, has a fine historical museum with good displays of its Hispanic origins.

San Mateo County. At Pacifica is the Sanchez adobe, now a park and museum run by the San Mateo County Parks and Recreation Department. There is a hiking trail up to Sweeney Ridge, offering the same view of San Francisco Bay as seen by Portola and his men in 1769; access is from Hassler Avenue off Highway 1.

At San Mateo the Allied Arts Guild has saved the out-buildings of Rancho Las Pulgas; the place is a center for local artisans. In the same town is the Casa de Tableta, a popular meeting place for Mexican Californians in the 1850s.

II. Central California

Santa Cruz County. In Santa Cruz there is a small-size replica of the original church of Mission Santa Cruz, close to the original site. Several blocks away is the only structural remnant from the Spanish period, a two-story soldiers' barracks. On Branciforte Street a schoolground marks the center of the failed Villa de Branciforte.

San Benito County. The rebuilt Mission San Juan Bautista faces the pueblo plaza, now a state historical park containing the Castro House, the Zanetta House, the Plaza Hotel (once a famous and luxurious place when San Juan Bautista was the main stagecoach stop, before the railroad bypassed the town). The effect is of a Mexican-period town. There are several old buildings in use as stores and restaurants on the main street only a block away.

Monterey County. At Salinas, the Boronda adobe.
The city of Monterey is one of the best places for a walking tour of California's Hispanic-period buildings and sites. Among the features on the "Path of History" are the Old Customs House, the Pacific Building, Casa de Oro, California's first theater, Colton Hall (where the state's first constitution was framed), Larkin House (origin of the Monterey Colonial style), Casa Gutierrez, Stokes Adobe, Casa Estrada. Near the entrance to the Presidio a plaque marks the spot where Portola originally founded it. Near-

by, a sign identifies the site of the old oak tree that stood at the place where both Vizcaino and Padre Serra came ashore. South of Fishermen's Wharf are two adobes: Casa Sanchez and Casa Alvarado. On Church Street is the Royal Presidio Chapel, originally started by Serra but rebuilt by Lasuen: the only remaining presidial church in California. The Catholic Cemetery of San Carlos was the burial place of many early Montereños. At the northern tip of Monterey Peninsula is Vizcaino's Punta de Pinos.

At Carmel is the much-visited Mission San Carlos Borromeo de Carmelo, or Mission Carmel, the restored headquarters and residence of Padre Junipero Serra and most of his padre-presidente successors. Sculptor Jo Mora created a sarcophagus for Serra's remains, kept in the church sanctuary; he is depicted slumbering prayerfully in death, with a recumbent grizzly at his feet, and three padres mourning him: his friends Crespi, Lasuen, and Palou. In the mission cemetery some three thousand neophytes were buried.

In the Salinas Valley, close to Highway 101, is Mission Nuestra Señora de la Soledad, now partially reconstructed. Nearby, in Soledad, is Los Coches Rancho campground.

Within the Hunter-Liggett Military Reservation is Mission San Antonio de Padua, about thirty miles west of Highway 101. It is one of the most impressive of the restored missions, showing the complete quadrangle layout followed by most of the missions in the chain.

San Luis Obispo County. Mission San Miguel Arcangel lies just east of 101, some miles north of Paso Robles. It is noted for its original mural decorations. Most of the original structure remains. Nearby, to the south, is the old Rios Caledonia adobe.

At Nipomo is the large adobe Casa de Dana, once famed for its Yankee ranchero's hospitality.

Mission San Luis Obispo de Tolosa is within the business district of San Luis Obispo. The restored church—unique for the round pillars on its collonade, the belfry, and the vestibule—includes a small museum with a collection of photographs of old adobe casas in California. A block away is the County Historical Museum with more Hispanic-period materials.

In Morro Bay there is the Canet adobe.

Santa Barbara County. Mission La Purisima Conccpcion, located west of Buellton, is regarded as the best of all mission restorations, reproducing faithfully the entire physical appearance of the Franciscan mission at its peak.

Mission Santa Ines, in Solvang, is partially reconstructed. Its chapel serves as a parish church.

The city of Santa Barbara has cherished and preserved its Hispanic buildings far better than most other places, in spite of the devastating earthquake of 1925. Mission Santa Barbara was in perpetual use as a parish church, so deterioration was not as severe as elsewhere; the altar light has been kept burning for almost two hundred years. The "Red Tile Tour" of history, within the central part of town, encompasses much of the presidial pueblo. The County Courthouse was supposedly built on the site of Portola's camp. The historical museum features many artifacts from the Hispanic period. El Cuartel and La Caneda Adobe were once part of the original presidio. The city has other adobe buildings and homes. Every August, Old Spanish Days Fiesta takes place; an historical parade, El Desfile Historico, presents events and personalities of the past. The mission, located at the base of Mission Canyon, has various ruins and restorations on its grounds, including waterworks, a gristmill, aqueducts, and a lavanderia where Indian neophyte women did laundry. Farther up the canyon are the small but excellent Natural History Museum, housed within a mission-style building, displaying the flora, fauna, and minerals of the coastal region that were known to the Spanish colonists, as well as Indian artifacts; and the Botanic Garden, where one can see the original dam site built for the mission's use.

III. Southern California

Ventura County.   San Buenaventura Mission, from which the city and county took their names, is now in the midst of a rapidly expanding metropolis. The church, rebuilt after an earthquake in 1812, was remodeled grotesquely by a well-meaning parish priest in the late 1800s but has now been restored to its original form. Nearby are remnants of its former reservoir and water system. Within the Ventura area are two adobes: Olivas and Ortega.

Los Angeles County.   Because of sheer size, the prosperity of various ranchos, and the predominantly Mexican population within the region until the land boom of the 1870s and '80s, this area has numerous historical sites and adobes.

At Calabasas, close to the Ventura County line, there is the Leonis family's adobe casa, open to the public.

In Placerita Canyon, a Los Angeles County Park and Nature Center near Newhall, one can see "the oak of the golden dream" still alive: the site of California's first gold strike in 1842, when the majordomo of a nearby rancho, Francisco Lopez, awoke from a nap, felt hungry, dug up some wild onions at the base of the tree and discovered gold flakes clinging to their roots. Visitors acquire some familiarity with the appearance of the oak and chaparral terrain of southern California ranchos.

On the northern side of San Fernando Valley, between Highways 5 and 405, is Mission San Fernando Rey de España. The entire mission and its grounds serve as a museum of mission living.

At Encino is the casa of Rancho de los Encinos, now a state historical park.

In North Hollywood, just south of Universal Studios, is Campo de Cahuenga, a replica of the six-room adobe where the peace treaty was signed by Fremont and Andres Pico in January of 1847, ending the Mexican War within Alta California.

A main attraction in the downtown area of Los Angeles is part of the original site of the Spanish pueblo, founded in 1781, now given over to El Pueblo de Los Angeles State Historical Park, still under refurbishment. During the 1930s, public-spirited people headed by Christine Sterling managed to save the few remaining historic buildings at Olvera Street, notably the Avila adobe—the city's oldest building. The street was then turned into a highly popular outdoor marketplace-mall, with stalls and shops selling Mexican goods and food to tourists. Nearby are the Old Plaza Catholic Church (restored from the original asistencia), the Plaza, the Pico House (an early hotel built by Pio Pico), and other sites and structures of interest, including part of the Zanja Madre (the old ditch that brought water to the pueblo from the Los Angeles River).

At the Southwest Museum in the Highland Park area there is a replica of a typical Californio home, La Casa de Adobe.

At Griffith Park (its 3,700 acres once part of a rancho) is the Feliz family adobe.

Rancho La Brea's adobe casa, ten blocks north of the tar pits and close to Farmers Market, was preserved by the Gilmore family as a private residence. The Page Museum at Hancock Park displays *la Brea* and its victims.

The Los Angeles County Museum of Natural History at Exposition Park, at the University of Southern California campus, features miniature dioramas portraying scenes of California history from the Indian-habitation and Spanish-settlement periods up to and including the American conquest.

At Glendale is the Verdugo family's Casa Adobe de San Rafael.

Mission San Gabriel Arcangel is in the suburb of San Gabriel, about ten miles east of downtown Los Angeles. Its unusual Spanish-Moorish design gives it an impressive appearance. The church itself remained almost intact through the years. On the other side of the mission wall is the Ortega-Vigare Adobe, the second oldest building in the area.

The Los Angeles County Arboretum in Arcadia contains the adobe casa lived in by Scottish ranchero Hugo Reid and his Indian wife at their Rancho Santa Anita.

In Claremont, the Rancho Santa Ana Botanic Garden displays the natural vegetation of southern California known to the Spanish and Mexican colonists.

Adobe de Palomares in Pomona is a restored hacienda. In Whittier, the Pio Pico Historical Monument shows the rancho casa of California's last Mexican governor, who remained a prominent citizen in the south even after the territory became part of the United States.

In Long Beach are two rancho casas open to public viewing: Los Cerritos (which belonged to Don Juan Temple) and Los Alamitos (Don Abel Stearns's country residence).

In Compton is the Dominguez family ranch house. (Dominguez Hill was the site of the nation's first air show, in 1910.)

In the City of Industry are remnants of William Workman's home at Rancho La Puente. In Montebello is the Soto-Sanchez adobe mansion.

San Bernardino County. At the town of Bryn Mawr, east of San Bernardino, is the asistencia mission and parts of its zanja and irrigation works.

At Yucaipa is an adobe house built by Diego Sepulveda, said to be the oldest house in the county.

At Chino is the Yorba adobe.

Riverside County. In the town of Riverside, the famous Mission Inn—which started out as an adobe guest house in the 1870s—was first built in the increasingly popular Mission style. It is now an apartment house.

At Hemet the annual *Ramona* outdoor pageant has taken place every spring since 1923.

Imperial County. Near the site of old Fort Yuma, across the Colorado River from Yuma, Arizona, are the separate sites of Missions La Purisima Concepcion and San Pedro y San Pablo, destroyed by Indians in 1781, a year after their founding. A Catholic church serving local Indians is close to the site of La Purisima, and contains a commemorative plaque and a statue of Padre Francisco Garces.

Orange County. At El Toro, the Serrano adobe. And in Estancia Park in Costa Mesa, the Sepulveda adobe.

In Santa Ana, the Charles W. Bowers Memorial Museum, built in the Mission style, displays the various phases of southern California's history, including the Indian and Hispanic periods. It contains historical documents, such as land-grant deeds and diseños.

Mission San Juan Capistrano, within the growing town of the same name, features the romantic ruins of an ambitious church felled by an earthquake, and the famous migratory swallows. It is among California's most popular tourist attractions. The old chapel, in which Padre Serra once said Mass, is still used for religious services. The town itself has several adobe casas, and one, several blocks from the mission, remains in a state of untenanted, forlorn neglect—which conveys the usual condition of abandoned adobes during the past century.

Dana Point southwest of the mission commemorates author Richard Henry Dana of *Two Years Before the Mast,* who worked in the hide trade here.

San Diego County. Mission San Luis Rey, inland from Oceanside, is an effectively restored mission, used partly as a seminary. It was the most prosperous of all Californian missions and had more neophytes attached to it than any other mission in the Americas, in good part due to the efforts and personality of Padre Peyri. The old peppertree planted by its padres is still alive. They used its spicy seeds as substitutes for peppercorns.

Mission San Antonio de Pala, an asistencia of Mission San Luis Rey built to serve the Indians living northeast, has been restored. Its chapel features an unusual bell tower.

Mission San Diego de Alcala, the first in the chain, is a restoration. It contains a small museum and a replica of an Indian rancheria. It lent its name to the highly commercial Mission Valley section of the city of San Diego.

In the increasingly renovated San Diego Viejo or Old Town section of the city, now a state historical park, a walking tour goes past such places as Plaza Vieja (whose flagpole has flown the flags of California's three governing nations), Casas de Estudillo, Machado, Lopez, Stewart, Cota, Carrillo, Bandini, and Pedroreña, and El Campo Santo —the old Spanish graveyard. Nearby is Presidio Hill, the scene of the first presidio and mission establishments in Alta California. The premises are now occupied by the handsome Serra Museum, founded by the San Diego Historical Society in 1929. It displays artifacts from all periods of city and state history and contains a research library. The Serra Cross on the hill was made from fragments gathered from the presidio's ruins.

Balboa Park, the city's main park and the location of two world's fairs (1915, 1935), has buildings left in various Spanish architectural styles which are now used as museums: the Museum of Man contains exhibits of the Mexican and Spanish periods in California, along with many Indian displays.

On the far west end of the city, on the Point Loma peninsula, are various early Hispanic sites, such as Ballast Point (Punta de Guijarros), where Spanish sailors took on cobblestones. The so-called Old Spanish Lighthouse at the tip dates from the American period. The Cabrillo National Historical Monument there memorializes Juan Rodriguez Cabrillo, the first Spanish-speaking navigator to see Alta California. (The statue of him was a gift from Portugal, his homeland.) The visitors' center is a small museum providing information about the Spanish period and the coastal region. This spot is reportedly among the most visited historical sites in the nation. On a clear day, the view from the high bluff is inspiring—though the city and its busy harbor would be wholly incomprehensible to a sixteenth century explorer.

For Further Reading

Abeloe, William N. *Historic Spots in California.* 3rd ed., 1966, based on Rensch and Hoover volumes published under the same title.

Bancroft, Hubert Howe. *California Pastoral.* Bancroft's Works, vol. 34: 1888.

Bolton, Herbert. *Outpost of Empire.* 1931.

California, State of (Department of Parks and Recreation). *California Historical Landmarks.* 1975.

Carrillo, Leo. *The California I Love.* 1961.

Caughey, John W. *California.* 1953.

Cleland, Robert G. *The Cattle on a Thousand Hills.* 1951.

———. *From Wilderness to Empire.* 1944.

Corle, Edwin. *The Royal Highway.* 1949.

Dana, Richard Henry. *Two Years Before the Mast.* 1840.

Denis, Alberta J. *Spanish Alta California.* 1927.

Dumke, Glenn S. *The Boom of the Eighties in Southern California.* 1944.

Eldredge, Zoeth S. *The Beginnings of San Francisco.* 2 vols. 1912.

Geiger, Maynard, ed. *As the Padres Saw Them.* 1976.

Gudde, Erwin G. *California Place Names.* 3rd ed.

199

———. *1000 California Place Names*. paperback, 1959.

Hanna, Phil T. *The Dictionary of California Land Names*. 1951.

Hart, James D. *A Companion to California*. 1978.

Heizer, Robert, and Almquist, Alan. *The Other Californians*. 1971.

Jackson, Helen Hunt. *Ramona*. 1884.

Johnson, Paul C. *Pictorial History of California*. 1970.

Kemble, John H. *San Francisco Bay: A Pictorial Maritime History*. 1957.

Lewis, Oscar. *San Francisco: Mission to Metropolis*. 1966.

McWilliams, Carey, *Southern California Country*. 1946; rev. ed. 1973 entitled *Southern California: An Island on the Land*.

Nadeau, Remi. *Los Angeles from Mission to Modern City*. 1960.

Nelson, Edna. *The California Dons*. 1962.

Pitt, Leonard. *The Decline of the Californios: A Social History of the Spanish-Speaking Californians, 1846-1890*. 1966.

Pourade, Richard. *The History of San Diego*. A series of pictorial histories commissioned by James S. Copley that includes: *The Explorers, The Call to California, Anza Conquers the Desert, Time of the Bells, The Silver Dons, Gold in the Sun*. 1960—.

Riesenberg, Jr., Felix. *Golden Gate: The Story of San Francisco Harbor*. 1940.

———. *The Golden Road*. 1962.

Robinson, Alfred. *Life in California*. 1846.

Robinson, W. W. *Land in California*. 1948.

———. *Los Angeles from the Days of the Pueblo*. 1959.

———. *Ranchos Become Cities*. 1939.

Sanchez, Nellie van de Grift. *Spanish and Indian Place Names of California*. 1914.

———. *Spanish Arcadia.* 1929.

Stewart, George R. *Names on the Land.* 1945.

Sunset Books. *The California Missions: A Pictorial History.* 1964; text by Paul C. Johnson.

Time-Life Books. *The Forty-Niners.* 1974; text by William Weber Johnson.

Treutlein, Theodore. *San Francisco Bay: Discovery and Colonization, 1769-1776.* 1968.

Weaver, John D. *El Pueblo Grande: A Nonfiction Book about Los Angeles.* 1973.

Introducing Spanish

SPANISH HAS FEWER pronunciation and grammatical rules than English. And they are more consistently applied. At the introductory level, when learning Spanish mainly from place-names, only the simplest rules are needed. California place-names can help you get acquainted with the sounds of Spanish. They are compounded of many basic words on which one can practice pronunciation. But they should also show agreement in gender (masculine or feminine) and number (singular or plural) between nouns and the words that modify them. They consist primarily of simple nouns—names for persons, places, things—plus articles (el, la, los, las) and adjectives; there are occasional prepositions, conjunctions, adverbs, a few verbs—but none that need conjugating. Not only do Spanish consonants and vowels follow regular patterns, so do those other essentials of speech: syllable division and stress.

Pronunciation varies from place to place, and people to people. The major difference is of course between the Castilian Spanish of the Old World, also spoken in various parts of the Americas, and the New World Spanish used in

Mexico and California. The primary distinction is the way they pronounce *c* before *e* or *i,* and *ll.* In Castilian the *c* is said like *th,* whereas in the New World it comes out *s.* The Castilian *ll* sounds like the *l'y;* New World like *y.* There are other regional differences and peculiarities. Even Spanish dictionaries prepared by linguistic scholars cannot agree on the precise pronunciation of many words.

The Spanish alphabet has twenty-eight characters. Except in foreign words, *k* or *w* are not used. (These sounds find near-equivalents in *c* and *qu-,* and combinations of consonants with *-ua.*) Spanish has four letters additional to the ones we have in English: *ch, ll, n,* and *rr.* When using a Spanish dictionary, remember that these letters are alphabetized separately, and follow after *c, l, n,* and *r.*

Spanish has the same vowels as English, but they each have only one pronunciation, and they are always voiced.

vowel	said like the
a	*a* in father
e	*a* in say
i	*ee* in see
o	*o* in oh
u	*oo* in booth

The pronunciation may change slightly, depending on their proximity to other vowels or their position in a word. The most marked change is in *e,* which gets clipped to an *eh* sound when followed by two consonants or when it occurs in the last syllable of a sentence in front of a single consonant. In the same situations, *o* is said less rounded.

I and *u* are considered weak vowels: they often combine with the other vowels or with each other to make a different sound—a diphthong or triphthong (two or three vowels sounded together). These compound vowels can be approximated by pronouncing each vowel properly in its place but running the result together quickly. When *i* is preceded in the same syllable by a vowel other than *u,* it is shortened slightly to an *ih* sound (like the *i* in it). When *u* precedes other vowels, it creates a sound rather like our *w:* *u* plus *a*—oo-ah or wah; *u* plus *e*—oo-ay or way; *u* plus *i*— oo-ee or wee. As in English, *y* functions as either a vowel or a consonant. When it is in a vowel positions, as in Ynez, it sounds like the Spanish *i.*

The consonants, too, behave in reasonable and regular ways. Some are rather different from the same English letters. *H* is usually silent, as in *hombre*—OHM-bray. *J* is pronounced with our *h* sound: *José* as hoh-SAY. *G* before *e* or *i* also makes an *h* sound: a Spanish *general* is hay-nay-RAHL. (Because of Aztec influence, Mexicans have various *x*s in their words, which are usually said like *h* too: Mexico is MAY-hee-koh.) *C* before *a, o,* or *u* sounds like our *k;* before *e* or *i,* like *s.* In Spanish, a *v* sounds very much like *b;* and *z* like *s.* (This is why certain place-names have varied spellings, such as Calabasas, Calabazas; Gabilan, Gavilan. *J, h,* and *g,* among consonants, and *i* and *y,* among vowels, often create similar spelling problems.)

One of the most distinctive consonants in Spanish is the *r,* which is formed differently than the English sound, by trilling the tongue tip against the roof of the palate front. The double consonant *rr* makes an even greater flourish. A single *r* in certain positions—at the beginning of a word, or in the middle of a sentence when following a syllable that ends in *l, n,* or *s*—is a similar double trill. As said before, the New World *ll* sounds like *y.* The *ñ* (an *n* with a tilde) is pronounced like the *n'y* in canyon. The rest of the consonants, including *ch,* are pronounced as they are in English.

Above and beyond the basic sounds of the letters, word pronunciation depends on the placement of stress. Syllable stress—highly erratic in English—is quite predictable in Spanish. Usually only one syllable is stressed, unless the word is very long or a combination of several words; it may then take a secondary stress. Words ending in vowels, except for *y*, and the consonants *n* or *s* are stressed on the next to the last syllable. Words ending in consonants other than *n* or *s*, and including *y*, are stressed on the last syllable. Any exceptions to these two basic rules should be accented (´) above the vowel in the stressed syllable. However, as mentioned in Chapter 2, many place-names in common and frequent usage have lost the accent—because it has become implicitly "understood."

Syllables are complete phonetic units consisting of a vowel sound alone or in combination with one or several consonants. When figuring syllable divisions in order to sound out words, remember that certain consonants occurring together are always treated as an indivisible pair: *bl*, *br*, *cl*, *cr*, *dr*, *fl*, *fr*, *gl*, *gr*, *pl*, *pr*, *tr*—and of course *ch*, *ll*, and *rr*. A vowel can begin or end a syllable. If it is followed by two consonants, the second one should begin the next syllable—unless it is part of an inseparable pair, in which case the vowel should end that syllable. When three consonants are together, the first two are attached to the preceding vowel while the third goes with the following vowel—except when the double-consonant pairs follow another consonant.

In combinations of *a, e,* and *o,* divide the vowels into separate syllables. If any of these are joined with *i* or *u,* or with *ui* or *iu,* they then form diphthongs or triphthongs—unless there is an accent mark on the *i* or *u* to indicate a separate syllable. If there is an accent on an *a, e,* or *o* within one of these multiple-vowel units, it only indicates that this syllable containing the vowels should carry the stress.

Plurals are generally formed from singular nouns by adding -s to nouns that end with unstressed vowels, or es to those that end with consonants or stressed vowels (except for e, which only takes an -s). Nouns ending in z are made plural by converting the z to ces: *nuez — nueces*. Usually any stressed syllable in the singular form is also stressed in the plural form, which may require the addition or subtraction of an accent mark in order to conform to the regular rules of syllable stress.

Almost all Spanish nouns have definite, assigned genders. This means that for grammatical purposes they are considered either "masculine" or "feminine." This gender identity is important to know, since both articles ("the" especially, as listed below) and adjectives — which can either precede or follow the noun they modify — must take forms appropriate to the noun's gender.

Most Spanish nouns ending in *o* have masculine gender; most ending in *a* are feminine. But there are many more possible endings, and rules — and exceptions to rules. Often one gets to know the right gender from familiarity with particular nouns and noun endings. When in doubt, a dictionary will tell you. Gender is sometimes vital in determining the right meaning of a word. For example, *puerto* is a port; *puerta* a door. When speaking of animals, if sex distinction is important, an *o* or *a — gato* or *gata* (cat) — can make it clear. And so can the appropriate use of the article *the*.

	singular	plural
masculine	*el*	*los*
feminine	*la*	*las*

Consider the word *gato* again. Add *the (el)* and *white (blanco)*. In singular and plural, masculine and feminine forms it would be:

	singular	plural
masculine	*el gato blanco*	*los gatos blancos*
feminine	*la gata blanca*	*las gatas blancas*

Some examples of California place-names with proper noun-adjective agreement in number and gender are El Segundo, La Mesa, Los Gatos, Las Trampas. Many other names, however, were concoted by Americans (after the Hispanic period had ended) with little regard for such basic rules of Spanish grammar. And 'double nouns were put together—as if one modified the other. Mar Vista is a typical result. Paso Robles began as Paso de Robles, but the connecting preposition was dropped.

A few prepositions appear in Spanish place-names. The most useful is *de* (of). "Of the——" is a frequent phrase. The masculine singular form becomes *del* by combining *de* and *el*. A similar contraction may be formed from *a* (to) and *el: al*.

Dictionary-Index

A

a [AH] *prep.* to, toward, at, in, upon, by, near, for

abadejo [ah-bah-DAY-hoh] *n.m.* codfish; yellow wren

abajeños [ah-bah-HAY-n'yohs] *n.m.* Southern Californians, 119–20, 152–53

abajo [ah-BAH-hoh] *adv.* under, below. *Abajo!, exclam.* Down with!

abanico [ah-bah-NEE-koh] *n.m.* fan

abedul [ah-bay-DOOL] *n.m.* birch tree

abeja [ah-BAY-hah] *n.f.* bee

abeto [ah-BAY-toh] *n.m.* silver fir tree

ablano [ah-BLAH-noh] *n.m.* hazel tree

abogado [ah-boh-GAH-doh] *n.m.* lawyer

abra [AH-brah] *n.f.* gorge, cove; opening

abrazo [ah-BRAH-soh] *n.m.* hug, embrace

abrevadero [ah-bray-vah-DAY-roh] *n.m.* watering place for cattle

abrigo [ah-BREE-goh] *n.m.* haven, shelter

Abril [ah-BREEL] *n.m.* April (month)

acampo [ah-KAHM-poh] *n.m.* common pasture; camp. Also a surname

acanto [ah-KAHN-toh] *n.m.* thistle

acaro [ah-KAH-roh] *n.m.* mite

acaso [ah-KAH-soh] *n.m.* chance; *adv.* maybe, perhaps

acebo [ah-SAY-boh] *n.m.* holly tree

aceituna [ah-say-TOO-nah] *n.f.* olive

aceituno [ah-say-TOO-noh] *n.m.* olive tree

aceña [ah-SAY-n'yah] *n.f.* water-driven flour or grist mill *acera* [ah-SAY-rah] *n.f.* sidewalk

acolito [ah-koh-LEE-toh] *n.m.* assistant, acolyte

acordarse [ah-kohr-DAHR-say] *v.* to remember

ácoro [AH-koh-roh] *n.m.* sweet grass, sweet flag

adelanto [ah-day-LAHN-toh] *n.m.* progress, forward

adelfa [ah-DEHL-fah] *n.f.* oleander

adobe [ah-DOH-bay] *n.m.* sundried brick, the basic building material of Spanish California, 17, 79-80, 100, 174, 183

Adobe, Casa de, 170, 183, 193

adorno [ah-DOHR-noh] *n.m.* adornment, decoration

aduana [ah-DWAH-nah] *n.f.* customs house

aeropuerto [eye-roh-PWEHR-toh] *n.m.* airport

agrado [ah-GRAH-doh] *n.m.* grace, agreeableness, pleasure

agriculture in California, 68, 79-80, 85, 86-87, 94, 99-100, 111, 151, 158-162

agua [AH-gwah] *n.f.* water; spring. (Water sources, essential to both travelers and settlers in early California, were often recorded on maps and later lent their names to places.) *See* water in Spanish place-names.

aguacate [ah-gwah-KAH-tay] *n.m.* avocado

aguaje [ah-GWAH-hay] *n.m.* waterhole or place; spring, reservoir

águila [AH-ghee-lah] *n.f.* eagle

aguilera [ah-ghee-LAY-rah] *n.f.* eagles' nest or aerie

aire [EYE-ray] *n.m.* air, wind

ajo [AH-hoh] *n.m.* garlic

al [AHL] contraction of *a* and *el; to the*

alambique [ah-lahm-BEE-kay] *n.m.* still (for distilling alcohol)

alameda [ah-lah-MAY-dah] *n.f.* poplar grove; mall; tree-lined walk

Alameda: city and county, 13, 61, 124, 188

álamo [AH-lah-moh] *n.m.* poplar; in California, usually its relative, the abundant cottonwood tree; *alamito*, small cottonwood tree

Alamitos, Los: rancho, 112, 124, 194

Alarcón [ah-lahr-KOHN] Spanish explorer, 29-30

alba [AHL-bah], *n.f.* dawn

alberca [ahl-BEHR-kah] *n.f.* pool, reservoir

albercón [ahl-behr-KOHN] *n.m.* large pond

alcalde [ahl-KAHL-day] *n.m.* mayor, judge, justice of the peace. (During the Hispanic period the *alcalde* was the civil administrator of a pueblo or larger settlement.) 17, 85, 148

alcatraz [ahl-kah-TRAHS] *n.m.* pelican, albatross *(pl. alcatraces)*

Alcatraz Island, 37, 181

alcázar [ahl-KAH-sar] *n.m.* castle, fortress

alcoba [ahl-KOH-bah] *n.f.* alcove, bedroom

aldea [ahl-DAY-ah] *n.f.* small village

alegre [ah-LAY-gray] *adj.* happy

alegría [ah-lay-GREE-ah] *n.f.* happiness

alemán [ah-lay-MAHN] *adj.* German

alforja [ahl-FOHR-hah] *n.f.* saddlebag

algarrobo [ahl-gah-RROH-boh] *n.m.* carob tree; honey mesquite tree

algodón [ahl-goh-DOHN] *n.m.* cotton

algoso [ahl-GOH-soh] *adj.* weedy

Alhambra Valley (formerly Arroyo del Hambre), 165

alicante [ah-lee-KAHN-tay] *n.m.* poisonous snake

alisal [ah-lee-SAHL] *n.m.* sycamore grove

aliso [ah-LEE-soh] *n.m.* alder tree; in California, usually a sycamore

alma [AHL-mah] *n.f.* soul

almadén [ahl-mah-DEHN] *n.m.* mine or mineral. (New Almaden in Santa Clara County was named after the quicksilver mine in Spain.) 150

almeja [ahl-MAY-hah] *n.f.* mussel, clam

almendra [ahl-MEHN-drah] *n.f.* almond, kernel

alomar [ah-loh-MAHR] *v.* to grow strong

alondra [ah-LOHN-drah] *n.f.* lark

Alta California—Upper California: as Spanish claim and colony, 7, 27–99; as Mexican province, 99–141

Altadena, 172

altanero [ahl-tah-NAY-roh] *adj.* soaring, proud

altivo [ahl-TEE-voh] *adj.* haughty, high-minded

alto [AHL-toh] *adj.* tall, high, loud; *n.m.* height, halt. *Alto!*, *exclam.* Stop!

altura [ahl-TOO-rah] *n.f.* height, level

Alturas, 173

Alvarado [ahl-bah-RAH-doh] Spanish surname, 59, 122, 190

Alvarado, Juan Bautista: Mexican politico, 97, 121, 125, 139

Alviso [ahl-BEE-soh] Spanish surname

amable [ah-MAH-blay] *n.m.* amiable, pleasing

amador [ah-mah-DOHR] *n.m.* lover, sweetheart

Amador, family, valley, town, county, 3, 13, 60, 145

amapola [ah-mah-POH-lah] *n.f.* poppy

amar [ah-MAHR] *v.* to love

amargo [ah-MAHR-goh] *n.m.* bitterness; *adj.* bitter

amargoso [ah-mahr-GOH-soh] *adj.* bitter

amarillo [ah-mah-REE-yoh] *adj.* yellow

amate [ah-MAH-tay] *n.m.* fig tree

ambiente [ahm-B'YEHN-tay] *n.m.* atmosphere, environment, ambience

Americano [ah-may-ree-KAH-noh] *n.m.* & *adj.* American. See *Yanqui*

American River (orig. *Río de los Americanos*), 95, 139, 141, 147

amigo [ah-MEE-goh] *n.m.* friend

amistad [ah-mees-TAHD] *n.f.* friendship

amo [AH-moh] *n.m.* master, owner, head of household

amor [ah-MOHR] *n.m.* love

amoroso [ah-moh-ROH-soh] *adj.* affectionate, gentle, pleasing

Ana, Santa [AH-nah] St. Anne (mother of the Virgin Mary) 14, 47, 48, 112–13, 195–96

Anacapa Island, 37

ánade [AH-nah-day] *n.m.* & *f.* duck

Andréas, San [ahn-DRAY-ahs] St. Andrew; town, 145

Andrés, San [ahn-DRAYS] St. Andrew; valley and fault, 62

anejo [ah-NAY-hoh] *adj.* annexed, attached

ángel [AHN-hehl] *n.m.* angel

Angel Island, 36, 164, 185

Ángeles, Los [lohs-AHN-hay-lays, but commonly pronounced loss AN-juh-luss or loss ANG-less] *pl. n.m.* the angels (city and county name abbreviated from *El Pueblo de Nuestra Señora la Reina de los Ángeles*), 13, 14, 16, 48–49, 86–87, 165–66, 192–95

Angeles River, Los, 48, 86. See also *Porciúncula*.

angelito [ahn-hay-LEE-toh] *n.m.* little angel

angosto [ahn-GOHS-toh] *adj.* narrow, close

Anián, Strait of [ah-nee-AHN] 30–31, 63, 130

anillo [ah-NEE-yoh] *n.m.* ring, circlet

ánima [AH-nee-mah] *n.f.* soul, spirit (*Las Ánimas* in a place-name usually refers to All Souls' Day.) 127

animals in Spanish place-names, 20, 124–25

Anita, Santa [ah-NEE-tah] rancho and town, 10, 127, 134, 194

año [AH-n'yoh] *n.m.* year

Ano Nuevo Point, 34, 37

Anselmo, San [ahn-SEHL-moh] town, 68

ante [AHN-tay] *n.m.* elk

antigua [ahn-TEE-gwah] *adj.* antique, old

anti-Mexican prejudice, 146–50. See also Chicano & Mexican immigrants in California

Antonio, San [ahn-TOH-n'yoh] St. Anthony; ship, 45, 75–76, 77; as place-name, 64, 113, 127; Mission San Antonio de Padua, 53, 78–79, 190

Anza, Juan Bautista de [AHN-sah] Hispanic explorer and soldier, 62–64, 65, 82–83, 86, 162

Amate

Anza-Borrego Desert State Park, 64

Anza Expeditions, 8, 62–64, 65

Anza Trail, 86, 136

Arabic words in Spanish, 17

arastradero: See arrastradero

árbol [AHR-bohl] *n.m.* tree

arbolado [ahr-boh-LAH-doh] *adj. & n.m.* wooded area

arboleda [ahr-boh-LAY-dah] *n.f.* plantation, grove

arcada [ahr-KAH-dah] *n.f.* arcade

architectural styles in California, Spanish, 5, 12, 79–81, 115–17, 134, 170–71, 183

arcilla [ahr-SEE-yah] *n.f.* white earth clay

arco [AHR-koh] *n.m.* arc, arch

ardilla [ahr-DEE-yah] *n.f.* squirrel

Ardo, San: contrived name, 68

arena [ah-RAY-nah] *n.f.* sand; arena

Arena Point, 38

argos [AHR-gohs] *n.m.* sharp-eyed person (from Greek mythological figure Argus, who had a hundred eyes)

argüello [ahr-goo-AY-yoh] *n.m.* faintness; emaciation

Argüello: Spanish surname, 38, 83, 95, 120, 185

Arguello Point, 38

arillo [ah-REE-yoh] *n.m.* small hoop, earring

armada [ahr-MAH-dah] *n.f.* fleet, squadron; town, 172

aromita [ah-roh-MEE-tah] *n.f.* odor, usually a peculiar one,

as of sulphur or pungent resin in wood

arrastradero [ah-rahs-trah-DAY-roh] *n.m.* drayman, hauler; worker at an arrastre (sometimes spelled *arastradero*)

arrastre [ah-RRAHS-tray] *n.m.* a large device used in crushing gold-bearing ores, 150

arriba [ah-RREE-bah] *adv.* up, above, overhead

arribeños [ah-rree-BAY-n'yohs] *n.m. pl.* Northern Californians, 119–20, 152–53

arriero [ah-rree-YAY-roh] *n.m.* muleteer, mule-driver

Arrillaga [ah-rree-YAH-gah] Spanish governor, 98

arroyo [ah-RROH-yoh] *n.m.* brook, creek. (In California, *arroyo* was also used for a riverbed that became dry in the summer season. *See* water in California place-names.)

arroz [ah-RROHS] *n.m.* rice

asilo [ah-SEE-loh] *n.m.* refuge, asylum

Asilomar, 21, 72

asistencia [ah-sees-TEHN-s'yah] *n.f.* assistance; in California, a chapel or "branch mission" in an outlying region that served local Indians or pueblo residents, 87, 95, 195, 196

áspero [AHS-pay-roh] *adj.* rough, harsh

Asunción [ah-soon-see-OHN] *n.f.* ascent of the Virgin Mary to heaven, 128

atascadero [ah-tahs-kah-DAY-roh] *n.m.* mudhole; a deep miry place

Atascadero: rancho and town, 4, 125, 181

atezado [ah-tay-SAH-doh] *adj.* darkened

átomo [AH-toh-moh] *n.m.* atom; something very small

atravesado [ah-trah-bay-SAH-doh] *adj.* crosswise; treacherous, mean

aurora [ah-oo-ROH-rah] *n.f.* dawn

avacado [ah-vah-KAH-doh] *n.m.* cowlike (or perhaps a misspelling of avocado)

avena [ah-BAY-nah] *n.f.* oats or oat

avenal [ah-bay-NAHL] *n.m.* oatfield

avenida [ah-bay-NEE-dah] *n.f.* avenue

aventura [ah-behn-TOO-rah] *n.f.* adventure

aviador [ah-bee-ah-DOHR] *n.m.* provider of supplies for a journey; aviator

Ávila [AH-bee-lah] Spanish surname, 193

avión [ah-bee-OHN] *n.m.* airplane

Avisadero Point, 37

avisador [ah-bee-sah-DOHR] *n.m.* adviser, admonisher

Ayala [ah-YAH-lah] Spanish navigator, 36–37, 185

ayuntamiento [ah-yoon-tah-M'YEHN-toh] *n.m.* town council, 148

azor [ah-SOHR] *n.m.* goshawk

azul [ah-SOOL] *adj.* blue

Azusa: an Indian place-name, 122

B

baca [BAH-kah] *n.f.* top or cover of cart, coach, or bus

bahía [bah-EE-ah] *n.f.* bay, harbor

bailarín [bye-lah-REEN] *n.m.* dancer

baile [BYE-lay] *n.m.* dance, ball, ballet, 118

Baja California [BAH-hah] 29–30, 35

bajada [bah-HAH-dah] *n.f.* slope, descent

bajío [bah-HEE-oh] *n.m.* sandbank, shoal

bajo [BAH-hoh] *adj.* low, short; mean, vile; *n.m.* deep place; *adv.* underneath, below; softly; *prep.* beneath, under

Bale, Edward: English physician and ranchero, 126, 186

balería [bah-lay-REE-ah] *n.f.* pile of bullets or shot

Ballast Point, 38, 197

ballena [bah-YAY-nah] *n.f.* whale, 20

Ballona [bah-YOH-nah] creek and land-grant title in L.A. County (named after the city of Boyona in Spain), 127, 173

balsa [BAHL-sah] *n.f.* raft; pool or lake

bancal [bahn-KAHL] *n.m.* terrace, garden

Bancroft, H.H.: Editor, bookman, founder of Bancroft Library, 167–69, 188

bandera [bahn-DAY-rah] *n.f.* banner, flag

bandido [bahn-DEE-doh] *n.m.* bandit. In California, 11, 22, 155–56

Bandini [bahn-DEE-nee] Spanish surname, 120, 134, 197

bandita [bahn-DEE-tah] *n.f.* small band

baño [BAH-n'yoh] *n.m.* bath, bathroom. (The town of Los Banos in Merced County got its name from pools at an arroyo where a padre bathed during missionary travels. It became the headquarters of the vast Miller & Lux cattle ranch in the San Joaquin Valley.)

baranda [bah-RAHN-dah] *n.f.* wooden railing

barata [bah-RAH-tah] *n.f.* barter, exchange

barato [bah-RAH-toh] *adj.* cheap, inexpensive

barbado [bahr-BAH-doh] *adj.* bearded; fenced

Bárbara, Santa [BAHR-bah-rah] St. Barbara of Rome, 74, 88

Barbara, Santa: Channel, 35, 88; county, 13, 191; city, 14, 191; island, 34; mission, 50, 89–90, 191–92; presidio, 50, 88–89, 191

barca [BAHR-kah] *n.f.* small boat, launch

barquero [bahr-KAY-roh] *n.m.* boatman

barquilla [bahr-KEE-yah] *n.f.* small boat

barraca [bah-RRAH-kah] *n.f.* barracks, hut, cabin

barranca [bah-RRAHN-kah] *n.f.* ravine, gorge (often replaced by gulch after the American takeover)

barrio [BAH-rr'yoh] *n.m.* ward or district of a city (now widely used to identify the Hispanic-American or Chicano communities within urban areas)

barro [BAH-rroh] *n.m.* mud, clay; earthenware

barroso [bah-RROH-soh] *adj.* muddy, spotted

Bartleson-Bidwell wagon train, 138–39

batata [bah-TAH-tah] *n.f.* sweet potato

batea [bah-TAY-ah] *n.f.* trough, tray; in California, a shallow bowl of wood or metal used in panning gold

batequito [bah-tay-KEE-toh] *n.m.* little "well" dug in the sand

bautismo [bowh-TEES-moh] *n.m.* baptism, christening

Bautista: Baptizer, Baptist. *See* Juan Bautista, San

baya [BAH-yah] *n.f.* berry

bayo [BAH-yoh] *adj.* bay-colored

Bear Flag Revolt & Republic, 10, 96, 140–41, 186, 187

becerro [bay-SAY-rroh] *n.m.* yearling calf; tanned calfskin. *Becerro marino:* seal or sea-calf

bello [BAY-yoh] *adj.* beautiful, pretty

bellota [bay-YOH-tah] *n.f.* acorn

Benicia [bay-NEE-see'yah] town, 3. (Planned on the north side of the Carquinez Strait, it originally took the first name of General Vallejo's wife, Francisca, but when Yerba Buena changed its name to San Francisco, the new town converted to her second personal name. As Benicia it briefly served as the state's capital in 1853.)

Benito, San [bay-NEE-toh] St. Benedict; county, 13, 189

Bernal [behr-NAHL] Spanish surname, 63

Bernardino, San [behr-nahr-DEE-noh] St. Bernardino of Italy; town, county, 13, 14, 68, 163, 195; mountains, 61, 64; rancho, 110, 127; asistencia, 195

berrendo [bay-RREHN-doh] *n.m.* antelope; *adj.* dappled, two-colored

berro [BAY-rroh] *n.m.* watercress

Berryessa, sometimes Berrelleza [bay-rrhee-EHS-sah] Spanish surname, 63, 152

Bidwell, John: American settler in California, 138–39, 142, 187

bienvenida [b'yehn-bay-NEE-dah] *n.f.* welcome

blanco [BLAHN-koh] *adj.* white; fair; blank

Blas, San [BLAHS] supply port on west coast of New Spain, 44, 45, 75, 81, 82

boca [BOH-kah] *n.f.* mouth; opening, entrance to a bay or river. (Because of the latter meaning, the word often appears in Spanish place-names.)

bocina [boh-SEE-nah] *n.f.* large trumpet

bodega [boh-DAY-gah] *n.f.* warehouse, wine cellar, grocery store. (Bodega Bay north of San Francisco did not get its name as a provision spot for mariners. It was named after the captain of a Spanish ship that entered the bay in 1775: Juan Francisco de la Bodega y Quadra.) 37

bola [BOH-lah] *n.f.* ball

bolero [boh-LAY-roh] *n.m.* an Andalusian dance; a loose, short jacket; *adj.* lying, fibbing

Bolinas: an Indian place-name, 122

bolo [BOH-loh] *n.m.* dunce

bolsa [BOHL-sah] *n.f.* purse, bag, pocket. (This word appears frequently in the titles of early California land grants, as the name for land "pockets"surrounded on three sides by water or difficult, steep terrain, therefore self-enclosed and not readily accessible.)

Bolton, Herbert: California historian, 169

bomba [BOHM-bah] *n.f.* pump

bonachón, -a [boh-nah-CHOHN, -CHOH-nah] *adj. & n.m. & f.* good-natured, easy person

bonanza [boh-NAHN-sah] *n.f.* fair weather; prosperity, success; in mining, a rich vein of gold or silver, 142–143

Bonita, Point, 38, 165

bonito [boh-NEE-toh] *adj.* pretty, handsome. (The name was also given to a California tuna prized by fishermen.)

Borica, Diego de [boh-REE-kah] Spanish governor, 98, 121

borrasca [boh-RRAHS-kah] *n.f.* storm; in mining, a barren site, 143

borrego [boh-RRAY-goh] *n.m.* yearling lamb. (In California, however, it usually refers to the bighorn sheep found around Borrego Valley and Anza-Borrego Desert State Park.) 62

bosque [BOHS-kay] *n.m.* forest, grove, park

bota [BOH-tah] *n.f.* boot; water container of leather; in California, a large rawhide bag,

esp. one used for shipping tallow from ranchos

Bouchard, Hipolito or Hippolyte: Pirate-revolutionist who attacked California colony in 1818, 131–32

bracero [brah-SAY-roh] *n.m.* strong-armed man; day laborer. (The word now means a worker admitted from Mexico by seasonal contract to work in agricultural areas in the U.S.) 12, 178–79

Branciforte, Villa de [brahn-see-FOHR-tay] 72, 90–91, 189

bravata [brah-BAH-tah] *n.f.* bravado, boasting

bravo [BRAH-voh] *adj.* brave; strenuous, wild; excellent; *Bravo!, exclam.* Well done!

brazo [BRAH-soh] *n.m.* arm; branch; division

brea [BRAY-ah] *n.f.* pitch, tar, asphalt, 48, 50, 124, 181

Brea, La: Tar pits, rancho, boulevard (Los Angeles), 48–49, 194

breña [BRAY-n'yah] *n.f.* craggy ground full of bramble bushes

breve [BRAY-vay] *adj.* brief, short

brillo [BREE-yoh] *n.m.* brightness, glitter

brío [BREE-oh] *n.m.* strength, courage, vim

Briones [bree-OH-nays] Spanish surname

brisa [BREE-sah] *n.f.* breeze

bronco [BROHN-koh] *adj.*
rough; rude; wild

bruno [BROO-noh] *adj.* dark
brown; *n.m.* plum tree

Bruno, San: German saint. Place-
name, 62

buaro [BWAH-roh] *n.m.* buzzard

Bucareli [boo-kah-RAY-lee]
Viceroy of New Spain, 82, 85

buchón [boo-CHOHN] *adj.* bulg-
ing, full-bellied; *n.m.* tumor,
goiter

Buchon, El, and Buchon Point,
37, 51–52, 58

buenaventura [BWAY-nah behn-
TOO-rah] *n.f.* good luck,
good health. (A legendary
river with this name, sup-
posedly flowing from the
Rocky Mts. to the Pacific
Ocean, was long sought by
American mountain men.)

Buenaventura, San: St. Bonaventure of Italy, 88; mission, 49,
87–88, 192

Buena Vista Valley, 61

bueno [BWAY-noh] *adj.* good,
kind; strong, healthy

buey, bueyes [BWAY, BWAY-
ehs] *n.m. sing. & pl.* ox,
steer, bull; oxen

bueyero [bway-YAY-roh] *n.m.*
cattle-herder or driver

bull-and-bear fights, 143–44

burro [BOO-rroh] *n.m.* jackass

busca [BOOS-kah] *n.f.* search,
hunt

butano [boo-TAH-noh] *n.m.*
spring; water canteen made
from cattle horn

Butterfield Overland Mail (stage-
coachline) 160

C

caballada [kah-bah-YAH-dah]
n.f. a rancho's herd of riding
horses, 107, 117

caballero [kah-bah-YAY-roh]
n.m. gentleman, horseman

caballeta [kah-bah-YAY-tah] *n.f.*
field cricket

caballo [kah-BAH-yoh] *n.m.*
horse

cabaña [kah-BAH-n'yah] *n.f.*
hut, cabin; flock of sheep

Cabazon, 165. *See cabezón*

cabeza [kah-BAY-sah] *n.f.* head

cabezón [kah-bay-SOHN] *adj.*
stubborn, big-headed

cabo [KAH-boh] *n.m.* end, ex-
tremity; promontory or cape;
haft, handle; chief of a group
(sometimes corporal)

cabra [KAH-brah] *n.f.* she-goat

cabrero [kah-BRAY-roh] *n.m.*
goatherd

cabrillo [kah-BREE-yoh] *n.m.*
small goat; also a Spanish surname

Cabrillo, Juan Rodríguez: Span-
ish-Portuguese navigator, 3, 7,
30–31, 33, 39, 197

Cabrillo National Historical Monument, 197

cacao [kah-KAH-oh] *n.m.* cocoa
or chocolate

cacera [kay-SAY-rah] *n.f.* irrigation canal

cadena [kah-DAY-nah] *n.f.* chain, link

Cahuenga [kah-WEHN-gah] Indian word; pass, 58, 119, 141

cajón [kah-HOHN] *n.m.* box, chest. (The name was often given to boxed-in canyons.) Cajon Pass, 61, 136

calabaza [kah-lah-BAH-sah] *n.f.* squash, pumpkin, gourd. (In place-names it is sometimes spelled *calabasa.* The English word calabash, meaning a hard-shelled gourd in which water can be carried, came from Spanish.)

calabozo [kah-lah-BOH-soh] *n.m.* dungeon, jail, jail cell, "calaboose," 162

calavera [kah-lah-BAY-rah] *n.f.* skull

caldera [kahl-DAY-rah] *n.f.* caldron; boiler

Calaveras creek and valley, 21–22

Calaveras river and county, 13, 21–22

caldero [kahl-DAY-roh] *n.m.* kettle

calera [kay-LAY-rah] *n.f.* limestone quarry; limekiln

caleta [kah-LAY-tah] *n.f.* cove, inlet, creek

calidad [kah-lee-DAHD] *n.f.* quality, condition

caliente [kah-L'YEHN-tay] *adj.* hot, fiery (applying to temperature only)

California [kay-lee-FOR-n'yah] as place-name, 14, 24, 27–29

Californio [kay-lee-FOR-n'yoh] a California settler during the Hispanic period, usually of Spanish ancestry; or a descendant of an early family

callado [kah-YAH-doh] *adj.* silent, quiet

calle [KAH-yay] *n.f.* street

calmar [kahl-MAHR] *v.* to calm, quiet, or soothe

Camarillo [kah-mah-REE-yoh] Spanish surname, 121

cambio [KAHM-b'yoh] *n.m.* change, exchange

caminata [kah-mee-NAH-tah] *n.f.* long walk, jaunt

camino [kah-MEE-noh] *n.m.* road, journey

Camino Real, El [EHL kah-MEE-noh ray-AHL] the "Royal Highway" or "King's Road." (This route connected the twenty-one Franciscan missions set up in late eighteenth and early nineteenth century Alta California. After Mexican rule began, the name was generally still used but the *real* came to mean "public" or "national" since monarchy was abolished.) 5, 46, 52, 70, 71, 92, 101, 117, 121, 156, 174

camisa [kah-MEE-sah] *n.f.* shirt, chemise

campana [kahm-PAH-nah] *n.f.* bell

campanero [kahm-pah-NAY-roh] *n.m.* bell-founder or -ringer

campesino [kahm-pay-SEE-noh]
n.m. peasant, rural inhabitant,
farmer
campestre [kahm-PEHS-tray]
adj. rustic, rural
campillo [kahm-PEE-yoh] *n.m.*
small field
campo [KAHM-poh] *n.m.* field,
country; mining camp. *Campo
santo*, cemetery
Campo Seco [KAHM-poh SAY-
koh] "dry diggings" gold
camp; town, 145
cañada [kah-N'YAH-dah] *n.f.*
small canyon, dell
Canada, La: town, 14, 123
canasta [kah-NAHS-tah] *n.f.*
basket
canción [kahn-see-OHN] *n.f.*
song
candela [kahn-DAY-lah] *n.f.*
candle
Cañizares [kah-n'yee-SAH-rays]
explorer of San Francisco
Bay, with Ayala
canoa [kah-NOH-ah] *n.f.* canoe
cañón [kah-N'YOHN] *n.m.* canyon; tube; cannon, gun barrel.
(Canon Perdido, a street in
Santa Barbara, received its
name from a lost cannon, not
a lost canyon.)
cántara [KAHN-tah-rah] *n.f.*
large pitcher
cantil [kahn-TEEL] *n.m.* cliff,
steep rock
Cantil Blanco (S.F.), 37, 83, 185
canto [KAHN-toh] *n.m.* song,
chant

capitán [kah-pee-TAHN] *n.m.*
captain. (The name El Capitan
was given, appropriately, to
the impressive sentinellike
rock in Yosemite Valley.)
carancho [kah-RAHN-choh]
n.m. hawk, buzzard; *adj.* ugly
carbón [kahr-BOHN] *n.m.* char-
coal, cinder
carbonera [kahr-boh-NAY-rah]
n.f. charcoal-making place
cárdeno [KAHR-day-noh] *adj.*
purplish, violet; livid
Carlos, San [KAHR-loce] St.
Charles, 77; ship, 36, 45, 75,
185; pass, 62; town, 175
Carlos Borromeo, Mission San
(Carmel Mission), 70, 77–78,
101, 190
Carlos III, King of Spain, 41–42,
77
Carmel River, town. Short for
Carmelo, the name given to
the *río* close to the modern
town and the mission, originally honoring several Carmelite friars on Vizcaino's
voyage, 35, 53, 57, 164, 190
carnadero [kahr-nah-DAY-roh]
n.m. butchering place
carne [KAHR-nay] *n.f.* meat,
flesh. *Carne seca*, dried beef
or jerky, 109. *Carne Humana,
Rancho de*, 10, 126, 186
carnero [kahr-NAY-roh] *n.m.*
sheep, ram
carona [kah-ROH-nah] *n.f.* sad-
dlepad or blanket
carpa [KAHR-pah] *n.f.* tent

carpintería [kahr-peen-tay-REE-ah] *n.f.* carpentry; carpenter's shop

Carpinteria, 50

Carquinez Strait: Indian place-word, 60–61, 65

carreta [kah-RRAY-tah] *n.f.* long, narrow, two-wheeled wooden cart used in Spanish California, 109–110

carrillo [kah-RREE-yoh] *n.m.* small cart; cheek

Carrillo [kah-RREEL-yoh] Spanish surname, 59, 89, 122, 134, 135, 197

carrizo [kah-RREE-soh] *n.m.* reed grass. (Having a sweet taste, almost like sugarcane, it was used as a sweetener by Indians.)

Carson, Kit: American explorer, 137

carta [KAHR-tah] *n.f.* letter, map, card

casa [KAH-sah] *n.f.* house, dwelling

cascada [kahs-KAH-dah] *n.f.* waterfall, cascade

cascarón [kahs-kah-ROHN] *n.m.* metal plate; niche for displaying sacrament in Roman Catholic churches; eggshell, 118

cascarrón [kahs-kah-RROHN] *adj.* rough, harsh

casco [KAHS-koh] *n.m.* cranium; cask; hoof

casino [kah-SEE-noh] *n.m.* club, social building

casita [kah-SEE-tah] *n.f.* small house

castaña [kahs-TAH-n'yah] *n.f.* chestnut; abandoned mine

Castilian Spanish, 17–18, 105–6, 203–4

castilleja [kahs-tee-YAY-hah] *n.f.* Indian paintbrush plant

castillo [kahs-TEE-yoh] *n.m.* castle, fortress, 83, 89

castor [kahs-TOHR] *n.m.* beaver

Castro [KAHS-troh] Spanish surname, 63, 120, 121, 122, 131, 134

Castro, José, 97, 189

Catalina, Santa [kah-tah-LEE-nah] St. Catherine. Santa Catalina Island (given its name by Vizcaíno in 1602 on the feast day of St. Catherine of Alexander) 34, 130

caudal [kowh-DAHL] *n.m.* assets, property, riches

Cavallo Point, 37

cayendo [kah-YEHN-doh] *adj.* falling

Cayetano [kah-yay-TAH-noh] from San Cayetano (St. Cajetan) 127

cayuco [kah-YOO-koh] *n.m.* kayak or small fishing boat

cazadero [kah-sah-DAY-roh] *n.m.* hunting place

cazador [kah-sah-DOHR] *n.m.* hunter

cebada [say-BAH-dah] *n.f.* barley

cebolla [say-BOH-yah] *n.f.* onion

cedro [SAY-droh] *n.m.* cedar

celeste [say-LEHS-tay] *adj.*
heavenly, celestial; sky-blue

centella [sehn-TAY-yah] *n.f.*
lightning

centinela [sehn-tee-NAY-lah] *n.f.*
sentry, guard, 126

Central Valley *(La Valle Grande)*,
61, 63, 65, 98–99, 154, 161

centro [SEHN-troh] *n.m.* center

Centro, El, 172

cerca [SEHR-kah] *n.f.* hedge,
fence; *adv.* near, close by

cerecita [say-ray-SEE-tah] *n.f.*
small cherry

cereza [say-RAY-sah] *n.f.* cherry

Cermeño [sehr-MAY-n'yoh]
sometimes spelled *Cermenho:*
Portuguese-Spanish navigator,
32, 56

cerrito [say-RREE-toh] *n.m.*
small hill

Cerritos, Los: rancho and town,
10, 112, 125, 163, 194

cerro [SAY-rroh] *n.m.* hill

Cerro Gordo, 150

chamisal [chah-mee-SAHL] *n.m.*
native California shrub

chaparra [chah-PAH-rrah] *n.f.*
scrub oak

chaparral [chah-pah-RRHAL]
n.m. grove of evergreen oaks.
(In California, the word came
to mean the thick, scrubby
vegetation on the slopes of
dry hills.)

Chapman, Joseph: American settler, 131–32

chapul [chah-PUHL] *n.m.* grasshopper

charro [CHAH-rroh] *n.m.* churl-
ish, ill-bred person

Chavez, Cesar: Mexican-American labor leader, 177–78

Chavez Ravine, 166

Chicano [chee-KAH-noh] *adj.* &
n.m. slang for Mexican American; culture, 177–80

chico [CHEE-koh] *adj.* small,
young

Chico: town, 142

Chili Gulch, Chileno Creek, 145

chiminea [chee-mee-NAY-ah]
n.f. chimney, fireplace

chino [CHEE-noh] *adj.* & *n.m.*
Chinese; half-breed or Mestizo

chiquito [chee-KEE-toh] *adj.*
very small, 145

chiripa [chee-REE-pah] *n.f.*
stroke of luck

cholla [CHOH-yah] *n.f.* skull; a
large southwestern cactus

cholo [CHOH-loh] *n.m.* half-
breed; scoundrel

chopo [CHOH-poh] *n.m.* black
cottonwood tree

chorro [CHOH-rroh] *n.m.*
stream, spurt

chualar [choo-ah-LAHR] *n.m.*
place where pigweed (lambs'
quarter) grows

Chula Vista, 21, 172

chulo [CHOO-loh] *adj.* handsome

Chumash Indians, 50, 87, 94

chupadero [choo-pah-DAY-roh]
n.m. brackish pool where animals drink

222 *Celeste*

cielo [S'YAY-loh] *n.m.* sky, heaven

cien [S'YEHN] *adj.* one hundred

ciénaga [see-AY-nah-gah] *n.f.* marsh, swamp. (La Cienega Blvd. in L.A. misspells the word, as did the rancho title originating it.)

ciento [S'YEHN-toh] *n.m.* one hundred

ciervo [see-EHR-boh] *n.m.* deer, stag, hart (sometimes spelled *cierbo*)

cima [SEE-mah] *n.f.* summit, peak; town, 173

cimarrón [see-mah-RROHN] *adj.* wild, unruly

cinco [SEEN-koh] *adj. & n.m.* five. (Cinco de Mayo, the Fifth of May, is a Mexican holiday commemorating the overthrow in 1867 by Juarez of the brief French rule by Emperor Maximilian. It is widely celebrated by the Mexican-American population in California.)

círculo [SEER-koo-loh] *n.m.* circle

cisco [SEES-koh] *n.m.* coal dust

Clara, Santa [KLAH-rah] St. Clare of Assisi, 84; county, 13, 69, 188; mission, 69, 84–85, 188; river, 49; valley, 69

claro [KLAH-roh] *adj.* clear, bright, light

clavel [klah-BEHL] *n.m.* carnation

clavo [KLAH-boh] *n.m.* nail (hardware)

Clemente, San [klay-MEHN-tay] St. Clement; island, 34

Coachella Valley: Indian name, 162

Coast Range, 33, 46, 61, 101

coche [KOH-chay] *n.m.* coach, car; hog, boar. (Hogs, like other domesticated animals not native to California, were brought by the Spaniards; often they broke loose and bred for generations in the wild. The *Cañada de los Coches* land grant is recalled in Coches Canyon in San Diego County.) *Rancho de los Coches* (Monterey County) 124, 190

cochino [koh-CHEE-noh] *n.m.* pig

coco [KOH-koh] *n.m.* coconut tree or nut; (slang) head

codorniz [koh-dohr-NEES] *n.f.* quail

cojo [KOH-hoh] *adj.* lame; *n.m.* lame man

Cojo Point, valley, 50

cola [KOH-lah] *n.f.* tail. (La Coleada was a competitive sport in which vaqueros and caballeros tried to "tail" a steer by grabbing his tail and pulling him over while riding by.)

colegio [koh-LAY-h'yoh] *n.m.* college

colina [koh-LEE-nah] *n.f.* hill

colmena [kohl-MAY-nah] *n.f.* beehive

colonization of California, Spanish, 2-3, 8-9, 35-36, 42-65

colorado [koh-loh-RAH-doh] *adj.* red, reddish. (*Palo colorado* is the Spanish name for the coastal redwood tree.) 54-55

Colorado Desert, 61, 62, 161-62

Colorado River, 29-30, 62, 64

comandante [koh-mahn-DAHN-tay] *n.m.* commander

comida [koh-MEE-dah] *n.f.* dinner, meal

commemorative place-names, 19, 22-24, 34, 38, 64-65, 101, 127-28, 156, 179-80

compadre [kohm-PAH-dray] *n.m.* godfather; benefactor; friend

compañero (kohm-pah-N'YAY-roh] *n.m.* companion, friend

concepción [kohn-sehp-see-OHN] *n.f.* conception; the Immaculate Conception

Conception, Point, 34, 37, 164

concha [KOHN-chah] *n.f.* shell, seashell, conch

condado [kohn-DAH-doh] *n.m.* county. (As in English, the word for the largest territorial division within a state came from the domain of a count or *conde.*)

cóndor [KOHN-dohr] *n.m.* vulture. (The two very large vulture species of the New World—one in the Andes, the other in California's southern coastal mountains—were of course called *cóndores* by the Spaniards. The California condor, numbering now only several dozen individual birds, lives in a protected preserve in Ventura County's Los Padres National Forest and is nearly extinct.)

conejo [koh-NAY-hoh] *n.m.* rabbit. (The word was often used in place-names, as in the El Conejo rancho and Conejo Creek and Mountain in Ventura County.) 113, 124, 181

conquista [kohn-KEES-tah] *n.f.* conquest

conquistador [kohn-kees-tah-DOHR] *n.m.* conqueror

consejo [kohn-SAY-hoh] *n.m.* advice, counsel; council

construction of buildings in Hispanic California, 43-44, 79-81, 115-17

Consumnes River, 98

contador [kohn-tah-DOHR] *n.m.* accountant

contra costa [KOHN-trah KOHS-tah] opposite coast. (The name of the county on the northeastern shore of San Francisco Bay. The Spaniards first applied it to the entire East Bay area, and also at first to the land north of San Francisco Bay.) 13, 61, 65, 92, 187

contrived place-names, 19, 68, 172-73, 175

copa [KOH-pah] *n.f.* cup, goblet. (*Copa de oro* is the name of a perennial vine bearing hundreds of large, open-throated, golden, cuplike flowers. Some streets are named after it. The Spaniards sometimes gave this name to the golden poppy which is the California state flower.)

corazón [koh-rah-SOHN] *n.m.* heart; benevolence; ardor

cordato [kohr-DAH-toh] *adj.* wise, considerate

cordero [kohr-DAY-roh] *n.m.* lamb; also a Spanish surname

cordillera [kohr-dee-YAY-rah] *n.f.* chain or ridge of mountains

corona [koh-ROH-nah] *n.f.* crown

coronado [koh-roh-NAH-doh] *adj.* crowned. (The name of the long sand spit south of San Diego, as well as of the nearby islands off the coast of Baja California, comes not from the famous explorer of the Southwest but from *Los Quatro Martires Coronados* — the Four Crowned Martyrs — whose feast day corresponded with the islands' discovery.)

Coronado: Spanish explorer, 28–29

coronel [koh-roh-NEHL] *n.m.* colonel

Coronel, Antonio: Hispanic settler, 120, 142, 168

correo [koh-RRAY-oh] *n.m.* mail, postman, post office

correr [koh-RREHR] *v.* to run

corrida [koh-RREE-dah] *n.f.* course, race, travel; *de toros*, bullfight

corriente [koh-rree-EHN-tay] *adj.* current, running

corte [KOHR-tay] *n.m.* cut; *n.f.* yard, court

Corte (de) Madera, 4, 116, 125, 186

Cortés, sometimes Cortez [kohr-TEHS] Spanish conquistador, 29

cortinilla [kohr-tee-NEE-yah] *n.f.* screen, shade

corto [KOHR-toh] *adj.* short, brief

corvina [kohr-BEE-nah] *n.f.* white California sea bass or corbina

costa [KOHS-tah] *n.f.* coast, shore; cost, expense

Costa Mesa, 172, 195

costanero [kohs-tah-NAY-roh] *adj.* coastal; sloping

Costansó, Miguel [kohs-tahn-SOH] Portola's cartographer, 46, 50, 53

costilla [kohs-TEE-yah] *n.f.* rib; barrel stave

Cota [KOH-tah] Spanish surname, 89, 120, 197

counties with Spanish names, 13

coyote [koh-YOH-tay] *n.m.* small wolf of North America; prairie wolf, 19

Coyote River Canyon, 62, 63

creole [cray-OH-lay] *n.* a person of Spanish descent in the

Creole

lands of the New World colonized by Spain

Crespí, Juan [krehs-PEE] Spanish priest-explorer, 46-59, 60-61, 63, 64, 75, 76, 90, 101, 190

cresta [KREHS-tah] n.f. crest, summit

Cristianitos Canyon, 47

Cristo [KREES-toh] Christ

crucero [kroo-SAY-roh] n.m. crossing, crossroads; town, 172

cruces [KROO-says] n. pl. of cruz, crosses

cruz [KROOS] n.f. cross. (A large santa cruz, usually made of crudely hewn wood, was a primary erection in the founding of a mission.)

Cruz, Santa: county, city, arroyo, 13, 54, 90, 91, 167, 189; island, 50; mission, 54, 90, 189

cuaderno [kwah-DEHR-noh] n.m. notebook

cuadra [KWAH-drah] n.f. stable; city block

cuadro [KWAH-droh] n.m. square; picture; schedule

cuarta [KWAHR-tah] adj. & n.f. quarter, fourth part

cuartel [kwahr-TEHL] n.m. military barracks

cuarto [KWAHR-toh] n.m. room

cuenca [KWEHN-kah] n.f. river basin, valley; wooden bowl

cuento [KWEHN-toh] n.m. story, tale

cuera [KWAY-rah] n.f. leather. Soldados de cuera, leather jacket soldiers, 43, 60, 71

cuerno [KWEHR-noh] n.m. horn

cuero [KWAY-roh] n.m. cattle hide; cuero crudo or cuero en verde, rawhide (Hispanic California's main commercial product)

cuervo [KWEHR-boh] n.m. crow, raven

cuesta [KWEYS-tah] n.f. hill, slope, ridge

culebra [koo-LAY-brah] n.f. snake

cumbre [KOOM-bray] n.f. summit, peak

cuna [KOO-nah] n.f. cradle; origin

Cupertino [koo-pehr-TEE-noh] derived from Arroyo de San José Cupertino, named by Anza and Font, 63

D

Dana Point, 38, 196

Dana, Richard Henry: American seaman and author, 38-39, 135, 196

Dana, William G.: American captain, ranchero, 134

de [DAY] prep. of

décima [DAY-see-mah] adj. tenth

del [DEHL] comb. prep. & article preceding masculine noun in singular form: de and el, of the

de la [DAY LAH] comb. prep. & article preceding feminine

noun in singular form: *de la*,
of the
de la Guerra [day lah GAY-rrah]
Spanish surname, 89, 113,
120, 122
Delano: town, 177–78
Delgada Point, 37
delgado [dehl-GAH-doh] *adj.*
thin, slender, delicate
delicado [day-lee-KAH-doh] *adj.*
tender, weak; delicious
Del Norte [DEHL NOHR-tay]
of the north. A county named
in 1857, 13
del rey [DEHL RAY] literally,
of the king or ruler. (After
independence from Spain, it
meant belonging to the nation
or to the public. Name-makers
add it to certain nouns to give
an "instant Spanish" effect,
as in Playa del Rey, Marina
del Rey.)
De Luz, 173
derecho [day-RAY-choh] *adj.* &
n.m. right-hand; right, just,
certain. (Like many other
languages, including English,
Spanish discriminates on the
issue of handedness. The opposite, *izquierdo*, is not only
left and left-hand; it can mean
crooked, sinister, degenerate,
wild.)
descanso [dehs-KAHN-soh] *n.m.*
rest
desconocido [dehs-koh-noh-SEE-
doh] *adj.* unknown
descriptive place-names, 19–21,
122–26

deshecho [dehs-AY-choh] *adj.*
undone, destroyed; *n.m.* sham
desierto [day-S'YEHR-toh] *adj.*
deserted; *n.m.* desert
destino [dehs-TEE-noh] *n.m.*
destiny, fate; destination
diablo [dee-AH-bloh] *n.m.* devil.
(Geographical names containing infernal references like
diablo have generally been inspired by curious, evil-looking
contortions in the landscape,
by strange or fiendish behavior
among humans there, or by
furious, hellish heat.)
Diablo, Monte del (Mt. Diablo),
61, 126, 138
Diablo Range, 61
diamante [dee-ah-MAHN-tay]
n.m. diamond; hardness
Diego, San [dee-AY-goh] St.
Didacus of Alcalá, 74
Diego, San: city and county, 13,
14, 196–97; mission, 58, 75–
76, 196; presidio, 46, 74–75
diez [D'YEHS] *adj.* & *n.m.* ten
Dimas, San [DEE-mahs] St. Dis-
mas, the penitent robber crucified alongside Christ, 127
diminutives in Spanish place-
names, 19–20
Dios [D'YOHS] *n.m.* God, supreme being
diseño [dee-SAY-n'yoh] *n.m.*
design, map (used in land
grants), 9, 114
divisadero [dee-vee-sah-DAY-roh]
n.m. divider; lookout. (San
Franciscans sometimes claim
that their street with this

Divisadero

name tends to divide the foggy west side of the city from the sunnier east side.)

Doak, Thomas: early American settler, 131

dolor [doh-LOHR] *n.m.* pain, sorrow

dolores [doh-LOH-rays] *pl.* usually refers to the sorrows of *Nuestra Señora*, as in Arroyo de los Dolores next to Mission San Francisco de Asis

domingo [doh-MEEN-goh] *n.m.* Sunday

Domínguez [doh-MIHN-gays] Spanish surname, 59–60, 112, 195

don [DOHN] *n.m.* a title of respect for a California caballero and ranchero, 105–7

doña [DOH-n'yah] *n.f.* the female counterpart of *don*

donoso [doh-NOH-soh] *adj.* witty, graceful, gay

dorado [doh-RAH-doh] *adj.* gilt, golden. (El Dorado, sometimes spelled Eldorado, was the fabled country of great riches whose chief was reputedly adorned with gold dust. It was avidly sought by the Spanish conquistadors of the 16th century in both Americas.)

Dorr, Captain: early American visitor, 130

dos [DOHS] *adj.* & *n.m.* two

Dos Pueblos, 125

Dos Rios, 20

Drake, Sir Francis, 31–32

Drake's Bay, 32, 56

dramatic place-names, 19, 21–22, 126

Duarte [DWAHR-tay] Spanish surname, 121

dueña [DWAY-n'yah] *n.f.* mistress; woman owner; duenna

dulce [DOOL-say] *adj.* sweet, gentle; fresh (as water)

dulzura [dool-SOO-rah) *n.f.* pleasantness, sweetness; town, 173

Dume, Point (orig. Dumetz), 38, 165

Dumetz, Padre, 38

Durán, Narciso [doo-RAHN, nahr-SEE-soh] padre at Mission San Jose, 91–92

durazno [doo-RAHS-noh] *n.m.* peach

E

earthquakes, 48–49, 84, 93, 100

Echeandía [ay-chay-ahn-DEE-ah] Spanish governor, 135, 136, 137

el [EHL] *m. sing. article,* the; *pl., los; f. la* and *las*

El Dorado: county, 13; 146–47. *See also dorado*

Eldredge, Zoeth: California historian, 169

embocadura [ehm-boh-kah-DOO-rah] *n.f.* opening; river mouth; mouthpiece of musical instrument

empino [ehm-PEE-noh] *n.m.* height, elevation

en [EHN] *prep.* in, into, on, upon

encanto [ehn-KAHN-toh] *n.m.* enchantment

encina [ehn-SEE-nah] *n.f.* evergreen oak, live oak

Encinitas, Las, 47

Encino [ehn-SEE-noh], 49, 113

enero [ay-NAY-roh] *n.m.* January

enramada [ehn-rah-MAH-dah] *n.f.* bower, arbor; brushwood shelter. (In Spanish colonial times, the first buildings were usually *enramadas*, with roofs of tule reeds and caked-mud walls.)

enselvado [ehn-sehl-BAH-doh] *adj.* full of trees

ensenada [ehn-say-NAH-dah] *n.f.* inlet, cove

ensueño [ehn-SWAY-n'yoh] *n.m.* fantasy, sleep

entidad [ehn-tee-DAHD] *n.f.* entity

entrada [ehn-TRAH-dah] *n.f.* entrance, admission

escala [ehs-KAH-lah] *n.f.* ladder; scale

escalón [ehs-kah-LOHN] *n.m.* stair, stepping-stone

escamilla [ehs-kah-MEE-yah] *n.f.* small scale

escarpado [ehs-kahr-PAH-doh] *adj.* steep, craggy

escolar [ehs-koh-LAHR] *n.m.* student, scholar

escolta [ehs-KOHL-tah] *n.f.* military guard (as at missions and presidios), 71

escondido [ehs-kohn-DEE-doh] *adj.* hidden (as water), 20; town, 172

escorial [ehs-koh-ree-AHL] exhausted mine site

escorpión [ehs-kohr-pee-OHN] *n.m.* scorpion

escrito [ehs-KREE-toh] *adj.* written, inscribed. (There is a Palo Escrito Mountain west of Soledad.)

escudero [ehs-koo-DAY-roh] *n.m.* shield-bearer; gentleman from an illustrious family

escuela [ehs-KWAY-lah] *n.f.* school

esmeralda [ehs-may-RAHL-dah] *n.f.* emerald

espada [ehs-PAH-dah] *n.f.* sword

Espada Creek, 50

España [ehs-PAH-n'yah] *n.f.* Spain

español [ehs-pah-N'YOHL] *adj.* Spanish

esparto [ehs-PAHR-toh] *n.m.* tough feather grass

espejo [ehs-PAY-hoh] *n.m.* mirror

esperanza [ehs-pay-RAHN-sah] *n.f.* hope

espinazo [ehs-pee-NAH-soh] *n.m.* spine, backbone

Espinosa [ehs-pee-NOH-sah] Spanish surname, 60

espinoso [ehs-pee-NOH-soh] *adj.* thorny, spiny

espíritu [ehs-PEE-ree-too] *n.m.* spirit, ghost; *Espíritu Santo:* the Holy Ghost

esplendor [ehs-plehn-DOHR]

n.m. splendor, glory, excellence

establo [ehs-TAH-bloh] *n.m.* horse stable

estación [ehs-tah-see-OHN] *n.f.* station; season; stay

estada [ehs-TAH-dah] *n.f.* sojourn, stay

estado [ehs-TAH-doh] *n.m.* state; condition, status; estate (*Estados Unidos de América* — the United States of America — is abbreviated E.U.A. in Latin America, not U.S.A.)

estancia [ehs-TAHN-see'ah] *n.f.* ranch; large room

estanciero [ehs-tahn-see-AY-roh] *n.m.* rancher

Estanislao [ehs-tah-nee-SLAH-oh] *See* Stanislaus

este [EHS-tay] *n.m.* east

estero [ehs-TAY-roh] *n.m.* estuary, inlet, marsh

Estero Americano, 95

estilo [ehs-TEE-loh] *n.m.* style

estrada [ehs-TRAH-dah] *n.f.* paved road

estrella [ehs-TRAY-yah] *n.f.* star

Estudillo [ehs-too-DEE-yoh] Spanish surname, 120, 134, 197

Expedición Santa. *See* Sacred Expedition

F

fábrica [FAH-bree-kah] *n.f.* building, factory; manufacture

faceta [fah-SAY-tah] *n.f.* facet of precious stone

faceto [fah-SAY-toh] *adj.* lively, witty

fada [FAH-dah] *n.f.* small apple; witch

Fages, Pedro [FAH-hace] Spanish officer, governor, 8, 46, 59, 60–61, 63, 65, 78, 80–82, 89, 98

falda [FAHL-dah] *n.f.* skirt; lap; fold; foothill

falena [fah-LAY-nah] *n.f.* moth

familia [fah-MEE-l'yah] *n.f.* family; *La Familia Sagrada:* the Holy Family

famosa [fah-MOH-soh] *adj.* famous; town, 173

fandango [fahn-DAHN-goh] *n.m.* a Spanish dance, 118

Fandango Valley, 143

farallón [fah-rah-YOHN] *n.m.* cliff, palisade; small, rocky sea island

Farallón Islands (Los Farallones), 32, 56, 150

faro [FAH-roh] *n.m.* lighthouse, beacon

farolito [fah-roh-LEE-toh] *n.m.* small lantern

fe [FAY] *n.f.* faith

Feather River. *See* Plumas, Río de las

felicidad [fay-lee-see-DAHD] *n.f.* happiness; prosperity

felicitar [fay-lee-see-TAHR] *v.* to congratulate, make happy

Felipe, San [fay-LEE-pay] St. Philip; place-name, 127

feliz [fay-LEES] *adj.* happy; *pl. felices*

Féliz, sometimes Félix [FAY-lees] Spanish surname, 63, 121, 167, 193

Fermin, Point, 38

Fernando, Colegio de San, 88, 100

Fernando, Mission San, Rey de España, 93–94

Fernando, San [fehr-NAHN-doh] St. Ferdinand, King of Spain, 93

Fernando Valley, San, 49, 94–95

Ferrelo [fay-RRAY-loh] Spanish ship's pilot, 31

ferro [FEH-rroh] *n.m.* anchor

ferrocarril [feh-rroh-kah-RREEL] *n.m.* railroad

fidel [fee-DEHL] *adj.* faithful, loyal

fidelidad [fee-day-lee-DAHD] *n.f.* faithfulness, loyalty

fierro [fee-AY-rroh] *n.m.* cattle brand showing ownership (sometimes *hierro*)

fiesta [fee-EHS-tah] *n.f.* party, celebration, festival, holiday. (Most fiestas in California life originated as saints' feast days that commemorated significant events in their lives.)

figuera [fee-GAY-rah] *n.f.* fig tree

Figueroa [fee-gay-ROH-ah] a surname; Mexican governor of California, 96, 99, 121

finito [fee-NEE-toh] *adj.* finite, limited

Fitch, Henry Delano: American ship's master and ranchero, 134, 135

flaco [FLAH-koh] *adj.* thin, weak

flecha [FLAY-chah] *n.f.* arrow; indicator of north on map

flor [FLOHR] *n.f.* flower

florero [floh-RAY-roh] *n.m.* flowerpot

Flores, José: Mexican bandit, 156

Flores Canyon, Las, 47

floresta [floh-REHS-tah] *n.f.* pleasant tree-filled place

foca [FOH-kah] *n.f.* fur-seal

fonda [FOHN-dah] *n.f.* inn, tavern, hotel

fondo [FOHN-doh] *n.m.* bottom; depth; back

Font, Pedro [FOHNT] Spanish padre and explorer, 62–64, 65, 86, 173

fontana [fohn-TAH-nah] *n.f.* fountain; town, 173

Foreign Miners' Tax, 149–50

Fort Ross: *See* Ross, Fort

fortuna [fohr-TOO-nah] *n.f.* fortune, chance; good luck; town, 173

fraile [FRY-lay] *n.m.* friar (abbrev. to *Fray* or Fr.)

Franciscan Order, 42, 45. *See also* missionaries in California

Francisco, Bahía de (first named) *See* Drake's Bay

Francisco, San: bay, 32, 36–37, 56–57, 59, 61, 82–83; city, 14, 65, 147–48, 185; peninsula, 56, 61; presidio, 82, 83, 185; streets, 64–65, 121, 169

Francisco de Asís, San [frahn-3EES-koh day ah-SEES] St.

Francis of Assisi, 83; mission, 83, 95, 185 (also called Mission Dolores)

Francisco Solano, San: St. Francis of Solano, 96; mission, 96, 186 (also called Sonoma Mission)

Francisquito Creek, San, 20, 62

Frémont, John C.: American explorer and military leader, 10, 36, 58, 125, 140-41

fresa [FRAY-sah] *n.f.* strawberry

fresco [FREHS-koh] *adj.* fresh, cool, just made

fresno [FREHS-noh] *n.m.* ash tree

Fresno (river, county, city) 13, 14, 160. (The ash, native to California, abounded in the San Joaquin Valley. Fresno River and County had been named before the city was founded in 1868 by a group of German immigrants.)

frío [FREE-oh] *adj.* cold, cool

frontera [frohn-TAY-rah] *n.f.* frontier, border

fruta [FROO-tah] *n.f.* fruit (edible)

fruto [FROO-toh] *n.m.* fruit (seed-container); town, 172

fuego [FWAY-goh] *n.m.* fire

fusco [FOOS-koh] *adj.* dark or dull brown

G

Gabilan Peak, 140, 165 (from *gavilán*)

Gabriel, San [gah-bree-EHL] St. Gabriel, the Archangel, 79; as place-name, 23; mission, 62, 64, 79, 87, 110, 132, 136, 194; river, 79; mountains, 173; valley, 58

galano [gah-LAH-noh] *adj.* gallant, elegant, lively

gallina [gah-YEE-nah] *n.f.* hen

gallineta [gah-yee-NAY-tah] *n.f.* sandpiper, grouse

gallo [GAH-yoh] *n.m.* rooster, cock

Gálvez, José de [GAHL-vays] official who launched the Sacred Expedition headed by Portolá and Serra, 12, 44-45, 57, 65, 71, 77

gama [GAH-mah] *n.f.* doe

gambling among Californios, 106, 118-19, 143-44, 151, 152

ganadero [gah-nah-DAY-roh] *n.m.* cattle drover, herder

ganado [gah-NAH-doh] *n.m.* herd of livestock

gándara [GAHN-dah-rah] *n.f.* low mountain range

Garcés, Francisco: Spanish missionary-explorer, 62, 64, 65, 86, 136, 195

garrapata [gah-rrah-PAH-tah] *n.f.* wood tick

garrote [gah-RROH-tay] *n.m.* cudgel; capital punishment by strangling; scaffold for same; in place-names, 145

garza [GAHR-sah] *n.f.* heron

garzo [GAHR-soh] *adj.* bluish;

232

blue-eyed (a frequent nickname for Americans)

gatera [gah-TAY-rah] *n.f.* hole cut in door for cats' use. (The padres kept cats to protect food supplies from rodents. One of Anza's chores was to transport a pair of felines from Monterey to Mission San Gabriel.)

gato [GAH-toh] *n.m.* cat. (In several geographical and rancho names *gatos* actually means wildcats.)

Gatos, Los, 10, 125

gaucho [GOW-choh] *n.m.* herdsman; man of humble birth

gaviota [gah-bee-OH-tah] *n.f.* seagull

Gaviota: pass, town, 21, 50, 181

gente de razón, la [HEHN-tay day rah-SOHN] people of reason; therefore, civilized beings or white settlers in California, 9, 97

gentil, gentiles [hehn-TEEL, hehn-TEE-lays] *n.m.* heathens; unbaptized Indians

geographical words in placenames, 19, 22, 122–24

George, Henry: quoted, 155

Gerónimo, San [hay-ROH-nee-moh] St. Jerome, 127

Gertrudes, Santa [gehr-TROO-days] St. Gertrude; sometimes spelled Gertrudis; rancho, 112

Gilroy, John: early settler, 132, 165

glorieta [gloh-ree-YAY-tah] *n.f.* summerhouse, arbor; plaza at the intersection of streets

gobernador [goh-behr-nah DOHR] *n.m.* governor, 72

gobernadora [goh-behr-nah-DOH-rah] *n.f.* a desert plant

gobernante [goh-behr-NAHN-tay] *n.m.* acting governor (as of California), 78

Golden Gate, 32, 36, 37, 60, 65, 185

Gold Rush, 11, 141–53, 158, 161

goleta [goh-LAY-tah] *n.f.* schooner

Goleta: point, rancho, town, 37, 126

golondrina [goh-lohn-DREE-nah] *n.f.* swallow. (*Las golondrinas* are the migratory birds that regularly return to San Juan Capistrano in the early spring.) 84

Gómez, Francisco: Spanish padre, 46, 47

Gonzales [gohn-SAH-lays] Spanish surname, 3, 121

gordo [GOHR-doh] *adj.* fat, thick

Gorgonio, San [gohr-GOH-n'yoh] St. Gorgonius; placename, 110, 127

gotera [goh-TAY-rah] *n.f.* gutter; leak

Graciosa: place-name, 51

gracioso [grah-see-OH-soh] *adj.* graceful, beautiful

Graham, Isaac: American settler, 139

granada [grah-NAH-dah] *n.f.*
pomegranate. (Granada is also
the name of the Spanish city
and province that were the
last stronghold of the Moors
before they were ousted in
1492.)

grande [GRAHN-day] *adj.* large,
great

"greaser": *See* anti-Mexican prejudice

Gregorio, San [gray-GO-r'yoh]
St. Gregory, 127

Griffith Park, 167, 193

grilllo [GREE-yoh] *n.m.* cricket

gringo [GRIHN-goh] *adj. & n.m.*
person from United States,
"Anglo," 141, 147

grulla [GROO-yah] *n.f.* crane

gruta [GROO-tah] *n.f.* grotto,
cave

Guadalupe [gwah-dah-LOO-pay]
a frequently occurring place-
name and personal name in
Hispanic countries. (The original shrine to Our Lady of
Guadalupe was in Spain but
was transferred to Mexico in
the 16th century after an
Indian had a vision of the
Virgin in a town that was
renamed Guadalupe. There is
a Guadalupe River in Santa
Clara County and a town by
the same name in Santa Barbara County.), 24, 85

Guadalupe River, 63, 84

guerra [GAY-rrah] *n.f.* war. (De
la Guerra was a well-known
Californio family name.)

guerrero [gay-RRAY-roh] *n.m.*
warrior; also a Spanish surname, 3, 121

guijarro [ghee-HAH-rroh] *n.m.*
pebble, cobblestone. (*Punta
de Guijarros* in San Diego Bay,
now known as Ballast Point,
furnished abundant stone ballast to Spanish mariners.)

guinda [GEEN-dah] *n.f.* wild
cherry

H

habra [AH-brah] *n.f.* mountain
pass, opening. (The Spanish
word is now spelled without
the *h*: *abra*.)

Habra, La, 48

hacienda [ah-see-EHN-dah] *n.f.*
large ranch, estate. (A Spanish
word that has been accepted
into English. At times, however, the name is misspelled
as "house." In Mexico an
hacienda was primarily a large
agricultural establishment. On
the California acreage largely
devoted to cattle raising, *rancho* was far more frequently
used.)

hada [AH-dah] *n.f.* fairy

hambre [AHM-bray] *n.f.* hunger.
(A land-grant title, *Cañada
del Hambre y las Bolsas* —the
valley of hunger and pockets
—seemingly originated when
some Spanish travelers were
trapped and nearly died of
hunger.)

Haro, De [AH-roh] Spanish surname, 120, 121, 185
Hartnell, William: English trader and ranchero, 133
hediondo [ay-dee-OHN-doh] *adj.* stinking. (Likely to be given to water sites that smelled foul because of sulphurous contents.)
helado [ay-LAH-doh] *adj.* frozen; *n.m.* ice cream
hermano [ehr-MAH-noh] *n.m.* brother
hermoso [ehr-MOH-soh] *adj.* handsome, beautiful
Hezeta, Bruno de [ay-SAY-tah] Spanish navigator, 37
hidalgo [ee-DAHL-goh] *adj.* noble; *n.m.* Spanish nobleman
hierro [ee-AY-rroh] *m. See* fierro
Higuera [ee-GAY-rah] Spanish surname, 188
Híjar-Padrés colonization, 120
hogar [oh-GAHR] *n.m.* hearth, home
hombre [OHM-bray] *n.m.* man
honda [OHN-dah] *n.f.* sling; slingshot
hondo [OHN-doh] *adj.* deep
Hondo, Río, 79
horizonte [oh-ree-SOHN-tay] *n.m.* horizon
hornito [ohr-NEE-toh] *n.m.* small oven or furnace; cavity in which bees lodge; a mudvolcano. (The town of Hornitos in Mariposa County is an example of frequent con-

fusion and conjecture over the origin of certain placenames.) 144–45
horno [OHR-noh] *n.m.* oven, furnace; bee-hive hole. (The earth oven, *hornitos* or *hornillos*, in which Mexicans baked bread were prevalent among the mining camps settled by Sonorans.)
hoya [OH-yah] *n.f.* hole, grave, pit
hueco [WAY-koh] *n.m.* hollow, hole
huero [WAY-roh] *n.m.* unfertilized egg; (slang) blond person (sometimes *güero*)
huerta [WEHR-tah] *n.f.* orchard
huevo [WAY-boh] *n.m.* egg
hybrid or contrived "Spanish" names, 172, 173, 175–76

I

Imperial County, valley, 13, 162
Indian place names in California, 2–3, 7, 10, 14, 25; 122 (list)
Indian words in Spanish, 18–19, 205
Indians at missions, 71, 88, 97–98
Indians on ranchos, 100–01, 107–09, 115
indio [EEN-d'yoh] *adj.* & *n.m.* Indian. (Among the American *vaqueros* or buckaroos, to be called an Indio was a high compliment, since it was acknowledged that the most

Indio

expert cattle-tenders were of Indian ancestry.)

Indio, 173

indo [EEN-doh] *n.m.* Indian (usually East Indian)

Inés, Santa [ee-NAYS] St. Agnes, 74, 94; river and mission, 51, 94–95 (also spelled Inez, Ynés, Ynez)

information conveyed in place-names, 19–21. *See also* geographical words in place-names, warnings

Irvine Ranch, 11, 162, 167

isla [EES-lah] *n.f.* island

islay [ees-LAY-ee] *n.* holly-leaf cherry shrub native to California. (Its fruit was eaten by the Indians.) 126

isleta [ees-LAY-tah] *n.f.* small island

-ito, -illo, -ijo diminutive endings added to nouns, modifying them to mean "little" or "small"; *see* diminutives in Spanish place-names

J

jabón [hah-BOHN] *n.m.* soap (sometimes misspelled *javón* in place-names)

jacal [hah-KAHL] *n.m.* shack, hut

Jacinto, San [hah-SIHN-toh] St. Hyacinth, who was honored in various California place-names: rancho, mountains, 14, 62, 110, 127

Jackson, Helen Hunt, 168

jardín [hahr-DEEN] *n.m.* garden

Jesuit Order, 42, 45

jinete [hee-NAY-tay] *n.m.* cavalryman; horse rider

Joaquín, Castillo de San (S.F.), 83, 141, 185

Joaquín, San [hwah-KEEN] St. Joachim, father of the virgin Mary. County, river, valley, 13, 61, 98, 136. *See also* Central Valley

Jolla, La [LAH HOY-yah] (town) Believed to be a misspelling of either *hoja* (mountain hollow) or *joya* (jewel). The name was used in the San Diego area in land records during the Spanish era. La Jolla, just north of San Diego, was officially named in 1869.

jornada [hohr-NAH-dah] *n.f.* march or journey performed in one day; journey or travel by land, as the padres did

José, San [hoh-SAY] St. Joseph, foster father of Jesus, 45, 85; ship, 45, 57; place-name, 127, 166; pueblo, city, 14, 69, 188; mission, 69, 91–92, 188

jota [HOH-tah] *n.f.* a Spanish dance

Juan Bautista, San [HWAHN-bow-TEES-tah] St. John the Baptist, 74, 92; mission, town, 92–93, 131, 189

Juan Capistrano, San [HWAHN kah-pee-STRAH-noh] St. John of Capistran, 74, 84; mission and town, 39, 84, 196

júbilo [HOO-bee-loh] *n.m.* joy,
    rejoicing, jubilee
juego [HWAY-goh] *n.m.* game,
    play, sport
junco [HOON-koh] *n.m.* rush
    plant; Chinese junk
junta [HOON-tah] *n.f.* meeting,
    council; junction
jura [HOO-rah] *n.f.* oath

K

Kings River, county (orig. Los
    Santos Reyes), 13, 98–99,
    147
Kino, Eusebio: Italian-Spanish
    priest and explorer, 41, 62

L

la [LAH] *f. sing. article*, the; *pl.,*
    las
ladera [lah-DAY-rah] *n.f.* slope,
    hillside, descent
lado [LAH-doh] *n.m.* side,
    direction
ladrillo [lah-DREE-yoh] *n.m.*
    brick, tile
ladrón [lah-DROHN] *n.m.* thief
lagarto [lah-GAHR-toh] *n.m.*
    lizard; (slang) sly, slippery
    person
lago [LAH-goh] *n.m.* lake
laguna [lah-GOO-nah] *n.f.* small
    lake, lagoon, pond
Laguna Beach, 175
lancha [LAHN-chah] *n.f.* boat,
    launch
Lancha Plana, 144

Land Act of 1851 and commis-
    sion, 151–53
land "booms," 154–55, 171
land grants, Spanish and Mexi-
    can, 9–10, 110–28
landscape features in place-
    names, 19–21. *See also* de-
    scriptive place-names and geo-
    graphical words in place-
    names
lano [LAH-noh] *n.m.* wool
largo [LAHR-goh] *adj.* long
Larkin, Thomas O.: American
    merchant and consul, 134,
    139–40, 189
las [LAHS] *f. pl. article*, the
Lasuén, Fermín Francisco de
    [lah-soo-EHN, fehr-MEEN]
    padre-presidente, successor to
    Serra, 38, 74, 89–94, 101, 190
látigo [LAH-tee-goh] *n.m.* whip
lazo [LAH-soh] *n.m.* loop, tie;
    lasso; trap
Leandro, San [lay-AHN-droh]
    St. Leander, 127
lechuga [lay-CHOO-gah] *n.f.* let-
    tuce
lechuza [lay-CHOO-sah] *n.f.* owl
Leese, Jacob: American trader
    and ranchero, 137
lejos [LAY-hohs] *adv.* far away
león [lay-OHN] *n.m.* lion; *leona,*
    n.f. lioness
Leonis: Spanish surname
leste [LACE-tay] *n.m.* east wind,
    east
libre [LEE-bray] *adj.* free
libro [LEE-broh] *n.m.* book
liebre [lee-AY-bray] *n.f.* hare,
    jackrabbit

Liebre

lima [LEE-mah] *n.f.* lime, lime
tree

limón [lee-MOHN] *n.m.* lemon
(fruit)

limonar [lee-moh-NAHR] *n.m.*
lemon grove

limpio [LEEM-p'yoh] *adj.* clean,
pure, limpid

lindero [leen-DAY-roh] *n.m.*
limit, boundary

lindo [LEEN-doh] *adj.* pretty

línea [LEE-nay-ah] *n.f.* line,
limit

Livermore, Robert: English settler, 132

llaga [YAH-gah] *n.f.* wound; *las
llagas*, the stigmata (wounds
of the crucified Christ dupli-
cated in devout followers,
such as St. Francis)

Llagas Creek, Las, 62

llanada [yah-NAH-dah] *n.f.* plain

llano [YAH-noh] *n.m.* level; flat
ground. (Often used in land-
grant titles. The town of
Llano in Los Angeles County
briefly harbored a socialist
colony in 1914, called *Llano
del Río*.)

lloron [yoh-RROHN] *n.m.*
weeper, mourner

lo [LOH] *neuter sing. def. article* the (a variant of *el* and *la*,
used for abstract nouns); also
can be a pronoun

lobo [LOH-boh] *n.m.* wolf; *lobo
marino*, seal or sea lion to the
early Spaniards, now usually
shortened to just *lobo*. (Anywhere near the coast, *lobo* is

apt to mean the marine
mammal.)

Lobos, Point, 37

loco [LOH-koh] *adj.* crazy. (The
word *loco* in a place-name
sometimes originated with
the name of a branch of the
Mono Indian tribe, *Loko*.)

loma [LOH-mah] *n.f.* small hill,
slope

Loma, Point, 38, 39, 131, 163,
197

lomata [loh-MAH-tah] *n.f.* hill
that arises in a plain

lomo [LOH-moh] *n.m.* animal's
back; ridge between furrows

Lorenzo, San [lo-REHN-zoh]
St. Lawrence, 127

los: See el

losa [LOH-sah] *n.f.* slab, flagstone

lote [LOH-tay] *n.m.* fortune,
chance, lot

lucero [loo-SAY-roh] *n.m.* morning star; splendor

Lucía, Santa [loo-SEE-ah] St.
Lucy; mountains, 33, 35, 52,
70, 78

luego [LWAY-goh] *adv.* then;
soon

Lugo [LOO-goh] Spanish surname, 61, 120

Luís: Louis or Lewis. (Note below the Spanish syllable stress
and the sounding out of the
s.)

Luís Obispo, San [loo-EES oh-
BEES-poh] St. Louis, Bishop
of Toulouse, 23, 81; mission
and town, 80–81, 170, 191

Luís Rey de Francia [loo-EES
ray day FRAHN-s'yah] St.
Louis King of France, 23, 81,
94; mission, 94, 111, 196
Luisito, San, 20
lumbre [LOOM-bray] *n.f.* bright
light; fire; splendor
Lummis, Charles F., 169–70
lunada [loo-NAH-dah] *adj.*
shaped like a half-moon
Lunada Bay, 37
luz [LOOS] *n.f.* light

M

machada [mah-CHAH-dah] *n.f.*
flock of male goats; (slang)
stupidity; virility or manliness
Machado [mah-CHAH-doh]
Spanish surname, 197
macho [MAH-choh] *n.m.* a male
animal, esp. a billy goat; *adj.*
masculine, robust
madera [mah-DAY-rah] *n.f.*
wood, lumber. (The place-
name *Corte (de) Madera* —
place where wood is cut — has
been used in various parts of
the state: one a land grant,
surviving in the town in Marin
County.)
Madera County: name given in
American period, thought appropriate because of wide-
spread lumbering done in
area, 13
madero [mah-DAY-roh] *n.m.*
beam, timber
madre [MAH-dray] *n.f.* mother;
source; riverbed. (Sierra

Madre was the name originally
given to the San Bernardino
Mountains, because the Sierra
Nevada and the coastal mountains appeared to have originated or been "born" from
them. *Zanja madre* was the
"mother ditch" of a pueblo;
it carried the main water supply from a nearby river
through the town and to
networks of irrigation channels in the fields.); *veta
madre*, mother lode
madroño [mah-DROH-n'yoh]
n.m. arbutus or madrone
shrub that grows in foothill
areas in many parts of California. Sometimes spelled
madrona
mal [MAHL] *adv.* badly, injuri-
ously, ill; *n.m.* evil, harm, hurt
Malaspina: Italian navigator serving Spain, 130
Malibu: Indian place-name, 113
malo [MAH-loh] *adj.* bad
malpaís [mahl-pah-EES] *n.m.*
badlands
malpaso [mahl-PAH-soh] *n.m.*
a difficult crossing or passage
mancha [MAHN-chah] *n.f.* stain
Manifest Destiny, 10, 139–41,
159
Manilla galleons, 7, 31, 32–33
manso [MAHN-soh] *adj.* gentle,
tame
manteca [mahn-TAY-kah] *n.f.*
tallow, lard, grease; butter
(also *mantequilla*)
Manteca. town, 172, 173

manzana [mahn-SAH-nah] *n.f.* apple; city block

manzanar [mahn-sah-NAHR] *n.m.* apple orchard. (The largest of the Japanese-American "relocation" camps during World War II was located at Manzanar in Owens Valley, which had thriving fruit-growing farms before the abundant water supply from the eastern Sierra was tapped for Los Angeles usage. The Japanese inmates tended some of the abandoned orchards, renewing their production. The site now is again neglected.)

manzanita [mahn-sah-NEE-tah] *n.f.* little apple; name of a shrub whose berries were eaten by the Indians and bears

manzano [mahn-SAH-noh] *n.m.* apple tree

mapache [mah-PAH-chay] *n.m.* raccoon

mar [MAHR] *n.m.* or *f.* sea

Mar Vista: town, 4, 173, 208

Marcos, San [MAHR-kohs] St. Mark, 127

Mare Island *(Isla de la Yegua),* 164

marea [mah-RAY-ah] *n.f.* tide

Margarita, Santa [mahr-gah-REE-tah] St. Margaret; river and valley, 47, 127

María, Santa [mah-REE-ah] one of several St. Marys. (The Virgin Mary was usually commemorated in place-names beginning *Nuestra Señora* and also in *La Purisima Concepción de Santísima María.*)

Marin County, 13, 37, 95, 185. (Marin County's name is probably shortened from Ayala's name for its largest bay, *Bahía de Nuestra Señora del Rosario la Marinera.* A variant story declares that Marin was the name of an Indian boatman who lived at Mission San Rafael and regularly transported Hispanic settlers.)

marina [mah-REE-nah] *n.f.* shore, coast

marinero [mah-ree-NAY-roh] *n.m.* mariner, seaman, sailor

marino [mah-REE-noh] *adj.* of or belonging to the sea; *n.m.* mariner, sailor

Marino, San, 68

mariposa [mah-ree-POH-sah] *n.f.* butterfly

Mariposa Creek, county, 13, 99, 125

mariscal [mah-rees-KAHL] *n.m.* blacksmith; marshal

marisma [mah-REES-mah] *n.f.* tidal lake

marriages between Americans and Californios, 134–36, 153

Marsh, "Dr." John: American ranchero, 126, 138, 186

Marshall, John: discoverer of gold, 141, 187

Martín, Cape San [mahr-TEEN], 39

Martínez [mahr-TEE-nehs] Spanish surname, 3, 121, 187

mártir [MAHR-tihr] *n.m.* & *f.*
martyr

Mar Vista, 172, 208

masa [MAH-sah] *n.f.* dough;
mass

matanza [mah-TAHN-sah] *n.f.*
slaughter-time on a rancho,
109

Mateo, San [mah-TAY-oh] St.
Matthew; place-name, 63,
127; county, 13, 188–89

matilija [mah-tee-LEE-hah] *n.f.*
large perennial poppy plant
with white flowers, native to
California

matorral [mah-toh-RRAHL]
n.m. field of brambles

mayordomo [mah-yohr-DOH-
moh] *n.m.* overseer of rancho; majordomo

médano [MAY-dah-noh] *n.f.*
dune, sand bank or bar

Medanos, Los, 125, 138, 187

medio [MAY-d'yoh] *n.m.* half,
middle

Melones, Los, 144

Mendocino [mehn-doh-SEE
noh] Cape, 32, 39; county,
13. (The cape's name was
given to honor Mendoza,
Viceroy of New Spain. The
county, however—one of the
first 27 named in 1850—does
not contain Cape Mendocino!)

merced [mehr-SEHD] *n.f.* grace,
mercy

Merced County, 13

Merced Lake, 63

Merced River, 4, 16, 98

merienda [may-ree-EIIN-dah]

n.f. outdoor feast or party;
picnic

mesa [MAY-sah] *n.f.* table, desk,
counter; flat-topped hill

mescal [mehs-KAHL] *n.m.* agave
cactus used by Indians for
food, fiber and drink

meseta [may-SAY-tah] *n.f.* stair-
way landing

Mestizo [mehs-TEE-soh] *n.m.*
half-breed

Mexican immigrants in California, 12, 119, 120, 142–50,
177–80

Mexican rule in California, 99–
101, 114–15

Mexican War, 140–41

Micheltorena, Governor, 119,
121

miembro [mee-EHM-broh] *n.m.*
member; limb of body

Miguel, San [mee-GHEHL] St.
Michael the Archangel, 93;
island, 31; mission, 93, 190

milagro [mee-LAII-groh] *n.m.*
miracle

military defenses, Spanish and
Mexican, 44, 71, 82, 83, 89,
95, 96, 98, 131–32, 141–42

Miller & Lux, 11, 162

milpa [MEEL-pah] *n.f.* field of
maize, cornfield

milpita [meel-PEE-tah] *n.f.* vege-
table garden; "truck farm"

Milpitas: rancho, town, 125

mina [MEE-nah] *n.f.* mineral,
mine

mira [MEE-rah] *n.f.* sight, lookout. (In American times this
word has been combined,

often erroneously, with other words to form place-names, such as Miraleste, Miramar, Mira Loma, Mira Monte, Mira Vista.) *Mira!*, Look! (verbal command)

mirada [mee-RAH-dah] *n.f.* look, view

mirador [mee-rah-DOHR] *n.m.* spectator; lookout, balcony

Miramontes [mee-rah-MOHN-tays] Spanish surname

mirasol [mee-rah-SOHL] *n.m.* sunflower

misión [mee-see-OHN] *n.f.* mission

missionaries in California, Franciscan (padres), 8, 45, 67–102

missions, secularization of: *See* secularization

mocho [MOH-choh] *adj.* cut-off, cropped; *n.m.* cattle with horns cut off

moda [MOH-dah] *n.f.* style, mode, fashion

modesto [moh-DEHS-toh] *adj.* modest

Modesto, 14, 173

mojado [moh-HAH-doh] *adj.* wet (hence the word *mojado* or "wetback" for illegal Mexican aliens)

Mojave [moh-HAH-vay] Indian word, 64

Mokelumne River (Moquelumne), 98, 147

molino [moh-LEE-noh] *n.m.* grist mill. (The word occurs in various place-names, the old ones dating back to times when grain-grinding mills were located along creeks or millstreams. A sawmill was not a *molino*; it was a *serrería*, at a *corte de madera*.)

mondo [MOHN-doh] *adj.* clean, pure

Mónica, Santa [MOH-nee-kah] St. Monica, the mother of St. Augustine

Monica, Santa: bay, 37, 76; city, 166, 171; mountains, 48–49, 76; rancho, 127, 166

mono [MOH-noh] *n.m.* monkey; *adj.* funny, cute. (In California place-names, *Mono* came from the name of a major Indian tribe living in the Owens Valley area of the eastern Sierra, called Mono or Monache. Hence, Mono Lake.)

Montalvo [mohn-TAHL-voh] Spanish author, 28

montaña [mahn-TAH-n'yah] *n.f.* mountain

montañoso [mahn-tah-N'YOH-soh] *adj.* mountainous, hilly

monte [MOHN-tay] *n.m.* woods or grove; tree-covered mountain. (The Americans often thought it meant "mount," as when they changed the name of Monte del Diablo to Mount Diablo. *Monte* was also the name of a fast-played card game popular among the miners and city gamblers.) 143, 163

Monte, El, 163

montecito [mohn-tay-SEE-toh]
n.m. small mountain, hill;
little woods. (The town of
Montecito was once part of a
land grant.)

Monterey [mohn-tay-RAY]
Name given by Vizcaino com-
memorating the Count of
Monterey, Viceroy of New
Spain in early 1600s

Monterey: presidial town, city,
76–77, 118, 131, 189–90

Monterey Bay, 31, 34, 35, 37,
44, 52–59, 76–77

Monterey County, 13, 189

mora [MOH-rah] *n.f.* mulberry;
blackberry

morada [moh-RAH-dah] *n.f.*
dwelling place

morado [moh-RAH-doh] *n.m.* &
adj. purple

Moraga [moh-RAH-gah] Spanish
surname, 63, 121, 187

Moraga, Gabriel: officer and explorer, 95, 98–99, 125

Moraga, José Joaquín: comandante (Gabriel's father), 63,
82–83, 84, 85, 98

morena [moh-RAY-nah] *n.f.*
brunette

moreno [moh-RAY-noh] *n.m.* &
adj. brown; town, 172–73

moro [MOH-roh] *n.m.* Moor;
adj. Moorish. (In California,
Mexicans used the word to
mean a dark gray or "blue"
roan horse, as at *Rancho Bolsa Nueva y Moro Cojo,* and
possibly at Moro Rock at
Sequoia National Park.) 126

morro [MOH-rroh] *n.m.* animal
snout; round hill, headland,
cliff

Morro Bay and Rock, 37, 52,
190

mosca [MOHS-kah] *n.f.* fly

mosquito [mohs-KEE-toh] *n.m.*
small fly, gnat

muchacho [moo-CHAH-choh]
n.m. boy

mucho [MOO-choh] *adj.* & *adv.*
much

muerto [MWEHR-toh] *n.m.* &
adj. dead. (*Muerto,* like Dead
Man, often occurred in Spanish geographical names, such
as *Cañada de los Muertos.*
Used as an adjective, however,
it may mean bare or barren,
as in Lomas Muertas in San
Diego County.)

Mugu, Point, 39

mujer [moo-HEHR] *n.f.* woman

mundo [MOON-doh] *n.m.*
world, earth

Murieta, Joaquín [moo-ree-AY-
tah, hwah-KEEN] Mexican
bandit, 155–56

muro [MOO-roh] *n.m.* wall

N

naba [NAH-bah] *n.f.* turnip

nacimiento [nah-see-M'YEHN-
toh] *n.m.* birth; the Nativity;
source of a river

Nacimiento River, 52

nada [NAH-dah] *n.f.* nothing

Napa: an Indian place-name,
122, 186

naranja [nah-RAHN-hah] *n.f.*
orange (fruit)
naranjo [nah-RAHN-hoh] *n.m.*
orange tree; *adj.* orange-colored; town, 172
Native American words: *see* Indian
Natividad [nah-tee-vee-DAHD]
n.f. the Nativity; birth of
Christ; river, valley, 63, 128
neblina [nay-BLEE-nah] *n.f.*
mist, light rain; confusion
negro [NAY-groh] *n.m.* & *adj.*
black
neófito [nay-OH-fee-toh] *n.m.*
neophyte; baptized Indian
Nevada County, 13
nevado [nay-BAH-doh] *adj.*
snow-covered. (The original
Sierra Nevada in southern
Spain is a high, snowy mountain range; it inspired explorers in the Americas to repeat
the name on similar ranges.
Inevitably, there were various
contenders for the title in
California. The Frémont map-
making party of 1845 used
the Spanish name for the long,
impressive chain of mountains
bisecting much of California,
helping to establish it among
the incoming Yankees.)
Neve, Felipe de [NAY-vay] governor of California, 85, 86,
88, 98, 179
New World Spanish, 18, 203–04
Nicasio [nee-KAH-see'yoh] a
saint's name

Nicolás, San [nee-koh-LAHS]
Island, 35
nido [NEE-doh] *n.m.* nest; home
niebla [nee-AY-blah] *n.f.* fog,
mist
nieto [nee-AY-toh] *n.m.* grandson
Nieto: Spanish surname, 112
nieve [nee-AY-vay] *n.f.* snow
Niguel [nee-GEHL] Indian word
used in a land-grant title, 22,
175
niño [NEE-n'yoh] *n.m.* child,
boy; *niña*, girl; *niños*, children
Nipomo [nee-POH-moh] Indian
place-name used in Dana family's land-grant title, 122, 190
noche [NOH-chay] *n.f.* night.
Noche Buena, Christmas Eve;
rancho, 128
Noé, José de Jesús [noh-AY]
San Francisco area Hispanic
landowner, 120, 121, 185
nogal [noh-GAHL] *n.m.* walnut
tree
Nordhoff, Charles, 164
Noriega [noh-ree-AY-gah] Spanish surname, 121
norte [NOHR-tay] *n.m.* & *adj.*
north
novato [noh-VAH-toh] *n.m.*
novice, beginner, greenhorn.
(Several land grants contained
this name. But the city of Novato in Marin County perhaps
commemorates an Indian
chief who converted to Christianity and at his baptism was
named after Saint Novatus.)

nube [NOO-bay] *n.f.* cloud

nublado [noo-BLAH-doh] *adj.* cloudy

nueces [NWAY-sace] *n.f. pl.* walnuts. (Walnut Grove took its name from a land-grant title, *Arroyo de las Nueces.*)

Nuestra Señora de ———: Our Lady of ———, refers to the Virgin Mary, 23-24

Nuestra Señora de la Soledad, Mission: *see* Soledad Mission

nuestro [NWAY-stroh] *adj.* our

Nueva California: new colony in Alta California, 42-45

Nueva Helvetia: rancho, 127, 139, 160

nueve [NWAY-vay] *n.m. & adj.* nine

nuevo [NWAY-voh] *adj.* new

nuez [N'WACE] *n.f.* walnut

nutria [NOO-tr'yah] *n.f.* sea otter. (Its pelt was first sought in California by the Russians. The fur was particularly prized by the Chinese, so American ships began to visit California ports to take part in this lucrative trade. By the 1840s the much-hunted mammal was almost extinct. Strict conservation laws have protected it since American times.)

O

o [OH] *conj.* or

Oakland, 14

obispo [oh-BEECE-poh] *n.m.* bishop

obrero [oh-BRAY-roh] *n.m.* worker

ocaso [oh-KAH-soh] *n.m.* setting of the sun or another heavenly body; death

océano [oh-SAY-ah-noh] *n.m.* ocean

ocho [OH-choh] *n.m. & adj.* eight

ocotillo [oh-koh-TEE-yoh] *n.m.* candlewood (a red-flowering, usually leafless, thorn-covered, many-branched shrub that grows in high desert areas of the Southwest)

oeste [oh-EHS-tay] *n.m.* west

Ojai [OH-hi] Indian place-name, 122, 164

ojitos [oh-HEE-tohs] *n.m. pl.* small eyes; spring

ojo [OH-hoh] *n.m.* eye; *ojo de agua*, spring

ola [OH-lah] *n.f.* wave

Old Spanish Days Fiesta (Santa Barbara), 104, 191

Old Spanish Trail (Santa Fe Trail), 64, 136, 137-38

óleo [OH-lay-oh] *n.m.* oil

olivera, olivo [oh-lee-BAY-rah, oh-LEE-boh] *n.f. & n.m.* olive tree. (The Mediterranean olive tree, useful for so many centuries in providing oil, food, and wood, was imported by the Franciscan padres for mission usage. It has thrived in warm areas, for

Olivera

both commercial and decorative purposes.)

Olivos, Los, 172

Olvera, Agustín [ohl—BAY-rah] Mexican colonist and judge, 120, 166

Olvera Street, 166, 193

onda [OHN-dah] *n.f.* wave (of water, light, sound)

Onofre, San [oh-NOH-fray] St. Onufrius of Egypt. (His name was given to a rancho attached to Mission San Juan Capistrano, which is now perpetuated at the nuclear power station.) 127

óptimo [OP-tee-moh] *n.m.* & *adj.* optimum, best

orca [OHR-kah] *n.f.* killer whale

oriente [oh-R'YEHN-tay] *n.m.* & *adj.* east

ornado [or-NAH-doh] *adj.* ornamented, decorative

oro [OH-roh] *n.m.* gold. (The precious metal, sought by both Spaniards and Yankees, was elaborated upon in many place-names, such as Orita, Oroville, Oro Loma, Oro Grande.), 144

Ortega [ohr-TAY-gah] Spanish surname, 59, 112, 132

Ortega, Juan Francisco: Spanish officer, 46, 56–57, 64, 84, 89

ortiga [ohr-TEE-gah] *n.f.* nettle

oso [OH-soh] *n.m.* bear. (*Oso pardo*—grayish brown bear—was the Spaniards' name for the grizzly, which once abounded in California, even near the coast.)

Oso Flaco, 21, 51, 181

Osos Valley, Los, 52, 80–81, 181

Osuna: Spanish surname, 59

otero [oh-TAY-roh] *n.m.* hill, height

ovante [oh-VAHN-tay] *adj.* victorious, triumphant

oveja [oh-VAY-hah] *n.f.* ewe, sheep. (Although most missions and many ranchos kept flocks of sheep, for both meat and wool, neither product could compare in quantity or interest with cattle.)

Owens River Aqueduct, 94

P

Pablo, San [PAH-bloh] St. Paul

Pablo Bay, San, 57, 97, 127. (First called *Bahía Redonda*, then *Bahía de Sonoma* by the Hispanic colonists. A rancho given the title of San Pablo was on the site of the city and river now bearing the name, which was also extended to the entire body of water northeast of San Francisco Bay. Saints Peter and Paul occupy opposite points in the bay.)

pacato [pah-KAH-toh] *adj.* gentle, peaceful

Pacheco [pah-CHAY-koh] Spanish surname, 63, 121

Pacifica, 56, 175, 188

pacífico [pah-SEE-fee-koh] *adj.* peaceful, pacific. (For several centuries, people have wondered why Magellan chose to call the vast, churning ocean west of the Americas *El Océano Pacífico*. Balboa and later Spaniards called it *El Mar del Sur*.)

Paco [PAH-koh] nickname for Francisco

padilla [pah-DEE-yah] *n.f.* small frying pan or oven

Padillo [pah-DEE-yoh] a Spanish surname

padre [PAH-dray] *n.m.* father; priest (generally used for the Franciscan friars who established and maintained the California missions)

Padres National Forest, Los, 101

país [pah-EES] *n.m.* homeland, country

paisano [pie-SAH-noh] *n.m.* fellow countryman

pájaro [PAH-hah-roh] *n.m.* bird

Pajaro River and Valley, 54, 97

pala [PAH-lah] *n.f.* shovel; oar blade

Pala: probably an Indian word—used for an *asistencia* of Mission San Luis Rey, whose complete name was Antonio de Pala, 196

paleta [pah-LAY-tah] *n.f.* shovel; shoulder blade; palette

palizada [pah-lee-SAH-dah] *n.f.* palisade, stockade

palma [PAHL-mah] *n.f.* palm tree

palo [PAH-loh] *n.m.* stick, wood; tree. (*Paloverde* is a shrubby, almost leafless tree that grows in the southwestern deserts and has green bark. The name Palos Verdes in Los Angeles County, however, may mean green trees.)

Palo Alto: place-name, town, 20, 62

paloma [pah-LOH-mah] *n.f.* dove, pigeon

palomar [pah-loh-MAHR] *n.m.* pigeon house

Palomares [pah-loh-MAH-rays] Spanish surname

palomino [pah-loh-MEE-noh] *n.m.* light-colored, Arabian-type horse; a young pigeon; (slang) bird excrement stain on clothing

Palos Verdes, 21, 124

Palóu, Francisco [pah-LOH-ooh] Spanish padre, explorer, author, 60, 61–62, 65, 89, 190

pampa [PAHM-pah] *n.f.* plain, prairie

pan [PAHN] *n.m.* bread

pana [PAH-nah] *n.f.* corduroy

panocha [pah-NOH-chah] *n.f.* sweet, candylike substance made by Indians from wild fruits and plant materials

panza [PAHN-sah] *n.f.* paunch; side of beef. (A *panza* was often used to bait bear traps in rancho days, not only to protect cattle from carnivorous grizzlies but also to obtain bears for the popular bull-and-bear fights.)

papagayo [pah-pah-GAH-yoh] *n.m.* parrot

papel [pah-PEHL] *n.m.* paper

parada [pah-RAH-dah] *n.f.* halt, stop; parade; herd of cattle

paraíso [pah-rah-EE-soh] *n.m.* paradise

paraje or *parage* [pah-RAH-hay] *n.m.* place, residence (a land-grant term meaning parcel)

parejo [pah-RAY-hoh] *adj.* level, equal, similar

parque [PAHR-kay] *n.m.* park

párroco [PAH-rroh-koh] *n.m.* parson, rector

partido [pahr-TEE-doh] *n.m.* party; interest; district; *adj.* free, liberal

pasada [pah-SAH-dah] *n.f.* passage, pace

Pasadena, 172

pasado [pah-SAH-doh] *n.m.* past time; *pl.* ancestors

pasajero [pah-sah-HAY-roh] *n.m.* passenger

pasatiempo [pah-sah-T'YEHM-poh] *n.m.* pastime

Pascual, San [pahs-KWAHL] St. Pascal Baylon of Spain; rancho, 134

paseo [pah-SAY-oh] *n.m.* walk; ride

paso [PAH-soh] *n.m.* pass, passage; ford (in river or stream); excursion

Paso Robles, 63, 124, 208

Pasqual Valley, San (Pascual), 141

pastoría [pahs-toh-REE-ah] *n.f.* pasture

patata [pah-TAH-tah] *n.f.* potato

patera [pah-TAY-rah] *n.f.* place containing ducks

patio [PAH-t'yoh] *n.m.* open courtyard, often in a building's interior

pato [PAH-toh] *n.m.* duck

Pattie, James O: American mountain man and author, 137

Paula, Santa [PAH-oo-lah] St. Paula (name originally given to a rancho attached to Mission San Buenaventura), 127

paz [PAHS] *n.f.* peace

pecho [PAY-choh] *n.m.* breast; courage or bravery

pedernal [pay-dehr-NAHL] *n.m.* flint

Pedernales Point, 51

pedregal [pay-dray-GAHL] *n.m.* stony place

pedregoso [pay-dray-GOH-soh] *adj.* rocky. Pedregosa Street and Park, 89

Pedro, San [PAY-droh] St. Peter. (One of the twelve apostles, Peter—who "founded Christ's church upon the rock of Rome"—has names in the Romance languages similar or equivalent to the word for rock or stone.)

Pedro, San, bay, rancho and city, 35, 37, 112, 171

Pedro, Mission San, y San Pablo: ill-fated mission on Colorado River, 85–86, 195

Pedro Point (San), 57

peligro [pay-LEE-groh] *n.m.* danger

peligroso [pay-lee-GROH-soh] *adj.* dangerous

pelono [pay-LOH-noh] *adj.* bald; bereft of vegetation

pena [PAY-nah] *n.f.* pain, sorrow, punishment

Peña [PAY-n'yah] Spanish surname

peñascal [pay-n'yahs-KAHL] *n.m.* mountain, rocky hill

peñasco [pay-N'YAHS-koh] *n.m.* large rock

peñasquito [pay-n'yahs-KEE-toh] *n.m.* small rock

penitencia [pay-nee-TEHN-s'ya] *n.f.* penance, penitence

peñón [pay-N'YOHN] *n.m.* rocky prominence, mountain

pequeño [pay-KAY-n'yoh] *adj.* small

pera [PAY-rah] *n.f.* pear (fruit)

peral [pay-RAHL] *n.m.* pear tree

Peralta [pay-RAHL-tah] Spanish surname, 63, 113, 121, 122, 152, 188

perdido [pehr-DEE-doh] *adj.* lost

perla [PEHR-lah] *n.f.* pearl; something precious

permanente [pehr-mah-NEHN-tay] *adj.* permament. (The word was used by the Spanish to characterize a river that did not dry up in the summer-time. Kaiser Permanente Cement Co. took its name from Permanente Creek in Santa Clara County.)

perro [PEH-rroh] *n.m.* dog

pesar [pay-SAHR] *v.* to weigh; to repent; *n.m.* grief

pescadero [pehs-kah-DAY-roh] *n.m.* fishmonger, fish shop

Pescadero Point, 38

pescado [pehs-KAH-doh] *n.m.* fish (caught); "catch"

pescador [pehs-kah-DOHR] *n.m.* fisherman

Petaluma: an Indian place-name; rancho, 122, 186

Peyri, Padre, 94, 196

pez [PACE] *n.m.* fish

picacho [pee-KAH-choh] *n.m.* peak, mountaintop

pico [PEE-koh] *n.m.* peak; pick, beak (in California place-names, most likely refers to a member of the famed Pico clan)

Pico: Spanish surname, 3, 63, 87, 113, 122, 134, 156, 166

Pico, Andrés, 63, 93

Pico, Pío, 63, 135, 193, 194

piedra [pee-AY-drah] *n.f.* stone, rock. *See* Pedro

Piedras Blancas Point, 20, 38, 125

pilar [pee-LAHR] *n.m.* pillar

pilarcitos [pee-lahr-SEE-tohs] *n.m. pl.* pillarlike rocks

pilita [pee-LEE-tah] *n.f.* waterhole in a rock

Pimería Alta: northern province of New Spain, 35

piña [PEE-n'yah] *n.f.* pine cone

piñata [pee-N'YAH-tah] *n.f.* pitcher, pot. (To most people nowadays a *piñata* is a breakable pot, often in the shape of an animal and decorated with colored paper shreds, which is filled with treats and suspended from a ceiling or branch. Blindfolded guests take turns trying to smash it with a stick: a Mexican and now a southwestern American custom at Christmastime and birthdays.)

pino [PEE-noh] *n.m.* pine tree

pinole [pee-NOH-lay] *n.m.* ground seeds; Indian-style cornmeal

Pinole: rancho and town, 10, 181

piñón [pee-N'YOHN] *n.m.* edible pine seed. (Pinion or pinyon nuts were regularly harvested by western Indians from the low-growing nut pines; in some tribes, they were an important food source.)

Pinos Point (Punta de Pinos), 34, 38, 53, 57, 76–77, 190

pintado [peen-TAH-doh] *adj.* painted

pinto [PEEN-toh] *adj.* spotted, mottled

pintoresco [peen-toh-REHS-koh] *adj.* picturesque

piojo [pee-OH-hoh] *n.m.* louse

Pismo: Indian place-word, meaning tar, 124

pita [PEE-tah] *n.f.* agave cactus or prickly pear

Pitas Point, 38, 49

pito [PEE-toh] *n.m.* Indian whistle or reed flute

place-names, Hispanic or Spanish: *see* commemorative, contrived, descriptive, dramatic, Indian, transported, ungrammatical

placer [plah-SEHR] *v.* to please; *n.m.* pleasure; in geographical names, place near riverbank where gold dust and nuggets are found, 142–43

Placer County, 13

Placerita Canyon: site of first "gold rush" in California, 93

Placerville, 145

planada [plah-NAH-dah] *n.f.* level ground; town, 173

plano [PLAH-noh] *adj.* flat, level; *n.m.* map, plan

plantel [plahn-TEHL] *n.m.* nursery; center for learning

plants in Spanish place-names, 20–21, 124

plata [PLAH-tah] *n.f.* silver

plátano [PLAH-tah-noh] *n.m.* plantain tree and its fruit; also banana tree; (Am.) plane or sycamore tree

platino [plah-TEE-noh] *n.m.* platinum

playa [PLAH-yah] *n.f.* beach, shore

Playa del Rey, 173

plaza [PLAH-sah] *n.f.* square, marketplace

Plaza Church (Los Angeles), 135, 193

pleito [PLAY'EE-toh] *n.m.* quarrel, lawsuit; contract; bargain (sometimes spelled *pleyto*)

pluma [PLOO-mah] *n.f.* plume, feather; pen

Plumas, Río de las (Feather River): Named during a scouting expedition by Luis Arguello because of the abundance of feathers in the area, 13, 147. The river's name was changed by the Americans but the county retained Plumas

Plumas County, 13

plumoso [ploo-MOH-soh] *adj.* feathery

poco [POH-koh] *adj.* little (in size or quantity)

political squabbles among Californios, 117–18, 119–20

polvadero [pohl-bah-DAY-roh] *adj.* dusty

polvo [POHL-boh] *n.m.* dust

poma [POH-mah] *n.f.* apple

pomar [poh-MAHR] *m.* orchard (particularly of apple trees)

ponderoso [pohn-day-ROH-soh] *adj.* heavy, ponderous. (*Ponderosa* is a pine species that is tall and heavy and yields good timber. It has very long needles.)

ponto [POHN-toh] *n.m.* sea (archiac, poetic)

Porciúncula [pohr-see-UHN-koolah] St. Francis's chapel at Assisi; added at the end of the first name given to the Los Angeles River, *El Río de Nuestra Señora la Reina de los Ángeles*

portada [pohr-TAH-dah] *n.f.* porch, facade

portal [pohr-TAHL] *n.m.* entrance, doorway

Portal, El (Yosemite), 173

Portolá, Gaspar de [pohr-toh-LAH] Spanish commander of colonization of California, 15, 45–59, 64, 74–77, 189

Portola Expedition, 8, 45–60, 65, 175, 188

Portola Valley, 64, 175

posada [poh-SAH-dah] *n.f.* home, lodgings

posita [poh-SEE-tah] *n.f.* small waterhole or pond (variation on *pozita*)

poso [POH-soh] *n.m.* sediment; repose. *See also pozo*

posta [POHS-tah] *n.f.* horse-relay or stagecoach express

potrero [poh-TRAY-roh] *n.m.* grazing field for horses (frequently misspelled and mispronounced as "Portrero.")

poza [POH-sah] *n.f.* pool, puddle

pozo [POH-soh] *n.m.* well

pozole [poh-SOH-lay] *n.* mush made of grain, vegetables and sometimes meat—the daily fare of the mission Indians

pradera [prah-DAY-rah] *n.f.* meadowland

prado [PRAH-doh] *n.m.* meadow, park

preciado [pray-see-AH-doh] *adj.* valued, esteemed; precious, valuable; proud

prenda [PREHN-dah] *n.f.* security, pledge

presa [PRAY-sah] *n.f.* dam, dike

presidio [pray-SEE-d'yoh] *n.m.* military garrison; barracks; prison. *See* Diego, Barbara, Francisco and Monterey for listings of the four California presidios

Presidio Hill (San Diego), 45, 46, 75, 197

prieto [pree-AY-toh] *adj.* dark; tight. (A *loma prieta* is a hill that looks dark from the distance.)

primavera [pree-mah-VAY-rah] *n.f.* spring (season)

primero [pree-MAY-roh] *adj. & n.m.* first, primary; the first, 172

primo [PREE-moh] *adj.* prime, first

púa [POO-ah] *n.f.* prick; sharp point

puebla [PWAY-blah] *n.f.* seed sown by gardener

pueblo [PWAY-bloh] *n.m.* village; people. (The pueblo was the official civilian settlement within a Spanish colony. Its residents were called *pobladores. See* Angeles, José, Branciforte.)

Pueblo de Los Angeles State Historical Park, El, 193

puente [PWEHN-tay] *n.m.* bridge

Puente, La, 48, 195

puerco [PWEHR-koh] *n.m.* pig

puerta [PWEHR-tah] *n.f.* door

puerto [PWEHR-toh] *n.m.* port, harbor; mountain pass

puesta [PWEHS-tah] *n.f.* setting; *Puesta del sol,* sunset

puesto [PWEHS-toh] *n.m.* post, shop, business

pulcro [POOL-kroh] *adj.* beautiful, graceful

pulga [POOL-gah] *n.m.* flea

Pulga Valley, 145

Pulgas, Las, 55, 125, 126, 189

punta [POON-tah] *n.f.* point, promontory. (The Spaniards gave many names to major and minor points of land along the California coast. A number of them still retain the original words, but preceded or followed by "Point" instead of Punta.)

Purísima Concepción, Mission La: destroyed post on Colorado River, 85–86, 195

Purísima Concepción de María Santisima, Mission La, 68, 89–90

Purisima Creek, 55

Purisima Point, 38

purísimo [poo-REE-see-moh] *adj.* purest, immaculate. (The mission of *La Purísima Concepción* — the Immaculate Conception — located close to present-day Lompoc, lent parts of its name to Purisima Point and the town of Concepcion.)

Q

quatro [KWAH-troh] *n.m. & adj.* four

que [KAY] *rel. pron.* who, what, that

quebrada [kay-BRAH-dah] *n.f.* gulch, ravine, deep pass

quebrado [kay-BRAH-doh] *adj.* broken

queda [KAY-dah] *n.f.* curfew, taps

quemado [kay-MAH-doh] *adj.* burnt

Quentin, San (properly *Quintin* —keen-TEEN) Like several other California place-names with San and Santa, this one acquired an illegitimate sainthood. Point Quintin was named after an Indian renegade by that name (who had been baptized with the name of St. Quintin of Rome), and after the American takeover the "San" was tacked onto both point and nearby settlement, and later to the state penitentiary located there— all misspellings of the original Spanish, 68, 181

queso [KAY-soh] *n.m.* cheese

quien [K'YEHN] *rel. pron.* who, whom, which; *¿Quién sabe?* Who knows? (a name given to a creek and land grant), 127

quinado [kee-NAH-doh] *adj.* bad-smelling

quinta [KEEN-tah] *n.f.* villa, country estate

quinto [KEEN-toh] *adj.* fifth

R

racial backgrounds of Hispanic colonists, 63-64, 105-06

rada [RAH-dah] *n.f.* roadstead, anchorage (naut.)

Rafael, San [rah-fah-EHL] St. Raphael the Archangel, 73, 95; mission, 95, 187; rancho, 112, 194

railroads in California, 160-61, 163-64, 171-74

rama [RAH-mah] *n.f.* offshoot (of plant or family)

ramada [rah-MAH-dah] *n.f.* a covering of branches for shade, a bower

ramal [rah-MAHL] *n.m.* offshoot; branch road

rambla [RAHM-blah] *n.f.* sandy ground; ravine

Ramón, San [rah-MOHN] St. Raymond, town, 68, 127, 145

Ramona [rah-MOH-nah] Novel by Helen Hunt Jackson, published in 1884, 11, 168-69, 171, 195

rana [RAH-nah] *n.f.* frog. (*Rancho la Ciénaga de las Ranas*— frog swamp—was a land-grant parcel of San Juan Capistrano.)

ranchería [rahn-chay-REE-ah] *n.f.* Indian village; small settlement. (Many present-day towns and other locales still use the Spaniards' versions of the Indians' words for themselves or their villages.) 7

ranchero [rahn-CHAY-roh] *n.m.* rancher

Rancheros Visitadores, Los (Santa Barbara), 95

rancho [RAHN-choh] *n.m.* large cattle-raising ranches based on land grants during the years of Spanish and Mexican rule in California and the Southwest, 9, 103–28; after American takeover, 150–56, 161–64, 166–67

rancho names and terms in place-names, 112–13, 122–28

ranura [rah-NOO-rah] *n.f.* groove, slot

rata [RAH-tah] *n.f.* rat

ratón [rah-TOHN] *n.m.* mouse

rawhide, uses for, 108–09

rayo [RAH-yoh] *n.m.* ray, light beam

real [ray-AHL] *adj.* royal; splendid; real; open; *n.m.* military camp; fairgrounds. (Like the expression *del rey*, the "royal" or "kingly" aspects of this word altered when Mexico and Alta California were no longer subject countries in a monarchy. *El Camino Real*, for example, began to mean an open "national" highway belonging to the public—not to any king.)

reata [ray-AH-tah] *n.f.* rope or tether usually made of rawhide, 107, 114

recado [ray-KAH-doh] *n.m.* message or gift sent to an absent person

recinto [ray-SEEN-toh] *n.m.* precinct, district

recodo [ray-KOH-doh] *n.m.* turn or bend in river or road

redondo [ray-DON-doh] *adj.* round

Redondo Beach, 124, 172

refino [ray-FEE-noh] *adj.* refined, very fine

reflejo [ray-FLAY-hoh] *n.m.* reflection; reflected light

refugio [ray-FOO-h'yoh] *n.m.* refuge, shelter

Refugio: rancho, beach, etc., 59, 112, 124

Reid, Hugo: Scottish ranchero, 134, 194

reina [RAY-nah] *n.f.* queen

rejado [ray-HAH-doh] *adj.* irrigated

religious place-names, 34, 69, 127–28. *See also* commemorative place-names and Sans and Santas

reliz [ray-LEES] *n.m.* landslide. (Sometimes spelled *reliez,* as in Reliez Valley in Contra Costa County. It was converted to Release Creek in Monterey.)

remolacha [ray-moh-LAH-chah] *n.f.* beet

remolino [ray-moh-LEE-noh]

n.m. whirlwind; disturbance; crowd

reno [RAY-noh] *n.m.* reindeer

repollo [ray-POH-yoh] *n.m.* cabbage

reposado [ray-poh-SAH-doh] *adj.* peaceful, quiet

represa [ray-PRAY-sah] *n.f.* restriction; repression; dam, sluice. (Is it strictly coincidental that the town of Represa in Sacramento County is the post office for Folsom Prison?)

reseda [ray-SAY-dah] *n.f.* mignonette (herb); town, 173

resplandor [rehs-plahn-DOHR] *n.m.* splendor, brightness

revuelta [ray-BWEHL-tah] *n.f.* return; second turn; revolt; change; delay; meditation

revuelto [ray-BWEHL-toh] *adj.* easily turned (as a horse); perverse, dissatisfied

rey [RAY] *n.m.* king. *See del rey*

Reyes, Los Santos, Río de (now Kings River), 13, 147

Reyes, Point, 32, 34, 38, 56–57

ribera [ree-BAY-rah] *n.f.* riverbank, seashore

Richardson, William: English merchant and ranchero, 133, 134

rico [REE-koh] *adj.* rich

riego [ree-AY-goh] *n.m.* irrigation

rienda [ree-AYN-dah] *n.f.* rein; restraint

riente [ree-EHN-tay] *adj.* laughing, cheerful

rincón [reen-KOHN] *n.m.* corner, nook; small district or country (a land-grant term)

Rincon Point, 38

rinconada [reen-koh-NAH-dah] *n.f.* angle; corner where two houses or roads meet (a land-grant term)

Rinconada Creek, 63

río [REE-oh] *n.m.* river

risa [REE–sah] *n.f.* laughter

rivera [ree-BAY-rah] *n.f.* creek, brook; town, 173, 175

Rivera y Moncada, Fernando [ree-BAY-rah ee mohn-KAH-dah] Spanish officer and explorer, 8, 45, 46, 59, 60, 61–62, 63, 65, 82, 83, 86–87, 120

Robinson, Alfred: American merchant and author, 134, 135

roble [ROH-blay] *n.m.* oak tree

Robles [ROH-blays] Spanish surname

roca [ROH-kah] *n.f.* rock, cliff

rodeo [roh-DAY-oh] *n.m.* enclosure where livestock are held; cattle roundup; roundabout way; cowboy contest (in America)

Rodeo de las Aguas, Rancho, 104

rojo [ROH-hoh] *adj. & n.m.* red

romero [roh-MAY-roh] *n.m.* pilgrim; rosemary plant

ronda [RON-dah] *n.f.* night watch, patrol

rosa [ROH-sah] *n.f.* rose

Rosa, Santa: St. Rose of Lima (used often in place-names), 22–23, 127

Rosa, Santa: city, 14, 22

rosario [roh-SAH-r'yoh] *n.m.* rosary

Ross, Fort *(Fuerto Ruso)*, 95, 96, 130, 139, 186

Roybal, Edward R., 179

rubio [ROO-b'yoh] *adj.* blond, fair

ruiseñor [rwee-say-N'YOHR] *n.m.* nightingale

Russian River *(Río Ruso* to the Spaniards, Slavianka to the residents at Fort Ross), 95, 165

Russians in California, 41. *See also* Ross, Fort

S

sabana [sah-BAH-nah] *n.f.* savannah or plain

sábana [SAH-bah-nah] *n.f.* bedsheet

sablón [sah-BLOHN] *n.m.* gravel, coarse sand; town, 173

sabroso [sah-BROH-soh] *adj.* salty, savory

saca [SAH-kah] *n.f.* exportation; extraction; *saca de agua:* lower dam for drawing off water for irrigation

saco [SAH-koh] *n.m.* sack

sacramento [sah-krah-MEHN-toh] *n.m.* sacrament

Sacramento: city and capital, 14, 149, 160, 187

Sacramento County, 13

Sacramento River, 61, 63, 98, 148, 160

Sacred Expedition, the *(la Expedición Santa)*, 44–60, 74–77

saga [SAH-gah] *n.f.* witch; long tale

saguaro, sajuaro [sah-GWAH-roh, sah-HWAH-roh] *n.m.* tree-size cactus with large branches growing outward and up from a single trunk. (Growing in the southwest deserts, its red fruits were eaten by the Indians.)

saints' names in English, 23–24

sal [SAHL] *n.f.* salt; wit

Sal: Spanish surname, 63

Sal, Point, 38

salado [sah-LAH-doh] *adj.* salty, briny

Salazar, Ruben, 179

salcedo [sahl-SAY-doh] *n.m.* damp spot of land covered with vegetation

salero [sah-LAY-roh] *n.m.* salt shaker

salida [sah-LEE-dah] *n.f.* departure; outlet, outcome; surroundings of a town

salina [sah-LEE-nah] *n.f.* salt marsh or pit

Salinas: city, 14

Salinas River and valley, 52–53, 76, 190

saloma [sah-LOH-mah] *n.f.* sea chantey

salsipuedes [sahl-see-PWAY-days] Get-out-if-you-can! (a popular term of warning on Spanish maps and in place-names), 21, 125

saltón [sahl-TOHN] *adj.* jumping, hopping; *n.m.* grasshopper. (The Salton Sea may have had no connection with hopping insects. A large dry lake bed and nearby railroad station in the Imperial Valley were probably given a coined name implying "salt." A saline lake was formed there later when the Colorado River overflowed.)

salud [sah-LOOD] *n.f.* health

saludo [sah-LOO-doh] *n.m.* salute, greeting

salvador [sahl-bah-DOHR] *n.m.* savior

salvia [SAHL-b'yah] *n.f.* sage (herb)

san [SAHN] *adj.* saint: used always in the masculine gender and before the Christian name. *See* separate entries under saints' Spanish Christian names.

Sánchez [SAHN-chays] Spanish surname, 63, 188, 190

sandía [sahn-DEE-ah] *n.f.* watermelon

Sandwich Islands (Hawaii), 106, 120, 131

sangre [SAHN-gray] *n.f.* blood

sano [SAH-noh] *adj.* healthy, sane, safe, sincere

Sans and Santas in California place-names, 22–23, 67–68, 72–74, 127. *See also* commemorative place-names

santa [SAHN-tah] *n.f. & adj.* saint. *See* entries under Christian names

Santa Fe Trail: *See* Old Spanish Trail

santanna or *santa ana:* A unique weather condition created in southern California when hot winds blow into the Los Angeles basin area from the desert country in the east, sharply increasing the probability of brush fires in the mountains

Santiago [sahn-T'YAH-goh] St. James, 23

Santiago Creek and rancho, 47, 112

santo [SAHN-toh] *n.m.* saint; *adj.* saintly, holy. (*Santo* instead of *San* precedes certain masculine names, such as Tomás and Domingo. For individual saints, *see* separate entries under their Christian names.)

sauce [SOWH-say] *n.m.* willow

saúco [sah-OO-koh] *n.f.* alder tree

sausal, sauzal [sowh-SAHL] *n.m.* willow grove

Sausalito: The town's name may have started out as Saucelito —little willow tree—rather than little willow grove. 10, 124, 134

sawmills, 116. *See also* Corte (de) Madera

sebo [SAY-boh] *n.m.* tallow, grease

seco [SAY-koh] *adj.* dry

secularization of missions, 9, 94, 96, 97, 98, 114–15, 136

segundo [say-GOON-doh] *n.m.* & *adj.* second

Segundo, El, 172

seguro [say-GOO-roh] *adj.* secure, safe, sure

seis [SACE] *n.m.* & *adj.* six

senda [SEN-dah] *n.f.* path, trail

sendero [sehn-DAY-roh] *n.m.* path

señor [say-N'YOHR] *n.m.* sir, mister; gentleman; master. (In the religious sense, *El Señor* refers to God.)

señora [say-N'YOH-rah] *n.f.* madam, mistress; lady. (*Nuestra Señora* was often embodied in place-names. "Our Lady" was the Virgin Mary.)

Sepúlveda [say-POOL-vay-dah] Spanish surname, 120, 166, 167, 195

Sepulveda Pass, boulevard, 49, 166

serenata [say-ray-NAH-tah] *n.f.* serenade, concert

sereno [say-RAH-noh] *adj.* serene

serpiente [sehr-P'YEHN-tay] *n.f.* serpent. (*Serpiente de cascabel* is the rattlesnake, which became familiar to the Spanish-speaking settlers in North America.)

Serra, Junípero [SAY-rrah, hoo-NEE-pay-roh] Spanish *padre-*

presidente, 45, 47, 58, 69–89, 101–02, 175, 190, 196

Serra Museum, 75, 183, 197

serrano [say-RRAH-noh] *n.m.* mountaineer; as Spanish surname, 121, 195

si [SEE] *conj.* if

sí [SEE] *adv.* yes

sierra [see-AY-rrah] *n.f.* saw; mountain range. (During colonial times, the word was frequently given to several peaks in a row, not just to a whole chain of mountains.) *Sierra Nevada:* snow-capped mountains. (The name also appeared in several land grants. Sierra Nevada was split to form two county names.) 61, 63, 98–99, 136, 141–50, 181

Sierra County, 13

Sierra Madre (town), 173

siesta [see-EHS-tah] *n.f.* hottest part of day; afternoon nap

siete [see-AY-tay] *n.m.* & *adj.* seven

signo [SEEG-noh] *n.m.* sign, mark

silla [SEE-yah] *n.f.* chair, movable seat; episcopal see; *silla de montar:* saddle; *silla vaquera:* Western-style saddle, with pommel, used by cowhands

sillero [see-YAY-roh] *n.m.* saddlemaker

Simeón, San [see-may-OHN], 127

Simi: Indian word used in Rancho San José de Gracia de Simi, 113, 122

sitio [SEE-t'yoh] *n.m.* site, location. (In the old days, one square league, it was used in land grants.)

Smith, Jedediah: American mountain man and explorer, 136–37

Soberanes [soh-bay-RAH-nays] Spanish surname, 59

sobrante [soh-BRAHN-tay] *n.m.* excess, leftover. (Contra Costa's El Sobrante comes from the land grant of that name, meaning surplus land.)

sobre [SOH-bray] *prep.* over, above; *n.m.* envelope

socorro [soh-KOH-rroh] *n.m.* help, aid

sol [SOHL] *n.m.* sun

Sola [SOH-lah] Pablo Vicente de: last Spanish governor, 98

solana [soh-LAH-nah] *n.f.* sunny place

solano [soh-LAH-noh] *n.m.* easterly wind

Solano, Chief, 96

Solano County (name derived from San Francisco Solano or his namesake, Chief Solano of the Suisun tribe living in Solano Valley), 13

solar [soh-LAHR] *n.m.* plot of ground, lot; heritage

soldado [sohl-DAH-doh] *n.m.* soldier; *soldado de cuera*

("leather-jacket" soldier), 43, 60, 71

soldado distinguido (distinguished or special soldier), 60, 105

soledad [soh-lay-DAHD] *n.f.* solitude, loneliness

Soledad Mission *(Nuestra Señora de la Soledad)*, 53, 68, 90, 190

solejar [soh-lay-HAHR] *n.m.* place exposed to the sun

solera [soh-LAY-rah] *n.f.* flat stone, flagstone

solo [SOH-loh] *adj.* alone, single, solitary

Solomon Canyon and Mount, 156

soltero [sol-TAY-roh] *n.m.* unmarried person

sombra [SOHM-brah] *n.f.* shade, shadow

sombrero [sohm-BRAY-roh] *n.f.* hat

Sonoma [soh-NOH-mah] an Indian word applied to Vallejo's settlement, then to the county, 96, 137, 140–41

Sonoma, Mission: an alternate name for Mission San Francisco Solano

Sonoma State Historical Park, 96, 186

Sonora, 144

Sonorans in California, 142–50

sonoro [soh-NOH-roh] *adj.* sonorous

sonriente [sohn-R'YEHN-tay] *adj.* smiling

sonrisa [sohn-REE-sah] *n.f.* smile

Soquel [soh-KEHL] an Indian place-name, 54, 122

sorpresa [sohr-PRAY-sah] *f.* surprise

soto [SOH-toh] *n.m.* grove, forest

Spanish place-names: Spelling errors in place-words, 25, 123, 165, 205; that look Spanish but are contrived or transported, 24–25, 172–73, 175–76; revived, 174; ungrammatical, 16, 172, 175–77, 208; using surnames, 3, 22, 25, 59–60, 63–65, 121–22, 166–67, 179–80

Spanish words in English, 16–17, 162

Stanislaus River, county (originally Estanislao), 13, 92, 147

statehood, California, 148–49

Stearns, Abel: American merchant and landowner, 122, 134, 139, 166, 194

subido [soo-BEE-doh] *adj.* elevated; strong-scented

sueño [SWAY-n'yoh] *n.m.* dream; sleep

suerte [SWEHR-tay] *n.f.* luck, fate; in pueblos, a nearby farming lot

Suisun Bay, 61

sumo [SOO-moh] *adj.* highest, excessive

Suñol [soo-N'YOHL] Spanish surname, 120, 121, 188

superbo [soo-PEHR-boh] *adj.* superb, proud

sur [SOOR] *n.m.* south. (Big Sur River was derived from *Río Grande del Sur*—big river of the south—south of the main settlement of Monterey. *Sur* was used in several land-grant names in the Monterey area.) 125

Sur, Point, 38

Susana, Santa: mountains, 49

Sutter, John Augustus: Swiss-American ranchero, 139, 160

Sutter's Fort, 140, 141, 148, 187

Sweeney Ridge (Pacifica), 56, 188

T

tabla [TAH-blah] *n.f.* board, slab, tablet

tajo [TAH-hoh] *n.m.* cut, incision; chopping board

taladro [tah-LAH-droh] *n.m.* bore hole; boll weevil

talega [tah-LAY-gah] *n.f.* sack, bag

Tamalpais: combining *Tamal* (Indian tribe) with *país* (land) for mountain and valley. (Other names had been *Pico y Cerro de Reyes, Picacho Prieto.*)

tambo [TAHM-boh] *n.m.* hotel, inn

tambor [tahm-BOHR] *n.m.* drum

Tanforán [tahn-foh-RAHN] Spanish surname, 121

tapia [TAH-p'yah] *n.f.* mud wall; also a surname

Tapia family, 113

Tarabal [tah-rah-BAHL] sometimes Taraval: Indian explorer, 62, 64, 65

tarde [TAHR-day] *n.f.* afternoon, evening; *adj.* tardy, late

tasajera [tah-sah-HAY-rah] *n.f.* place for drying meat (a word often used by the Spaniards in place-naming, with variations in spelling, such as Tassajara), 109, 165

tasajo [tah-SAH-hoh] *n.m.* beef jerky (also *charqui*)

tecolote [tay-koh-LOH-tay] *n.m.* owl

Tehachapi Mountains, 61, 119

tejón [tay-HOHN] *n.m.* badger. (The Tejon Ranch in San Joaquin Valley was one of the largest in the American West; it had 50,000 head of cattle at its peak.)

Tejon Canyon and Pass, 61, 124

temblor [tehm-BLOHR] *n.m.* earthquake. (Mission San Gabriel used a T for temblor on its *fierro* or cattle brand; it stood for *de los Temblores*, an addition to the mission's name because of frequent earthquakes there.)

temescal [tay-mehs-CAHL] *n.m.* sweathouse (from the Aztec word), 19

Temple, John and Francis: American landowners, 134, 138, 166, 194

tinaja [tay-NAH-hah] *n.f.* large jar or crock; waterhole; also *tinaja*

tercero [tehr-SAY-roh] *adj.* third

término [TEHR-mee-noh] *n.m.* end, limit

terneza [tehr-NAY-sah] *n.f.* softness, tenderness

terraza [tay-RRAH-sah] *n.f.* terrace; glazed pot

tesorero [tay-soh-RAY-roh] *n.m.* treasurer; treasure hunter

tesoro [tay-SOH-roh] *n.m.* treasure

tía [TEE-ah] *n.f.* aunt; elderly woman. (The Mexican border town Tijuana was once on the Tia Juana, or Tiajuana, landgrant rancho. It was apparently a Spanish corruption of an Indian word.)

tibio [TEE-b'yoh] *adj.* warm

tiburón [tee-boo-ROHN] *n.m.* shark

Tiburon (peninsula, rancho, town), 10, 125

tiempo [T'YEHM-poh] *n.m.* time

tierra [T'YAY-rrah] *n.f.* earth, land, ground

tijera [tee-HAY-rah] *n.f.* scissors, shears; stretcher; drainage channel. (As a California landname it doubtless has the latter meaning.)

timba [TEEM-bah] *n.f.* bucket

Timoteo, San [tee-moh-TAY-oh] St. Timothy

tinaja [tee-NAH-hah] *n.f.* large earthenware jar; waterhole

tirador [tee-rah-DOHR] *n.m.*
marksman, sharpshooter
tiro [TEE-roh] *n.m.* shot, throw
todo [TOH-doh] *adj.* all
Tomales: a place-name whose
origin is questionable. It may
be an Indian word for bay or
west, or a misspelling of the
Spanish food, *tamales.*
tonada [toh-NAH-dah] *n.f.* tune
Topanga: Indian place-name,
113, 122
topo [TOH-poh] *n.m.* gopher,
mole
torcido [tohr-SEE-doh] *adj.*
twisted, bent
toro [TOH-roh] *n.m.* bull
Toro, El, 124, 195
torre [TOH-rray] *n.f.* tower,
turret, steeple
tórtola [TOHR-toh-lah] *n.f.*
turtle-dove
tortuga [tohr-TOO-gah] *n.f.* tor-
toise, turtle
trabuco [trah-BOO-koh] *n.m.*
blunderbuss
Trabuco Valley, 47, 175
trade, foreign, 10, 104–05, 129–
40
trampa [TRAHM-pah] *n.f.* trap,
snare
tranca [TRAHN-kah] *n.f.* bar
across a door or window to
prevent entry; barrier to prevent cattle from escaping
translations of original Spanish
place-names, 147, 164–65
transported place-names, 19, 24,
25, 127, 172, 174

travesía [trah-bay-SEE-ah] *n.f.*
passage; crossroad
Treaty of Guadalupe Hidalgo,
141
trébol [TRAY-bohl] *n.m.* clover
trees in Spanish place-names,
20–21, 124
tres [TRAYS] *n.m. & adj.* three
trigo [TREE-goh] *n.m.* wheat
trinidad [tree-nee-DAHD] *n.f.*
trinity
Trinidad Bay, town, county, 13,
37
Trinity River (originally Río de
Trinidad. The river was at
first believed to flow into
Trinidad Bay.) 13, 147
triste [TREE-stay] *adj.* sad,
gloomy
triunfo [tree-OON-foh] *n.m.*
triumph
Triunfo Canyon and Pass, 58
trópico [TROH-pee-koh] *adj.*
tropical
Tujunga [too-HOON-gah] Indian
place-name
tulare [too-LAH-ray] *n.m.* place
where bulrushes grow
Tulare: county, town, 13, 61
tule [TOO-lay] *n.m.* reed, bul-
rush. (The word was brought
from Mexico by the Span-
iards. Today it appears in the
news as the notorious "tule
fog" of the Central Valley
which causes extreme hazards
to drivers.)
tuna [TOO-nah] *n.f.* prickly pear
cactus; its fruit *(tunita)*

Tirador

Tuolumne River, 98
turquesa [toor-KAY-sah] *n.f.* turquoise
Two Years Before the Mast, 38, 135, 196

U

Ulloa [oohl-L'YOH-ah] Spanish navigator, 29
último [OOL-tee-moh] *adj.* last, ultimate; remote
umbroso [oom-BROH-soh] *adj.* shady
un [OON] *sing, article* a, an; *unos* [OO-noce] *pl.* some
una [OO-nah] *f. sing. article* a, an; *unas* [OO-nahs] *pl.* some
ungrammatical Spanish place-names, 16, 172, 175–77, 208
único [OO-nee-koh] *adj.* single, only
uno [OO-noh] *pronoun & adj.* one, someone; one (number)
usado [oo-SAH-doh] *adj.* used, worn-out
usted [oo-STEHD] *sing. personal pronoun* you (abbreviated as *Vd.*); *ustedes* [oo-STEH-dehs] *pl. personal pronoun* you; they (abbreviated as *Vds.*)
uva [OO-vah] *n.f.* grape. (*Cañón* or *Cajón de las Uvas* was Pedro Fages's name for the deep cleft he passed through in the Tehachapi Range. This is now the famous Grapevine grade on Highways 99 and 5 be-

tween Bakersfield and Los Angeles.) 165

V

vaca [BAH-kah] *n.f.* cow; also a surname
Vaca family and Vacaville, 121, 138
vado [BAH-doh] *n.m.* ford; a broad, level, shallow part of a river
vago [BAH-goh] *n.m.* vagabond; uncultivated plot of ground
val [BAHL] *n.m.* vale, valley
válido [BAH-lee-doh] *adj.* valid; binding, obligatory
valla [BAH-yah] *n.f.* fence, stockade
valle [BAH-yay] *n.m.* valley. (*La Valle Grande* was the Spaniards' name for the great Central Valley lying between the Cascade and Klamath ranges in the north and the Tehachapi and Tranverse ranges in the south and encompassing the Sacramento and San Joaquin rivers and deltas, which received water from the Sierra Nevada runoff. *See* Central Valley.)
vallecito, vallejo [bah-yay-SEE-toh, bay-YAY-hoh] *n.m.* small valley
Vallejo: city, 14
Vallejo: Spanish surname, 61, 97, 116–17, 120, 122, 126, 134, 137, 186

Vallejo, Mariano Guadalupe: Mexican landowner and military leader, 92, 96–97, 137, 139, 140–41, 150, 186

Vancouver, George: English navigator, 8, 38, 130

vaquero [bah-KAY-roh] *n.m.* cowboy or cow tender (from the word *vaca*), 103, 107–09, 114, 115, 162

vaso [BAH-soh] *n.m.* vase, glass

Vásquez, Tiburcio [BAHS-kays, tee, BOOR-s'yoh] Mexican bandit, 156

vecindad [bay-seen-DAHD] *n.f.* vicinity; population

vecino [bay-SEE-noh] *n.m.* neighbor

vedado [bay-DAH-doh] *n.m.* game park

vega [BAH-gah] *n.f.* open plain or meadow

vela [BAY-lah] *n.f.* vigil, watchfulness; pilgrimage

velador [bay-lah-DOHR] *n.m.* watchman, keeper; spy

veloz [bay-LOHS] *adj.* active, swift

venablo [bay-NAH-bloh] *n.m.* javelin

venado [bay-NAH-doh] *n.m.* stag; venison

venida [bah-NEE-dah] *n.f.* arrival, return; *bienvenida:* welcome

venta [BEHN-tah] *n.f.* sale

ventana [behn-TAH-nah] *n.f.* window

ventura [behn-TOO-rah] *n.f.* fortune, chance, luck

Ventura: city (name shortened from San Buenaventura) 14, 49, 88

Ventura County, 13

vera [BAY-rah] *n.f.* edge, border

verano [bay-RAH-noh] *n.m.* summer

veras [BAY-rahs] *n.f.* truth, fervor, fact

verdad [behr-DAHD] *n.f.* truth

verde [BEHR-day] *n.m. & adj.* green

verdugo [behr-DOO-goh] *n.m.* young shoot of tree; torment; executioner

Verdugo: Spanish surname, 3, 60, 112, 194

verdura [behr-DOO-rah] *n.f.* foliage, greenery; garden vegetables

vergel [behr-HEHL] *n.f.* flower or fruit garden

verruga [bay-RROO-gah] *n.f.* wart; pimple

Verruga Canyon, 21

veta [BAY-tah] *n.f.* vein in ore or wood; *veta madre:* mother lode

vía [BEE-ah] *n.f.* way, route, path

viajante [bee-ah-HAHN-tay] *n.m.* traveler

víbora [BEE-boh-rah] *n.f.* viper

Vicente, Point, 38

Vicente, San [bee-SEHN-tay] St. Vincent; rancho, 127

Victoria, Governor, 119, 121

vida [BEE-dah] *n.f.* life

viejo [B'YAY-hoh] *adj.* old. (Viejas Valley in San Diego

County supposedly got its name because everyone in an Indian settlement fled from the Spaniards except the old women.)

viento [B'YEHN-toh] *n.m.* wind

vigía [bee-HEE-ah] *n.f.* lookout; reef

villa [BEE-yah] *n.f.* village; country house

Villa de Branciforte: *See* Branciforte

viña [BEE-n'yah] *n.f.* vineyard. (In place-names, however, it usually appears as *Vina.*)

vino [BEE-noh] *n.m.* wine

virazón [bee-rah-SOHN] *n.f.* sea breeze

virgen [BEER-hehn] *n.f.* & *adj.* virgin. (In Catholic sainthood, chastity is a high virtue, and religious women were to uphold the purity of the Virgin Mary before the birth of the Messiah. Both Santa Barbara and Santa Monica were *martires* and *virgenes.* But in place-names such as Las Virgenes Creek, the essential meaning may relate to a source of pure water.)

Virgin Mary, 23–24. *See* María, Santa.

visitación [bee-see-tah-S'YOHN] *n.f.* visitation. (In place-names, it undoubtedly refers to religious visitations by saints or holy spirits.) 127

Visitacion: Rancho and valley, 127

víspera [BEES-pay-rah] *n.f.* prelude, vesper; evening before a festival

vista [BEES-tah] *n.f.* view. (One of the highly favored Spanish words for Anglo use in making new place- and street-names—which often end up ungrammatical, as in Rio Vista and Mar Vista. Properly, it should be modified by a feminine adjective, as in Linda Vista, or be followed by a *del* or *de la* and then by another noun, as with Vista del Mar.)

¡viva! [BEE-vah] *exclam.* Long live! Hurrah!

vivienda [bee-B'YEHN-dah] *n.f.* dwelling house

Vizcaíno [bees-kah-EE-noh] Sebastián: Spanish mariner-entrepreneur, 7, 15, 33–35, 39, 44, 190

volcán [bohl-KAHN] *n.m.* volcano

vuelta [BWEHL-tah] *n.f.* turn; recompense; wrong side

W

Walker, Joseph: American explorer, 137

Warner, Jonathan Trumbull: American ranchero, 139

warnings in Spanish place-names, 21, 125

water in Spanish place-names, 20, 123

Wilkes, Charles: American surveyor, 140

Wilson, Benjamin D.: American ranchero and businessman, 138

Wolfskill, William: American ranchero, 137

Workman, William: English-born trader, ranchero, businessman, 137–38, 195

Y

y [EE] *conj.* and

Yang-Na: Indian settlement in Los Angeles basin, 48

Yanqui [YAHN-kee] *n.m. & adj.* Yankee or American. (Most early visitors to California from the U.S. came in New England sailing ships.) 10, 128–74

yegua [YAY-gwah] *n.f.* mare. *See* Mare Island.

yerba [YEHR-bah] *n.f.* herb. (*Yerba Buena* was the Spanish name for a white-flowered wild mint growing in the San Francisco Bay area. The name was given to a small cove and then to a port settlement founded by William Richardson on the peninsula, between the presidio and the mission. In 1847 the pueblo's name was changed to San Francisco.)

Yerba Buena (orig. name for Sàn Francisco), 37, 120, 134, 147

Yerba Buena Island. (The island, located between San Francis-

co and the East Bay area, on which the Bay Bridge pauses, was first called *Isla de las Alcatraces.* For many years Anglo settlers called it Goat Island, because it was overrun by wild goats descended from a domesticated flock set there by townspeople.) 37

yermo [YEHR-moh] *adj.* barren, desolate

Ynés, Ynez, Santa. *See Inés, Santa*

Yorba [YOHR-bah] Spanish surname, 60, 112, 121, 195

Yorba Linda, 121

Ysabel, San [ee-sah-BEHL] St. Elizabeth (Queen of Portugal)

Ysidro, San [ee-SEE-droh] St. Isadore; rancho, 127

Z

(Sometimes *s* and *z* are interchangeable in Spanish placenames, especially early ones.)

zafiro [sah-FEE-roh] *n.m.* sapphire

zanja [SAHN-hah] *n.f.* trench, ditch. (*La Zanja Madre* was the main water-conveying ditch. A remnant of the one at El Pueblo de los Angeles can still be seen at Olvera Street.), 80, 87

zanjon [sahn-HOHN] *n.m.* channel, slough (sometimes *sanjon zanjonero* [sahn-hoh-NAY-roh] *n.m.* ditch-keeper in a pueblo (one of the most important and respected jobs)

zapatero [sah-pah-TAY-roh] *n.m.* shoemaker

zapato [sah-PAH-toh] *n.m.* shoe

zarzito [sahr-SEE-toh] *n.m.* bramble patch

zorilla [so-REE-yah] *n.f.* skunk, polecat

zorra [SOH-rrah] *n.f.* female fox; low cart

Zuniga, Point, 38

Barbara and Rudy Marinacci are a Los Angeles-based book production team. Barbara is a writer and editorial consultant; Rudy, a writer and graphic designer. They have researched, written, and designed books on a wide variety of subjects, but with a particular interest in West Coast topics. The Marinacci's guide to Sunset Boulevard will be published in spring 1981.

NOTES

NOTES

NOTES

NOTES

NOTES

NOTES

NOTES

NOTES